9993

Mansfield
Handbook of English
costume in the
twentieth century

DATE DUE

NO 21 '84			
AP 15 '86			
AP 30 '86			
MY 1 '87			
MY 2 - '88			
NO 20 '92			

HANDBOOK OF ENGLISH COSTUME
IN THE TWENTIETH CENTURY,
1900–1950

1923.—Woman's evening gown of an embroidered and beaded sleeveless tunic-dress of flesh-coloured net over a cream satin underdress. Tunic and overdress with an orange ribbon border and bead fringe. Callot Soeurs, Paris. Brick red velvet evening cloak stencilled in gold. The crêpe de Chine lining bears the signature of the designer, Maria Galenga, Rome. Ostrich feather fan.

Man's dress suit by Henry Poole of London. Corded silk lapels and silk basket buttons. Braided trousers. White waistcoat.

Courtesy: Museum of Costume, Bath

Handbook of English Costume in the Twentieth Century, 1900-1950

ALAN MANSFIELD
and
PHILLIS CUNNINGTON

illustrated by Valerie Mansfield

Publishers
PLAYS, INC.
Boston

Published 1973 in USA by
PLAYS, INC., Boston, Mass.

© Copyright by Alan Mansfield and Phillis Cunnington
1973

Library of Congress Catalog Card No. 73-42
ISBN 0-8238-0143-8

Printed in Great Britain by
Robert MacLehose and Co. Ltd.
The University Press, Glasgow

To C. Willett Cunnington
with love and gratitude

CONTENTS

ACKNOWLEDGEMENTS

The Authors wish to express their grateful thanks to the following individuals, institutions and firms for their help and co-operation; especially for permission to reproduce material as acknowledged in the text and in the Sources of Illustrations.

Aero Zipp Fasteners Ltd and Mr. D. Evans, *Ambassador*, Army and Navy Stores Ltd., Mr. S. H. Baker, Mr. P. Blatch, British Man-Made Fibres Federation, and Mr. P. N. Rowe, Miss Patricia M. Butler, Central News, Miss Pamela Clabburn, Mr. D. T.-D. Clark, Colchester and District Chamber of Commerce, Colchester Public Library and Staff, the Costume Society, Courtauld's Ltd., *The Daily Mail*, Essex County Library, *Essex County Standard*, Mrs. D. Fahie (loan of photos), Messrs. Foster Bros. Ltd., Solihull, Miss Zillah Halls, Mr. R. A. Harrison, Harrods Ltd., International Wool Secretariat, Ipswich Public Library and Staff, Mrs. N. Keen (photos), Lightening Fasteners Ltd. and Miss Christine Jenkins, Mr. A. J. Linnel, Messrs. A. J. Lucking & Co. Ltd., Colchester. The Staffs of the following museums: Holly Trees Museum Colchester, London Museum, Central Museum Northampton, Christ Church Mansion Ipswich, Gallery of English Costume Manchester, Stranger's Hall Museum Norwich. Mrs. Nevard (photos), Miss Brenda Nevard (photos and typing), Frank H. Page & Sons Ltd. Colchester, The Proprietors of *Punch*, Mrs. John Purdon (typing), Mrs. M. Rossiter, Mrs. Ruffell (photos), Mr. Cyril Smith, Mrs. John Smith (photos), Miss June Swann, Syndication International I.P.C. Services Ltd. (*Weldon's* publications, *Wife and Home, Women's Own, Woman's Pictorial, Woman's Weekly*), *Tailor and Cutter, Vogue*, Messrs. Wallis & Linnel Ltd. Kettering,

Owen Ward Ltd. Colchester, Mr. A. A. Whife, Messrs. Williams & Griffin Ltd. Colchester, The Zip Fastener Manufacturers Association.

The Authors are especially indebted to Susan Luckham for typing the manuscript and for her most helpful advice, and to Valerie Mansfield for her constant help and encouragement and the majority of the drawings.

Also those many people whose recollections have helped the Authors.

A great debt is owed to those firms and periodicals which no longer survive and whose heirs, if any, it has not been possible to trace.

INTRODUCTION

The aim of this book is to present as concisely as possible the changes in fashion during the first half of the present century and to indicate some of the factors which appear to have brought these changes about.

The increasing tempo during these years has presented problems that do not appear in studying the history of costume of past ages when the pace of life was slower and technology was so much less advanced.

Examples from contemporary advertisements and from actual garments themselves are quoted from a variety of sources, both national and local, and the illustrations attempt to show representative clothes as worn by a wide cross-section of the men and women of the time. As is normal in all periods, women's clothes have survived and been collected in far greater numbers than have those of men, and perhaps, paradoxically, the earlier years are better represented, in the case of both sexes, than the later.

Men's clothes moved slowly during the half century: women's clothes present a bewildering variety in each decade. In both cases fashions overlapped considerably, and although general overall patterns of fashion can be discerned, not every woman achieved *le dernier cri*, and in many cases trends in male fashion were resisted by the majority of men. Jeeves' attitude to soft-fronted dress shirts and white mess jackets was based on good conservative grounds common to all classes of society, and the fate of Bertie Wooster's innovations was that of the majority of dress reforms. Nevertheless, a steady movement away from stiffness and formality marks the male dress of the period. The clothes considered have been the general run of everyday dress, with brief notes on clothes for special occasions and for sport. These categories, especially sports clothes, which developed prodigiously during the half century, need volumes to themselves to do them justice and only the most common tendencies have been noted. Similarly children's clothes require a separate study and have not been described.

Underclothing has not been included, but its effects in the case of women should be borne in mind. The curves of the Edwardians and the flatness of the girls of the Twenties were alike conditioned by the corsets they wore as much as by the cut of the outer garments.

The effects of two world wars, the emancipation of women, economic conditions, the increase in ready-to-wear clothing and of the multiple shops have all to be evaluated in considering costume in the present century. So too must the influence of the cinema be considered, noticeable particularly in the later Twenties and Thirties, when the glamour of the film stars, and their techniques, often emphasized in the fashion journals, was a powerful factor in the lives of many. It was in hair-do and hats and accessories, rather than in actual new designs of dress that this influence was greatest.

Looking back one discerns some interesting minor features: the strange similarity of men's and women's bathing dresses in the 1920's and early 1930's, and the tendency for hair to grow longer as skirts shorten during the later Thirties and early second war years, a tendency contrasting with the shingles and Eton crops of the short skirt days of the Twenties. These are but two examples.

Did the similarity in bathing dress designs accord with the theory of female reluctance to assert her sex in a world which had been deprived of so many young men, or did it presage the concept of Unisex? Did the lengthening hair indicate that as artificial means of covering the body were to become scarcer, the natural clothing of the hair was to be exploited to the full?

These and other such questions are not easy to answer in a simple phrase – it is for the historian to record them, the psychologist to explain.

The Authors owe much to the late C. Willett Cunnington's *English Women's Clothing in the Present Century*, and where the name 'Cunnington' appears after a quotation or illustration it refers to that work. However, much additional contemporary material has been studied and employed, and for the later periods the present Authors' perspective is lengthened by nearly a quarter of a century.

ALAN MANSFIELD

SECTION ONE

WOMEN

1900-1910

INTRODUCTORY REMARKS

The lines of the late 1890's passed into the new century, changing in 1908 to a line which began to tip the balance of fashion away from the mature woman in favour of the charms of youthfulness. From the same year dates also the commencement of a steady diminution in the amount of clothes worn by the average woman. Contemporary writers claim the early years of the century based their clothes on the 1830's and, in a way, there is in sleeves and other features an echo of those times.

The bodice at the beginning of the decade was still lined and boned: the skirt of a soft and pliable line with deep curved gores and, in many cases, with skilfully cut flounces giving a fluted effect. By 1909 skirts were generally close-fitting and often, in evening dresses at least, showed distinct signs of shackling below the knee – the beginnings of the hobble skirt period which lasted some five years, until the outbreak of war in 1914. This five-year period was also, significantly, the time of the greatest activity of the militant Suffragette movement. By 1910 bodices were still close-fitting, but the high boned collar was rapidly giving place to the Peter Pan or turn-down collar, and the fashion for a long, un-covered throat and neck is spoken of, and although many day dresses, according to contemporary illustrations, keep the familiar high-necked look; the bodices seem less aggressive than they were at the beginning of the century.

From 1906 onwards there is a tendency for the waist line to rise from its natural level which accentuates, especially in evening dresses, the Empire and Directoire lines being revived in 1909.

The influence of contemporary arts and events was, of course, reflected in the fashions of the day, and the South African war and Art Nouveau, *inter alia*, contributed to the design and colouring of women's dress. In 1900 it was written that 'Khaki hats, blouses, and cloth are rampant in the shops, mostly trimmed with red' and in 1903 an evening dress was advertised 'in Art Nouveau style; low blouse with full elbow sleeves and three-tiered skirt in canary yellow satin, lined with red and set off with reed-like leaves in green satin . . . and a huge butterfly motif in green velvet . . .'

The quasi-Oriental tastes of Diaghilev's ballet in Paris also affected the fashions to a degree, but less in England than in France, although Paul Poiret who exploited Diaghilev and the Oriental in his designs, claimed that over here 'both day and evening clothes showed its influence'. This occurred at the very end of the first decade and what results there were did not really become evident until 1911 or later.

The Edwardian age saw a new understanding and approach to the subject of underclothes among women; an approach markedly different from the 19th-century attitude, and an understanding which apparently suddenly awoke to the sex attraction that they were capable of displaying. 'The endless frou-frou of lace,' and 'there is something very attractive about the elaborate petticoat with its frou-frouing mysteries. Our countrywomen realise at last that dainty undergarments are not necessarily a sign of depravity,' are among the opinions of lady journalists; and in 1902 Mrs. Pritchard even wrote 'dare I whisper also of a strong fancy amongst many immaculate people for black undergarments?' During this period two great dressmakers, Lucille in London, and Poiret in Paris, both claim to have pioneered the new concepts in underclothes, but they were rather sensitively aware of the undeclared but nevertheless deep needs of the hour, than really leaders of a liberating movement.

DAY DRESSES

Three types are included under this heading:
(i) The two-piece dress of separate bodice and skirt.
(ii) The blouse and skirt, the skirt being a costume skirt or a skirt of the type worn with a bodice. The blouse of different material from the skirt.

1901 'In the ordinary style of blouse the length of skirt [of the blouse] is simply arranged to slip under the waist band of the costume skirt.

    In other styles of blouses the bottom is finished on more precise lines, until the distinction between them and the bodices becomes merely infinitesimal'.

Thornton's Sectional System

(iii) The one-piece dress.

SEPARATE BODICE AND SKIRT

This was a prevalent pattern, and the 'tailor-made' in costume materials was a firm favourite for morning wear.

Bodices
Lined and boned generally, the boning becoming lighter after 1908. Often with a yoke. Boleros and bolero effects popular. Pouching of the bodice, starting in about 1898 became more pronounced in 1900 and began to go out in 1906. A long bodice, worn over the skirt, was a new fashion of 1910. Throughout the decade the Zouave style of jacket-bodice, like the bolero, remained in favour.
Collars were high, whalebone supports largely being replaced by silk covered wire and a host of patent devices. In 1901 collars higher at the back. Medici collars in the early years and 'Toby' ruffles (from the well-loved dog of Mr. Punch then appearing weekly on the magazine cover) from about 1908 were variations. In 1909 the turn-down or Peter Pan collar began to come in. In some cases light silk yokes or muslin or lace chemisettes gave a transparent appearance at throat and neck.
Sleeves were generally long and mostly close fitting for part of their

length, but many very full below the elbow and puffed or pouched
at the wrist until 1905, when the fulness tended to be more above
the elbow, and the 'semi-gigot' evoked a line of an earlier day.
Elbow sleeves or sleeves with wide ends would be enriched by
undersleeves or 'sleevettes' or ruffles. From about 1903 to 1908
the Kimono-cut sleeve opening was to be found; in the latter year
also were cape sleeves over undersleeves. Throughout the decade
variations of the upper- and under-sleeve theme appear.

Fastenings were generally hooks and eyes or hooks and bars, and
press-studs (poppers) from 1905.[1] Bodices were fastened at left or
centre front, or centre back. Linings independently fastened in a
similar manner. Yokes fastened at left side, shoulder, and neck,
as a rule. Button fastening at the front, or false, decorative buttons,
sometimes found. At centre back of the bodice were one or two
hooks or eyes to attach the skirt. These might also occur at sides
and front. Bodice construction was very complicated at this
period. Waistbands, attached at the back and fastening in the
front, were usual inside the bodice. This waistband often bore the
label of dressmaker or tailor.

Skirts

Usually touched the ground in front, and four inches longer at the
back for the earlier years, but

> 'are so directly influenced by the fashion of the moment that it is impossible to
> give any permanent instructions for their precise regulation'.
>
> Thornton, op. cit.

Gored and flared patterns were usual. They began to get fuller in
1904 when gathering round the hips in groups of small tucks was
popular. Waists began to dip in front in 1903 and in 1904 the
back of the skirt was hooked on to the bodice in such a way as
'to let the front droop in the fashionable manner'. Many varieties
of skirts: skirts pleated to the knee and then flowing free; close
fitting to the hips skirts; flounced skirts; the *waterfall* skirt with
tucks round the hips, pleated into a waistband at the back with the
fulness falling down 'waterfall fashion'; the *mermaid* skirt hugging
the hips and thighs and then flaring out from the knees at the back

[1] But at least as early as 1901 across the Atlantic.

in a fish-tail effect. The *sunray* was a pleated circular skirt; the *umbrella* cut in two semi-circles shaped to the hips and full below the knees. The old favourite seven, eight, or nine gored skirt was still much in service, as was the five gored, straight fronted *eel* skirt. 'Foundations' – an underskirt joined at the waist to the main skirt – were worn with most types to give added substance; heavy material skirts tended to be lined also. Skirts of light materials were weighted around the hem. In 1905 it was said 'the ornate skirt has pleats, box-pleats, tucks, or braid trimming'. Pockets were still sometimes to be found in the side of the foundations, somewhat low down. By 1905 skirts were touching the ground all round for day wear. *Corselet* skirts of 1906 extended several inches above the waist on boned waistbands. *Yoked* skirts were popular during the years 1903–08.

During 1907 the skirt became more clinging and with softer lines: hips were played down and the rising waistline evened up the former frontwards dip. Decorative borders of various types were features of many skirts up to 1908, after which they became rarer. In 1908 and 1909 *peplum overskirts* cut into three points and mounted on the same waistband as an underskirt, and *tunic skirts*, with just-below-the-knee tunics, rivalled close-fitting wrap-over and buttoned models bordered with fur or heavy braiding. Few skirts now had foundations. By 1910 the flare had disappeared from fashion, and skirts were of varying degrees of skimpiness and straightness. By the end of the year the tightness at the knees, caused by a band of material at that level, or at the ankles, by narrowing the hem, despite efforts to ignore it or talk it away by the fashion journals, had become fixed to present a tubular outline for the up-to-date dress. Heavy bands of fur or velvet above the hem were also fashionable in this year.

Throughout the decade walking skirts were always shorter than 'indoor' skirts – from just clear of the ground in 1900 to fairly high up the instep in 1910.

Fastenings Generally hooks and eyes at the centre back or left front. At the back were one or more hooks or eyes to attach the skirt to the bodice; sometimes with additional ones at sides and front.

*1. 1905   House frock of
silk ornamented with lace.*

*2. 1910   Frock of royal
blue cloth trimmed matching
braid and velvet.*

EXAMPLES

1900   Grey watered silk dress. Bodice boned and lined throughout. Buttoned at
front. Close fitting sleeves with wings and cuffs. Pearls and silver embroidery
on shoulders, cuffs, and front of bodice, which are all of pleated chiffon.
Bodice slightly pouched. Six-inch lace-edged guaze frill inside hem of
skirt.

London Museum specimen

1905   'Summer toilette of embroidered linen, the pouched bodice banded with
broderie anglais, tucked yoke and collar, with vest of coloured linen
studded at intervals with worked silk buttons; the elbow sleeves have bands
of broderie and are finished with lawn ruffles; the full pleated skirt is tucked
over the hips and inlet with broderie down the front.'

Dickens & Jones

1909 'Gown of pale blue figured foulard with original draped skirt with two
large motifs of guipure and silk, draped bodice with cross-over back; vest
and cuffs of fine lawn inlet with Valenciennes lace'.

Swan & Edgar
(Both quoted Cunnington)

BLOUSES

The separate blouse and skirt ensemble was much worn, either
with or without a coat or jacket. Like the dress bodice it was
pouched up to 1906, and was also often lined. The neck could
be high and boned, or low and square or V-shaped with or
without a collar. Some had sailor collars and some had the collar
square in front and rounded at the back – the 'American Yoke'.
Sleeves followed the fashion as for the bodice. From the 1890's
summer blouses were known as 'shirts'.

1900 'Ladies American Shirts'.

Advertisement in *Essex County Standard*

     a   b

3. Blouses: (a) 1901 Gathered on to shoulder yoke. (b) 1905   Shirt of coloured Delaine.

In 1902 the *Russian blouse* had a short basque and an ornamented waistband wide behind and narrow in front.

1902 'Suit of new Russian blouse, lined silk, and with fancy velvet collar, flounced skirt lined linenette, in pastel shades of all wool Vicuna serge. 73/6'

Peter Jones (quoted Cunnington)

The revival of a somewhat similar garment in 1909 was the Russian blouse tunic, a long over-the-skirt blouse which had appeared in the 1890's.

A transparent blouse of muslin and lace with a small collar was known as the Pneumonia blouse – in 1902 it was described as 'neither sufficient, appropriate, nor becoming'. Camisoles were necessary wear with transparent blouses or those with transparent yokes, which by 1906 had become known as 'peek-a-boo' blouses.

Towards the end of the decade short, square yokes continued into a point over the sleeves. Some of these models had frilled collarless necks. Magyar sleeves and falling collars went together, and in 1910 the one-piece Magyar-sleeved frock was ousting the blouse and skirt as morning wear.

In 1901 it was declared blouses must be white, or of the same colour as the skirt; in 1903 white with 'dainty touches of colour' was admissible, but the blouse must still 'harmonize with the skirt'.

Decoration in a wide variety of tucking; pleating; insertions; vertical or inward slanting bands or strips of velvet or galloon; false revers; silk trellis work; lace, lawn or cambric collars with or without jabots. Embroidery and other trimming in the shape of false bolero fronts.

1901 'Ladies Blouses from 1/6½ to 3/11'.

Advertisement, *Jersey Evening Post*

1902 'The demi-toilette or afternoon blouse . . . is ofttimes made on a lining and is therefore quite as dressy as, or even more so than, the regulation dress bodice'.

Mrs. Eric Pritchard, *The Cult of Chiffon*

1909 'Vieux bleu cloth skirt with blouse of ninon to match'.

Cunnington

THE ONE-PIECE DRESS

Although not common during this decade various types of one-piece dress were seen from time to time, increasing in numbers after the years 1907–08 as lighter and more delicate materials became popular, thus making this style of construction easier to carry out.

The type most often seen was undoubtedly the familiar 'Princess' cut – without a waist seam, bodice and skirt cut in one, with the skirt gored. The Empire style was also fashionable during the decade.

In 1906 a sleeveless Princess dress with a square-cut top was worn over a blouse: this was the *Pinafore gown*. This fashion was again seen in 1909.

In 1908 high-waisted muslin dresses 'en princesse', 'slightly Empire at the back' were described for summer wear.

c. 1908–9   A silk ninon dress, high waisted, lined bodice with a square neck and lace collar and short sleeves, decorated on collar and sleeves with ribbon flower motifs. Narrow skirt, slightly trained. Back fastening from neck to waist with hooks and eyes and thence press studs to hip level.

Holly Trees Museum, Colchester

The *Soutane* frock was a one-piece garment, buttoned through on the left-hand side from shoulder to hem, and worn with a silk girdle, fashionable in 1909, as was *the Mrs. Noah day jumper frock,* a back fastening model, with the bodice-skirt junction defined by a band of embroidery.

COSTUMES (COAT AND SKIRT, SUIT)

Continued as popular in the early years of the new century as they had been in the 1890's. The century opened with coats of many designs: double breasted or bolero shape, or Eton jacket fronts with swallow tails and oval revers, or three-quarter sacs or slightly basqued rounded jackets. Often worn with the above were long waistcoats with high-necked collar bands with a velvet stock.

4. 1901   Jacket designs.

Skirts narrow above and flaring below, lined or with founda-tions. Decorations in the form of strapping, pleating, cording and flounces on skirts.

Box pleating was fashionable in coats of 1903, as was the basqued 'Russian' coat. High belts and large buckles.

1903   'Russian blouse and Sac costumes in Fashionable Tweeds'.
Advertisement, Essex County Standard 28th February

In 1907 half-length cutaway coats with waisted, bolero-shaped coatees. Short waisted 'semi-Empire' coats with plain circular skirts. Lines slimmer and more vertical.

The higher waist and narrower skirts of 1908 were often not reflected in the coat and skirt, and tailor-made dress. Coats and skirts frequently differed in material and colour; well defined borders to skirts were going out. Sleeves often pleated into arm-holes with a slight gigot effect.

Skirts of 'sports' costumes were shorter and fuller than the walking skirt. Wrap over skirts, buttoned left side, for sport and walking, in 1909. By now few skirts with foundations.

By 1910 the narrower skirts were evident, worn with fairly close-fitting long 'Russian' jackets, front open to waist with velvet revers and turn-back collar: or jackets to knee, buttoned one side, with high waist. A marked feature of many 1910 costume jackets was long rolling lapels and fronts buttoning over below the waistline.

5. 1901 (a) Mermaid costume skirt. (b) Box pleated and flounced skirt. (c) Strapped and pleated skirt.

a   b

6. 1901   (a) Tailor-made walking costume. Three-quarter-length coat. Astrakhan collar.
Worn with a Toque. (b) Tailor-made costume with short jacket.

EXAMPLES

1900   'Black and Navy Serge plain cloth and covert coating costumes 29/6–49/6'.
                                                    A. & E. Baker, Colchester

1901   'Ladies Tailor Made Costumes in New Shades 6/11½–19/11
            „   „   „   „   to Measure 21/-–45/-'
                                    Advertisement, *Jersey Evening Post* 12th March

a

b

7a. 1905 *Walking costume, short skirt, waistcoat, leather cuffs and collar.*

7b. 1910 *Tailored costume of white cloth decorated with large buttons.*

8. 1901 *(a) Double-breasted bolero jacket. (b) Open front bodice.*

a   b

1907 'Tailor made Suit of Fine Facecloth, semi-Empire coat and long plain
       circular skirt. 7 gns.'

                                                        Redmayne & Co.
                                                    (quoted Cunnington)

THE TEAGOWN, etc.

One piece in Princess style with long free lines from neck to hem,
or Empire, with tiny loose bodice or a sack worn high under arms.
Some bodices with bolero effect. Necks low and sleeves long.
Accordian pleating and lace trimmings often featured.

In 1904, 'A teagown is only worn when one is alone, for
dinner. For afternoon tea, a bridge-frock is the proper thing'.
Bridge frocks were elaborate afternoon dresses, or skirts worn with
'bridge coats' or blouses of lace or net, brocade, velvet or silk.

The apparent casual and easy lines of a teagown, originally
worn in the boudoir only, and uncorsetted, by the period under
review, concealed an elaborate and intricate construction.

EXAMPLES

1901 'Teagown in rose pink accordian pleated nuns veiling voile and ecru lace.
       Tucked sailor collar surrounded with guipure. Soft knotted sash of cream
       crepe de chine surrounds the figure and trails to the foot. Bishop sleeves, with
       tight band at the elbow and expanding into angel sleeves, edged with lace.
       Lace flounce to hem of skirt. 4 guineas.'

                                                              Cunnington

1902-3 Cream and white silk with a corded pattern. The back darted and
        shaped, the sides and front lose. Hook and eye fastenings to knee in
        front. Square cut half-sleeves and a square collar trimmed with lace.
        An inner silk bodice boned all round.

                                                          London Museum

1906 Black silk overdress over fine black wool underdress, shaped bodice with
      vertical tucking. Silk chiffon undersleeves. Ornamented all over with
      black lace.

                                          Stranger's Hall Museum, Norwich

9. 1910   *Teagown decorated with guipure lace. £5. 19. 6.*

EVENING DRESSES

These followed the same general lines as the day dresses, in more sumptuous and richly ornamented materials. Separate bodice and skirt generally; one-piece dresses less popular until after *c.* 1907.

Bodice lined and boned, and pouched in the early years of the century. Low cut, square or round or V (from *c.* 1903) décolletage with bertha or fichu in lace or some flimsy material. Shoulders often exposed with shoulder straps, or band enclosing shoulders, and with transparent sleeves or lace elbow sleeves. Flounces, puffs and ruffles also appear in sleeves, as does the angel sleeve, a long square panel floating from the arm-hole and reaching almost to the ground. In 1904 the 'decency frill' was of spotted net or chiffon 'which draws up tightly over the bust when an evening dress is at all low'. Wide boned waistbands and Directoire styles were popular in 1905, and the Princess gown regained its place in fashion, also three-quarter-length tunic dresses; and Empire lines with lace or net over satin underdresses. Waist lines were generally natural in front but raised five or six inches at the back from 1906; mostly round or slightly pointed. Skirts were of flimsy materials over silk or satin underskirts, sewn in at the waist. Flared and very full at the feet, and frilled, flounced or scalloped; generally trained, the train often lined at the bottom with a 'froth' of lace or chiffon.

From 1907 a classical revival with décolletage cut very low, generally square, filled in with embroidery lace or tulle. Top of arm bare or a transparent covering, rest of sleeves very draped. Empire line increasingly fashionable from 1908, with draped bodice and shoulder sleeves of folds of material. High waisted. Corselet bands studded with stones, with skirt tight round hips and falling in folds of drapery from the front waist. Skirts generally plain but embroidered, often with gold or silver motifs or with beads.

In 1909 evening dresses were described as of 'sumptuous extravagance' with Empire and Directoire styles general. Skirts somewhat narrower with the over skirt caught below the knee level to the foundation, often with a horizontal band of embroidery,

11. *1909 Winter gown of white mousseline decorated with silvery lace and ribbon of silver tissue.*

10. *1902 Evening gown of sky blue silk. Striped with spaced tucks. Skirt decorated with artificial flowers. Bertha and epaulettes of cream silk and deep blue velvet, decorated with beads, spangles and artificial flowers.*

for example, showing elementary hobble. One-piece dresses gained favour in the last years of the decade. In 1910 bodices in many cases no more than shoulder straps from a high waisted belt, crossed at the back with the ends falling on to the skirt. Dresses now of very light materials, e.g. ninon mounted on chiffon. The train was often a separate oblong panel. Hobbling quite distinct in many cases, sometimes the overskirt ending just above the feet and gathered into a buckle, or with a knotted effect tied below the knees at the back. Some had sashes.

'Semi-evening' or 'restaurant' gowns for the theatre and restaurant wear had the décolletage with a high transparent yoke and sleeves of tulle or chiffon, in the earlier years of the decade, ending at the elbow and worn with lace mittens.

Dance frocks were just clear of the ground in 1903 with pleated or sunray skirts, ground length in 1908 in Princess, Greek, Empire or Directoire style with embroidered chemisette and lace sleeves, and in 1910 were showing signs of the hobble. Evening dresses had a multitude of decorative motifs in appliqué, embroidery, etc. At the beginning of the decade bolero effect appliqué was in the fashion, and tassels were popular in 1902. Guaging, pleating and flounces and, in the middle of the decade, a revival of jet trimming. Bead embroidery on various parts of the dress was also in evidence in the early years and also from about 1907. The end of the decade saw rouleaux trimmings, fringes, galloons and tiny rosettes.

The popular blouse also occurred occasionally in an evening form, of chiffon, etc.

Flimsy skirts were often weighted at the hem with lead shot.

EXAMPLES

1903   'Evening dress of soft soi-de-chine with accordian pleated top skirt over
        plain skirt of same material . . . The bodice off the shoulders with van-
        dyked lace bertha and pouched front. Angel sleeves. The upper skirt yoked,
        and pointed at the foot in front and back, the points just touching the hem
        of the lower skirt which is trained. 6½ guineas.'

                            Advertisement, Peter Robinson (quoted Cunnington)

1907-8   '. . . a pale heliotrope chiffon gown'.

                                            G. G. Whyte, Nina's Career

         '. . . a gown of soft white satin, with white jewelled embroidery glittering
         on her bodice and sleeves and . . . skirt'.

                                                                        Ibid.

c. 1910 White silk, one piece evening dress. Bodice and front of skirt at hem
         embroidered with green silk and gold metal thread. Bodice boned and
         lined, square cut with cross-over effect. Sleeves of gold and silver machine
         made lace. Skirt not lined.

                                                              London Museum

CLOTHES FOR SPECIAL OCCASIONS

WEDDINGS

1901   'The bride may enter the church with her veil thrown back'.

Veils were lighter than formerly.

White satin wedding dress. Separate back-fastening bodice and skirt: small puff sleeves. Skirt padded at hem and gathered into small train. Small swathed waist.

London Museum

1903   White silk and lace with separate bodice with hanging yoke of lace, and a trained skirt.

London Museum

1906   Cream alpaca with chiffon yoke to bodice and panel at front of skirt. Horizontally pleated waistband. Trimmed with white Honiton lace.

London Museum

MATERNITY

c. 1910   Black crepe satin one-piece dress with lined bodice. The skirt front shaped into a pouch below waist with a flying panel over and a matching panel at the back, both from waist to knee. Machine embroidered appliquéd motifs and tasselled fringe. Elbow-length sleeves with narrow gold braid trimming.

Stranger's Hall Museum, Norwich

MOURNING

Widows all in black: skirt entirely of crape or crape from hips down: crape yoke and collar.

Crape worn for a year and a day, then plain black for another year (1900).

1900   'Mourning orders executed at a few hours notice'.

Albert Scorfe, Colchester

National mourning for Queen Victoria, e.g. 'black alpaca, voile, a smooth cloth with pinpoints of black silk' (1901).

1903   'Black gowns are so charming that they alone could reconcile one to a widowed state'.

1909 'Mourning much reduced'. Widows in black for fifteen months and half
      mourning for another three months.

                                                                    Cunnington

COURT

For débutantes a white dress was essential. Court dresses were
cut low, unless ill-health required a high neck, when the Queen's
permission had to be obtained. White gloves and white feathers
(two for unmarried ladies, three if married) and veil (1900).

1908 'Ladies attending Their Majesties' Courts will appear in full dress with
      trains and plumes. For half mourning black and white, white, mauve, or
      grey should be worn. Feathers should be worn so that they can be clearly
      seen on approaching the presence, with white veils or lappets. Coloured
      feathers are inadmissible, but in deep mourning black feathers may be worn.
           The King has been pleased to permit that a High Court Dress . . . may
      be worn . . . by ladies, to whom, from illness, infirmity, or advancing age,
      the present low Court dress is inappropriate'.

                                            Regulations for dress worn at Court

           For this last, permission had to be obtained via the Lord Chamberlain.
      White gloves were *de rigueur*, except in the case of mourning when black
      could be worn.

1908 White satin dress embroidered white and silver. Green velvet train 109
      inches long, pleated at shoulders and hooked to dress. Low V-neck separate
      bodice with elbow-length chiffon sleeves. Three white ostrich feathers and
      net veil mounted on a hair clip.

                                                              London Museum

SPORTS CLOTHES

BATHING

Red or navy serge, often braided in white. Knee-length skirt,
knickers, and basqued tunic, or combination type with separate
skirt (1900).

Elaborate examples include white tunic-style with black braid,
scarlet embroidery and satin bow and black buttons (1907).

Figure-fitting woven bathing dresses caused some comment
(1909). Black or white bathing stockings, and bathing shoes

with criss-cross lacing up to the knee were fashionable during this decade.

SKATING

Blue cloth dress, short, flared skirt, double-breasted coat with habit-basque. Fur collar and cuffs: black braid trimming on skirt (1901).

The Russian tunic was knee length in one piece from neck to hem worn over a close-fitting skirt. Tight sleeves. Tunic and skirt edged with fur (1910).

Gloves, hats, and muffs were, of course, indispensable.

GOLF

Norfolk jackets and skirt about 6 inches off the ground, or flannel jacket, or jersey. Skirts often with strip of leather round hem.

12. 1901 Bicycling costume with skirt having a saddle piece pleat to allow it to fall vertically. Straw 'boater'.   *13. 1909 Knitted golf jersey. 16/11d.*

15. 1902 Yachting dress of serge decorated with strapping. Yachting cap.

14. 1902 Muslin summer gown suitable for river wear.

Blouses or shirts worn with coats and jackets, generally with a tie, sometimes with a stiff collar, but high collars and stiff shirts declining in popularity.

Hats of homburg type, tam o'shanter, and cloth caps, but sometimes hatless from *c.* 1909. Boots or shoes and cloth gaiters.

TENNIS

Dress or skirt and blouse or shirt of linen, holland, etc. in white or natural colour. From 1903 white was the rule and skirts shortened to above ankles.

High collars going out of fashion by 1902; soft collars, cuffs and ties. *Hats*: straw 'boater' very popular.

RIDING

Habits of jacket and apron-skirt worn over breeches. Some divided skirts or breeches worn with calf-length coats for riding astride.

SHOOTING

Tweed coats and skirts, with skirts leather edged as for golf. Leather also used for trimming the coat, which could be long or of Norfolk or bolero style. Felt or tweed hats, or tweed caps. Often shirts with collars and ties. Boots or shoes and gaiters.

16. 1909   Travelling or motoring coat of face cloth lined squirrel and nutria collar and cuffs. 7 gns.

MOTORING

Long fur-lined leather or cloth coats. In summer long linen, alpaca, etc. dust coats. Flat hats, tied on with large veil. Goggles, or hoods with mica masks.

BICYCLING

Blouses or jackets and skirts. Skirts often specifically cut to allow the back to hang straight down over the wheel. Knickerbockers rarely worn.

OUTDOOR CLOTHES

At this period 'Ulster' was a generic name applied to a wide variety of top coats. Three-quarter and full-length capes and cloaks were also common. High Medici collars and very wide revers characterized many coats and jackets of the opening years of the decade.

Long paletots with triple capes; pelerine effects; fitted long or three-quarter-length coats; large buttons; Raglan coats; basqued jackets with revers and high collars; fitted or sac tailor-made half-length coats, were all popular in 1900–02.

Travelling cloaks and Ulsters in reversible tweed, with a short cape and velvet collar mentioned in 1903, as was a military-style navy-blue three-quarter-length coat piped in red and with brass buttons, and a vogue for collarless coats.

In 1907 a coat cut like a man's morning coat was in fashion, and the following year saw styles cut very long behind and with a bolero front appearance. Ground-length coats again fashionable in 1908, although shorter styles still appear. The full-length or half-length 'Russian' coat was popular in 1909: this had a belt and an embroidered border. Horizontal bands of decoration fashionable on all types of coat. The last year of the decade saw long, double-breasted coats with big buttons and a fashion of three-quarter-length cloaks.

17. 1901   *Semi-sac Inverness.*

18. 1901   *Dolman Ulster.*

19. 1909   *Ladies Chesterfield type fly-fronted coat of
tweed.*

21. 1901 Three-quarter-length showerproof 'absolutely odourless'. Black, fawn, drab. £1. 2. 6.

20. 1901 Single-breasted long raincoat, in black, drab and fawn. Rainproof material. £1. 9. 6.

*22. 1901   Cape, in various shades of boxcloth, with collar of
Japanese fox. Grey and white squirrel lining. £3. 8. 6.*

Fur coats, capes and wraps: full length and boleros and jackets.
Sable most chic and expensive. Mink, sealskin, chinchilla, camel,
astrakhan, Persian lamb, musquash, pony, bear, skunk, Tibetan
goat, beaver, otter, and nutria also in use. In 1902 the Coronation
brought a demand for minever and ermine 'at fabulous prices'.
Some coats and wraps lined with another type of fur in 1901 and
1902, but usual lining white or grey satin. Short semi-sac just
covering waist and with vandyked edges in 1907.

Day mantles were declared in 1903 to be 'worn only by the
elderly'; in 1908 they were cut into points at the sides, simulating
the effect of a peplum; in 1910 there was a fashion for large fur
shawl collars.

Various raincoats and waterproofs, including full or three-quarter-length Aquascutums in single-breasted and double-breasted styles. Dust coats for motoring.

Evening wear in the form of wraps and cloaks of silk, velvet, and fine cloth in a bewildering variety of styles. Fur, feathers, ruching, embroidery, appliqué, sequins, lace, guipure etc. ornaments and trimmings. High collared and flounced evening capes were a distinctive feature of the earliest years of the century. Large tasselled evening cloaks in 1908.

EXAMPLES

1902   'Brown cloth, heavily strapped travelling coat with loose sleeves and big pockets'.

Mrs. E. Pritchard, *The Cult of Chiffon*

1903   'Collarless coats, the feature of the Season in new Donegal Tweeds'.

Alfred Scarfe, Colchester

1905   'Novelties in strapped and pleated backs in new seven-eighths style'.

Horwood & Co., Colchester

1905   'Parker's Nonwetto waterproofs. Proofed with best rubber which will not crumble off, and free from smell and stickiness. Cut full to allow for ventilation and easy movement. 10/6 to 21/-.'

Advertisement, *The London Magazine*

1908   'Handsome tweed coats 50″ long in new striped designs. Collar real opposum. 23/9.'

Ibid.

HAIR

Generally, during the years 1900–10, the hair was dressed full and loose; wide rather than high, although some raised 'Pompadour' styles appeared. Young ladies in their teens until coming out or putting their hair up would wear it loose or plaited and tied with a ribbon bow, often of very wide black ribbon, a fashion popular in the USA.

By 1908 the hair 'conforms more to the shape of the head';

23. Hair styles: (a) 1901.
(b) 1910.

it was dressed even wider, sometimes with a centre parting, the hair carried back in waves, a fillet confining the back hair.

There was a profusion of false hair – fringes, wigs and pieces known coyly as 'transformations'; and of pads and wire frames, combs and pins. Tortoiseshell combs and pins very popular.

Permanent waving was introduced by Karl Nessler, working in London, in 1904.

MILLINERY

Indoors the small lace or lace and velvet caps of a former day lingered on the heads of unfashionable old ladies. For evening wear Juliet caps of pearl beads; tulle bows are spoken of by an American journal in 1908.

Outdoors the bonnet had been replaced by the hat except by a few women of conservative tastes. A revival of a small model, worn with untied strings, was attempted in 1903. Hats ranged from the brimless toque to the cartwheel picture hat, increasing in size as the decade passed.

In 1900 small hats were fashionable in black – a colour which in 1902

'is economical, and never fails to be becoming and in good style'.

Mrs. E. Pritchard

Brims curved upwards in 1901 and became wider until 1905 when the smart hat once more became small, but was, next year, of even larger size; the hat worn well forward with trimming behind, and the toque, by contrast, tilted back off the face. Large, full crowns, with drooping brims in 1907 and 1908, became enormous in 1909 and 1910. A tricorne style was fashionable about 1904.

In summer, straw, crinoline, lace, tulle and chiffon were all popular. Some leghorn picture-hats had tulle drapery from the back brought forward to fasten on the front of the bodice. 'Watteau' hats had a dozen and a half roses and leaves on top and a similar number under the brim. Breton and French-sailor shapes in straw in 1904 and 1905. Mushroom shapes popular in the middle years of the decade.

With tailor mades and for sporting dress the trilby shaped felt was worn in the early years: for games there was an increasing tendency to go bare headed. The straw 'boater' less popular than previously.

TRIMMINGS

Veils on smart hats in 1904, gaining popularity until 1908, returning again in 1910. They were of plain, spotted, or patterned net, usually black but sometimes coloured.

Feathers, birds' wings, artificial flowers and foliage, ribbons, buckles, lace and tulle all helped to decorate hats and toques.

Trimming under the brim was out of fashion by 1909.

Tall feathers in front of the hat were a feature of 1907.

EXAMPLES

1900   'French flowers, fruit blossom and fruits, Osprey, paradise feathers, ostrich flats, Barretter pins and buckles etc.'

F. Fish, Ipswich

1905 'Chip hats. Crinoline Hats. Coarse Plait Hats. Flowers in soft pastel shades'.

G. Pretty, Colchester

FOOTWEAR

High cut shoes replacing boots for dressy occasions.

SHOES

High cut: Cuban or Louis heels, generally waisted, 2–2½ inches.

American 'toothpick' pointed toe appeared at end of 19th century: long slim fit, fashionable by 1909, when the Boston or Bull-dog toe, which had an upwards swell or bulge, was also to be seen occasionally.

Fastenings
   Laces – Oxford and Derby styles.
   Buttons – some cloth topped models.
   Straps and large buckle – 'Cromwell'.
   Bar and button, single or multiple.

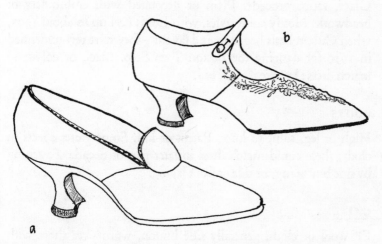

24. 1905   *Shoes: (a) Black box calf. (b) White satin bar shoe, with bead embroidery.*

D

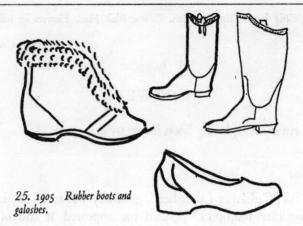

25. 1905 *Rubber boots and galoshes.*

Materials

Glacé, patent or tan leather.
Satin, late in decade. Buckskin in summer.

Colours

Mostly black; white for summer and with white dresses; some brown; a few coloured.

EVENING SHOES

Glacé, satin, brocade. Plain or decorated with embroidery or beadwork. Mostly court styles, with Louis heel up to about 1908, when Cuban heels began to find favour – they were recommended in 1910 for dancing the Boston Two Step. Black or colour to match dress: bronze if glacé kid.

BOOTS

High in leg, some to knee. Patent or kid. Some gaiter effects in cloth; these could match dress in later part of decade. Fastening by side buttoning, or side or front lacing.

GAITERS

Of wool or cloth, generally side button, worn over shoes with elastic or strap under the foot.

EXAMPLES

1902 'Fashionable bootmakers today . . . copy the lovely Louis XV shoes, especially for indoor wear . . . in Kid, leather or brocade'.

Mrs. E. Pritchard

1906 Deep red kid shoes, high front, tie with five holes each side: decorated in gold design. 2″ heels.

Northampton Museum

c. 1910 Black patent brogue-style Derby, with 2″ uncovered painted wooden heel. Tie with four metal-eyeletted holes each side. Patent leather lining. Probably American made.

Northampton Museum

STOCKINGS

Fine ribbed silk or lisle thread. In winter plain or ribbed spun silk, or cashmere. Merino for country wear.

COLOURS

Black, white, brown or bronze, but some of colours matching the dress or shoes. Decorated with self coloured clocks or with lace insertions up the instep, and perhaps up the leg.

About 1908–9 a fashion for brighter colours – greens, purples, etc. often with matching neckties.

ACCESSORIES AND JEWELLERY

MUFFS

Fur or velvet, large, flat and broader at the base than at the top. Heads and tails of animals often the decoration for muffs. In 1904 small round models also in fashion.

In 1906 muffs became wider. Muff chains round neck to support muff and free the hands.

1900   'Choice fur in necklets, muffs, trimmings, etc.'
Advertisement, Essex County Standard

GLOVES

Suede or leather. Brown, white, grey, black: light tan and lavender very popular. Four buttons for day gloves. Some gauntlets. Evening gloves in suede, kid, or silk; twelve buttons. Elbow length in 1906.

PARASOLS AND UMBRELLAS

Lace lined with chiffon: silk: moiré.
Long handles. Gold, silver, jewelled knobs and hand grips: china and 'Art Nouveau' enamel for less expensive: also plain wood. Fringes around edge in 1909. Black lace; scarlet or dress-matching silk recommended in 1902.

Umbrellas with similar but less decorative handles; generally black silk.

When not required for immediate use umbrellas and sunshades were carried tightly rolled.

HANDBAGS AND PURSES

Bags of suede or leather on metal frame. Brocade and beadwork bags. 'Dorothy' bags with draw strings at the neck for evenings.

Gold, silver, or gun-metal chain also very popular.

About 1910 very long cord handles reaching almost to the ground.

Although never as popular as today, the handbag became more common as the decade advanced.

HANDKERCHIEFS

Small, white linen the rule, but also coloured, bordered, floral, etc. Lace handkerchiefs for evening wear 'out' by 1902 in smart circles.

26. 1901 *Ermine tie or stole. Toque*   27. 1910 *Feather ruffle or boa, with silk*
decorated with egret feather.   *tassels. Black and grey.*

1905   'All pure linen handkerchiefs, ladies size, hemstiched. 4/6 dozen'.
                                        Advertisement, *London Magazine*

RUFFLES, BOWS, CRAVATS, BOAS, ETC.

In lace and chiffon, also indoor capes in lace and knitwear.

1900   'Charming effects in Ladies Cravats, Bows, etc. Made up lace goods, lace
        scarves, chiffons, etc.'
                                        Advertisement, *Essex County Standard*

1902   'There never was a better finish to a morning or afternoon toilette than a
        dainty cream or white tulle bow'.
                                        Mrs. Pritchard

1905   'Ladies, avoid chills. Knitted wool capes for 3/- post free'.
                                        Advertisement, *London Magazine*

FEATHERS

For hat decoration, boas, stoles, muffs.

In 1900 many of the boas reached almost to the ground; in 1905 knee-length of ostrich feathers.

BELTS

Elastic, leather, material. Some widening in front to diamond shape. Silver buckles and clasps. Boned sashes.

FANS

Small, of gauze with spangles or sequins, feathers, Spanish lace, hand-painted material. Some large black or white ostrich feathers.

JEWELLERY

1902   'If in doubt wear pearls'.

Mrs. Pritchard

All precious stones if financially available. Clasps, brooches, pendants, necklaces, chains. Silver very popular, often combined with enamel in 'Art Nouveau' designs. Dog collar necklets of pearls or diamonds; long necklaces of semi-precious stones or beads.

Earrings, including screw-on type; long drops, and single stones.

Brooches etc. generally small.

Aigrettes and jewelled combs in hair for evening.

Much artificial jewellery, including 'French jet' – black glass imitating Whitby jet.

HATPINS

Became longer as hats became bigger. Steel with heads ranging from gold and jewel to home-made ones of sealing-wax. Lucky girls with a boy friend in one of the Services had naval or regimental buttons mounted on hatpins.

MATERIALS

Alpaca, bouclé, brocade, Cashmere, chiffon, cloth, crêpe de Chine, delaine, foulard, hopsack, lace, linen, merve, moiré, mousselaine de soi, muslin, net, ninon, panne, piqué, plush, poplin, satin, serge, silks, taffeta, tulle, tussore, tweeds, velour, velvet, velveteen, voile, Vyella.

Artificial silk, later known as rayon, was first made in this country by Courtaulds in 1904, but little is heard of it at this period.

COLOURS

Pink, blues, reds (especially in 1902 a rich ruby was launched in honour of the Coronation), browns, mauve, greens, grey, orange, tan, khaki (especially in years of and after Boer War), pastel shades popular: yellow fashionable. Black, white, navy always.

Designs floral or spots, mostly rather small. Some stripes, especially in summer.

1910-1920

INTRODUCTORY REMARKS

The years under review in this chapter were marked by the death of Edward VII and four years later the outbreak of the Great War of 1914–18. Changes in women's clothes which had commenced before the death of King Edward were in turn superseded by the new fashions born of the war years. It is interesting also to note that the immediate post-war reaction of fashion was to attempt to put the clock back to 1913.

The woman's suffrage movement, so militant and vehement in the years leading up to the war, was overtaken by that greater event and when the vote was given to women in 1918 it was as much man's appreciation of their work during a conflict which affected those at home in a way no previous war had ever done, as it was the result of protest and demonstration.

A phenomenon coinciding with the climactic years of the suffragette movement was the popularity of the hobble skirt. The hobble skirt has been explained as an intuitive device by women agitating for freedom to ensure that they did not obtain too much. Nineteen-eleven and 1912 saw the high water mark of the hobble skirt, first appearing in 1909, and with it went a masculine air in day clothes. But the harem skirt, a Turkish-trouser garment, accepted by Parisian fashion, did not achieve success in Britain. Perhaps it offended the feminists by reminding them of the subjection of the harem, and their opponents because of its overt mannish connotations in a culture where only men were two-legged creatures.

The fashion of tight tube-like dresses had reduced the bulk of underclothes that could be worn, as it had done in the early years

of the nineteenth century, and a revelation of the anatomical outline was a feature, as was an increasing lowness of neckline. The
introduction of the brassière during the years 1913–16 added
emphasis to the breasts in evening dresses: 'gowns of utmost . . .
softness have made a bust-support essential'.

Bakst's designs for Diaghilev's ballets and his use of colour
generally had less effect than was thought at the time. To quote
Willett Cunnington his 'influence as a colourist was much
diluted by the time it reached these shores. . . . As for form, it is
evident that this had been developing towards a style to which
Bakst was himself being drawn; in other words it was a widespread influence affecting him together with various art forms'
(*English Women's Clothing in the Present Century*). At the end of
this decade and into the 'twenties this developed into an 'almost
flamboyant brilliance of colours', as the fashion correspondent of
Pan wrote in March 1920, and an Oriental influence in embroidery
designs for coats and wraps and an attempted revival of the harem
skirt are noted in the same year.

In 1914 a peg-top was developing alongside the tube-like form
and angles began to return. The outbreak of war in that year saw
a reflection by 1915 of military styles in a more waisted, youthful
silhouette. Later, skirts became wider and shorter and the cut of
jackets and coats, with large side pockets, echoed the army
officer's tunic. Also at this time the jumper was being introduced.

By 1918 cloth was scarcer (in October 1917 a Colchester
tailor's advertisement referred to the 'great scarcity of wool') and
skirts became skimpier. In this year also waists and breasts began
to be played down and a 'barrel' outline, swelling towards the
middle of the figure, appeared.

The attempt to introduce the pattern of a 'National Standard
Dress' adaptable for all purposes, including that of a nightgown,
was as unsuccessful as it was unpopular.

The post-war phase, beginning in 1919, was, like Macbeth,
infirm of purpose, with backward looking designs of longer skirts
and a hesitant return to hobble effects. The barrel-line persisted in
evening dresses, but by 1920 an increasing shapelessness in day
clothes was eliminating both barrel and peg-top, and signs of a

lower waist foreshadowed the style to be followed in the next decade.

Some of the effects of the war years were seen in the fashion for short hair – more and more set in the popular 'permanent waves' – and the final legitimization of make-up.

The increase in the use of artificial silk and the triumph of the ready-made dress were added to the decline in class distinctions, largely attributable to the war, to ensure the spread of fashions over a much wider social area than in earlier ages.

DAY DRESSES

During the years 1910–20 the separate bodice and skirt design was generally superseded by the one-piece dress, increasingly bought ready made. In the opening years of the decade, however, the casual-appearing drapery of the bodice concealed a boned and fitted lining or underbodice. The most elaborate construction of bodice, lining and underbodice was reached about the year 1912; from then on bodice construction became considerably less elaborate as skirts became plainer. Nevertheless the custom of lining bodices, or building an overbodice onto a foundation or underbodice, persisted into the early 1920's. In the case of the flimsier materials the skirts also were mounted on foundations or underskirts.

Necklines in some cases still had high collars during the years 1910–12, but from then on most fashionable was a modest V or round line, with or without a 'fill-in', and generally with a turn-down collar, such as the Peter Pan, or with a standing collar at the back.

1911 'Collarless bodices in daytime are only becoming to the very young . . . as also are the Peter Pan and Claudine collars'.

The Woman's Book

(The 'Claudine' collar was a pleated version of the Peter Pan.)

1913 'Fashions decree that our necks shall be bare'.

Cunnington

28. 1912 *Tailor-made wool cloth button-through dress.*
Underbodice with longer sleeves and high neck.

A high-waisted Empire line was in fashion until 1915, but side by side with it went a more natural waist level which triumphed during the war years, and even dropped slightly, although evening gowns exhibited a tendency to higher waists in 1917 and 1918.

SEPARATE BODICE AND SKIRT

(a) Bodices high necked and boned. Bolero coatees and bolero bodice tops worn with blouses and corselet skirts (1911).

(b) Wrap-over bodices with deep frilled V opening with stand-up collar at back. Or draped bodices over underbodices (1913). Some tunic effects in skirts.

(c) Cross-over tunic or long overblouse continuing into a tunic skirt, worn with a separate lower skirt (underskirt) (1911).

A variation was the 'chemise' dress of 1918, or 'pull-over' style bodice and tunic in one over a separate underskirt. Popular as no fasteners required.

Similar was the 'jumper' dress of 1919, a sleeveless overdress with a tasseled sash worn over a skirt supported by shoulder straps.

(d) Basqued bodice, frilled neckline or overlapping fronts forming a V, or a wide fichu fastened at the waist; worn with a fluted skirt and loose, front-fastened sash (1916).

(e) 'Lingerie' dresses of summer-weight materials with jumper tops and accordian-pleated skirts (1920).

ONE-PIECE DRESSES

(a) Double, or tunic over-dress style
Skirts. Hobble to 1914–15, then widening; narrowing again in 1919. In 1911 the upper skirt (tunic) often caught in by a band below the knees. Some underdresses with steel hoop at hem and overdress ruched at the foot, for afternoon gowns.

In 1912 some attempts at pannier effects by bunching up tunic skirts at sides, below the hips. Knee-length tunics shaped into an inverted V in front, or wrapped across with front folds of drapery. Drapery effects particularly noticeable in afternoon frocks from

*29. 1914 (a) Day dress with jacket-like bodice and open tunic overskirt.
(b) Travelling gown.*

1912, obscuring the basic straight, tight skirt. In 1913 flared-flounced dresses, some with three-tiered skirts; waists generally high and indefinite. Panelled skirts and skirts with buttons popular. By 1914 a distinct one-sided effect is seen in the drapery on the hips; tunics are kilted over a narrow underskirt, or are long and flat in effect. Widening hip line with narrow hem producing a peg-top silhouette.

In 1915 the influence of the war on fashion began to be seen. Skirts enlarged considerably in hem circumference, from one and a quarter yards in the 1914 hobble up to five yards. They also became flared or bell-shaped and much shorter – by 1916 they were six inches off the ground. Multiple flounces appeared in 1915 and the tunic was less popular. Where tunics were employed some came to a point in front in 1916; and in 1918 were pointed at the sides, below the knees, the front of the tunic forming a knee-length apron.

In 1919 it was said that 'over-tunics and over-blouses are still very smart, though the straight unbroken lines are newer,' and skirts were longer and skimpier again, but full at the hips, some with flounces or drapery. Gaping hip pockets were also seen by 1920.

Bodices. In 1910 many dresses were still high-necked, but from 1911 they generally became lower. Afternoon gowns often with full bodices with *tablier* tunics of lace and a sash with bow on left side and fringed ends hanging down. Some bodices arranged with fichu effect. Yokes with a band at high-waist level. V necks with turn-down collars, with or without revers, or with high Medici collars at the back (1914–16); deep, frilled V necks, or deep square or round collars for summer. Frilled tulle or feather ruffles. Neck frills on wane in 1916, but some ear-high collars with frilled top in 1920.

In 1910–13 deep cross-over Vs with fill-in or chemisettes. Some pouched or bloused effects. Coatees and zouaves. Afternoon gowns with plastrons and pleats. Bretelles, sashes and stole-effects. Some fur edging.

(b) Single Dress style

Popular as morning, sports and summer wear. They followed the general fashion line, and there were a number of distinct varieties: house frocks, coat frocks, lingerie frocks, tub frocks (washing frocks).

HOUSE FROCKS, HOME GOWNS, HOUSE GOWNS

Button through at front. V neck at first worn with vest and ruff frill or with high flared lace collar, then becoming plainer without frills: sometimes with a square neckline.

COAT FROCKS

In 1915 'it can be worn over a waistcoat, petticoat, or princess slip'. In 1917 it was single or double breasted, buttoning down to the waist, generally high, where there was a belt or sash. Skirts usually pleated, straight or flared. May have large gaping pockets

30. 1918 One-piece day dress. 'Barrel' outline.

at side hip. Close-fitting sleeves. High closed collar, or turn down
flat sailor collar, or round collar with revers or lapels. Generally
with the look of a tailor-made dress with vaguely military undertones. Made of cotton or shantung in summer or heavy woollen
cloth in winter.

LINGERIE FROCKS

For summer wear of delicate materials, such as georgette, voile
and muslin, with lace and embroidery. Some with skirts gathered
on to hip yokes.

TUB FROCKS

An American name for washable dresses, current from about the
turn of the century. A 1913 example in linen has frills at V neck,
and frilled elbow sleeves, with three narrow matching frills round
bottom of its tight skirt. Box pleated or front buttoned skirts
1914–15. Some pinafore style or matching blouse and skirt.

AFTERNOON GOWNS

In 1910 the 'princess robe' with lower part of skirt pleated, cross-
over V or square neckline. Some sleeveless dresses worn over a
chemisette. Elbow sleeves; some with wrist-length undersleeves.
Single or multiple flounces on skirts in 1915. 1916, sashes with
ends hanging down in front, basques to bodices, frilled neckline,
which could be V or square.

Much drapery from about 1917, tending to accumulate at the
hips. Some square trains. In 1918 a square tabard-like overbodice
from shoulders to hips could be removed for 'afternoon dances'.
The barrel line appears. In 1920 square loose panels from waist at
back and front of skirt.

Throughout the decade necklines were generally low, cross-over
V style, or square collarless, or some round with a sailor collar, or
no collar at all, or V with revers and large sailor collar.

Waistcoats worn with some of these dresses, of contrasting
colour or material.

THE TEAGOWN

Less prominent than in previous years. By 1915 some are of pinafore-dress form, in crêpe de Chine or ninon. 'Home gowns' and 'rest frocks' (also in pinafore style) and in 1917 'the new rest gown has no fastenings, but is slipped on over the head' – a possible result of the war-time stringencies.

Illustrations of rest gowns in 1919 show the barrel line in formless draperies, ankle length, with wide Magyar elbow sleeves and V necks. Some have detachable trains, and tassels are a favourite decoration. Another model was described as in accordian pleated crêpe de Chine, with a yoke trimmed with ninon frills, as were the cuffed elbow sleeves. It had a self-plaited girdle.

The altering social habits caused by the war, the rise of the dance frock, and the increasing habit of dining in an afternoon dress, all contributed to the decline of the teagown.

EXAMPLES

1911   'Morning dress of washing material cut just long enough to clear the ground or even shorter. It should fit the figure neatly, yet loosely enough to allow free movement. Composed of a blouse bodice, front fastened with row of buttons, wrist length close sleeves, Peter Pan collar, attached to a plain seven-gored skirt in semi-princess style. Skirt may be finished off with a flounce at the foot, or left plain. Skirt may have inverted pleats at back, finished with gathers, or left plain. For a 36" bust, 4⅞ yards 44" material: 1¼ yards extra for flounce. The dress may be made up with or without a lining.'

The Woman's Book, T. C. & E. C. Jack

1911   'Cotton Dress Materials, Cambrics, Zephyrs, Cotton Voiles at 6¾d. per yard.'

A. & E. Baker, Colchester

1911–12 'Lingerie' afternoon dress of white muslin, self embroidered, with lace and netted silk insertions. Plain collarless round neck to bottom of throat; sleeves just below elbows. Skirt just touching ground, straight, rather full at back.

Gallery of English Costume, Manchester

1912   'Afternoon gown of limpet grey taffeta, double line of buttons running down skirt to meet double ruching of silk; bodice with Magyar sleeves; finished with ruching; bertha collar of lace falling from clear net guimpe. 6 gns.'

Advertisement, quoted Cunnington

E

1912   'Dainty cotton frocks. Ready to Wear from 10/6. Charming zephyr morning gowns 10/6–21/-.'

[Ready to Wear]

1914   'Black silk Merveilleux. 1/4¾ per yard.'

1915   'Cotton poplin 1/6¾.'

All A. & E. Baker, Colchester

1915–18   Peach silk one-piece dress with brown net overdress. Unlined. Hook and eye fastenings neck to waist at back. Drawstring at waist finished off with tassels.

Holly Tree Museum, Colchester

c. 1916   Simple one-piece unlined thin silk dress with overtunic. Ornamented with white beads. Black velvet sash.

London Museum

1917   'Grafton Cotton Voile 1/11½ per yard double width.'

F. Fish, Ipswich

1919   'House and evening gowns from 35/9.'

H. S. Horwood, Colchester

'Fashionable up-to-date coat frocks in gabardine, coatings, poplin, etc. 45/9– 6 gns.'

F. Fish, Ipswich

1919   'Afternoon dress of black satin with overdress of blue georgette bordered with thick ropy double fringe that is so popular this year.'

Advertisement, quoted Cunnington

1920   'Coat frock of gabardine, accordian-pleated skirt joined to the bodice five inches below the waist. Sleeves with line of buttons from shoulder ending just above elbow.'

Advertisement, quoted Cunnington

COSTUMES: COATS AND SKIRTS: TAILORED SUITS (from 1918)

As popular as ever when the decade opened, and seeming to gain in popularity as the war years advanced. The costume was generally worn with a blouse or shirt.

31. 1912.   *Tweed tailor-made walking costume faced with contrasting material. High neck, side buttoning jacket, short skirt. £4. 14. 6.*

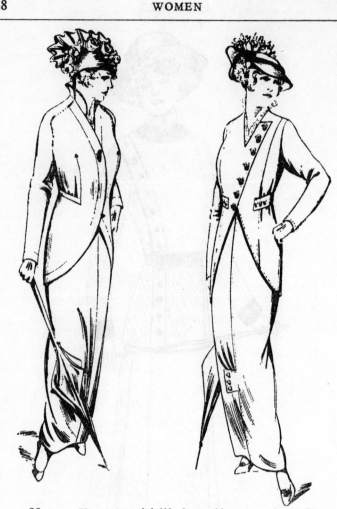

32. 1914   Town suits with hobble skirts and 'morning coat' cut jackets.

COATS

In 1911 and 1912 long to knees or hips, single or double breasted, sleeves close with cuffs. Velvet collars with lapels of contrasting materials, or wide, deep revers to waist level, with velvet or embroidery. Large decorative buttons.

Shorter waisted in 1913 and 1914, some with 'morning coat' fronts, cut away and fastened with one or more buttons: these

33. 1916   *Costume in tweed or serge, short, wide flared skirt.*
Jacket with flared basque and shoulder yoke. 5 gns. Also a
summer version in piqué or drill. £2. 12. 6.

34. 1917 (a) Tailor-made costume with 'military' jacket. Laced boots. (b) Pleated coat frock, wide skirt with hip pockets. Buttoned gaiters over shoes.

worn with waistcoat or with simulated waistcoat effects. Or rounded fronts, or reefer style, single or double-breasted. Magyar and kimono sleeves. In 1915 comparatively long for morning wear, shorter for afternoons. Some three piece with sleeveless or sleeved bolero, and short jacket. Braid trimming and military style cuffs with buttons and braid by 1915. Hip length sac, reefer and Norfolk styles in 1916, some with basques and defined waists. Some belts and half belts back or front. Turn-down collars with revers or collars standing high at the back. Military styles in

1917 with belts and large hip-level patch pockets. Belts buckled or fastened by buttons either side of front centre. Some shorter. Some loose and semi-fitting. Some box pleats. In 1917 and 1918 the waistcoat is revived. In 1919 waistless and following lines of man's lounge jacket, straight hanging: or with flat flounces and basques, accentuating the hips. Pleating common; or with half belts and closer fitting. Some detachable sailor-collars with long stole-ends in front. The 'Batswing style' was a sleeved cape worn open over a waistcoat. The 1920 suits with somewhat longer coats, often contrasting colours. Some buttoning closely round the throat. Often belted.

From 1916 onwards fur was very frequently used as a trimming.

SKIRTS

At first straight, tubular, to instep or just above ground. Decorated by banding or strapping just above hem, or with vertical row of buttons up side. Some split at side for about twelve inches and partly buttoned, or slightly open at bottom of front seam. Let-in side panels common, giving impression of the skirt being buttoned across. Rows of decorative buttons down skirts.

Wrapping across in 1913 or buttoning centre front. Splits up from hem now rare. Some tunic skirts. Some skirts have attached braces of self-material or patent leather (a similar example dated 1920–22 is in the London Museum).

Skirts plainer by autumn 1914 and become moderately full and shorter in 1915. In 1916 skirts were six inches off the ground and in the following year were full, fluted, and rose to 8 inches clearance.

By 1918 they were becoming straighter, some with a stitched seam up back and front. In 1919 skirts were straight and narrow, some with pleats, and this line held generally for the next year also.

EXAMPLES

1912   'Navy coating ready-to-wear coats and skirts, trimmed braid. 32/6–3½ gns.'
                                        A. & E. Baker, Colchester

1913–14   Fine pink face-cloth suit of skirt and bolero with matching pink velvet
          jacket with face-cloth undersleeves. Skirt directoire style with foundation
          of pink satin and under-flounce at hem of pink chiffon. Bolero has long
          tight sleeves and a chiffon fill-in and lace collar: decorated with gold-
          worm embroidery. Jacket has wide sleeves and black fur collar: fastening
          by braid frog and self-covered button.

                                                             London Museum

1917   Summer costume of fine worsted mixture in narrow black and white stripes.
          Short thigh-length coat single breasted, turn-down collar, square at back,
          with revers. Large patch pockets at hips. Front centre buttoning with self
          covered buttons and belt crossing over at front and buttoning either side of
          centre. Skirt fairly full and above-ankle length shaped over hips.

                                                 Holly Trees Museum, Colchester

1916   'Smart tailor made costumes 47/6 to 4 gns.'

                                                     A. & E. Baker, Colchester

          But also, in the same town:
          'Newest costumes in serges and cloths from 14/11½'.

1918   '"Park Lane" costumes, tailor made to your measures, 45/- to 60/-.' [Mail
          order]

                                                           Hartley & Co. Leeds

1919   'Sale. Smart Costumes 29/6 to 10 gns.
          Usually 39/6 to 12 gns.'

                                                      H. S. Horwood, Colchester

1920   'Strictly tailored walking-suit in fine navy serge, with a three-quarter coat
          flaring ever so slightly at the hips, and with revers cut almost down to the
          waist . . . belted with black moire ribbon threaded through carved ivory
          slots. The skirt was very slim and short, showing high boots of navy-blue
          suede.'

                                            Fashion correspondent, *Pan*, March

BLOUSES

Worn with coat and skirt suits or with a skirt alone. Most styles
worn inside skirts, and a belt was normal. Black skirt and white
blouse was a popular combination.

In 1911 and 1912 the high boned collar was still in fashion, but
yielding to low, round necklines with or without a flat collar.

35. *1912   Blouse with low neck, crêpe de Chine.* £1. 11. 9.

36. *1912   Blouse in Jap silk. 16/9d.*

Sleeves in general were long, close fitting, with cuffs or wrist-bands: some elbow sleeves with small turn-back cuffs, or a frill, and sometimes with undersleeves. Fronts tucked, pleated and embroidered at yoke or with embroidered panels in front: in 1913 a variety worn open in front over a tucked vest. In this year bare necks or Medici frills popular. Blouses often lined or worn over a blouse slip or underslip. Most of the pre-1914 blouses were back fastening and worn inside the skirt. Jerkin blouses, Russian blouses and basqued shirt blouses were, however, worn belted, in most cases, over the skirt. The blouse-coat, introduced about 1913, fell to just below the hips and buttoned through from the left shoulder to the hem.

In 1914 sleeves were wider and looser with a long shoulder line: some sleeves and yokes made in one, with body slightly gathered into the yoke. The neck line became V shaped with a stand-up Medici collar at the back, or a standing-up ruff in 1915 and this style continued side by side with flat collars and revers with a deep décolletage in 1916. The V and revers continued throughout 1917, 1918 and 1919, although the sailor collar shared its popularity in 1917, and there were also a number of round or square necklines. Chemisettes or fill-ins sometimes employed in the décolletage, and in 1917 a vogue for rolled over collars of georgette or ninon on dressy blouses.

In 1915 it was said 'the leg-of-mutton sleeve with the lowered shoulder line is the right thing for many of the blouses', and in

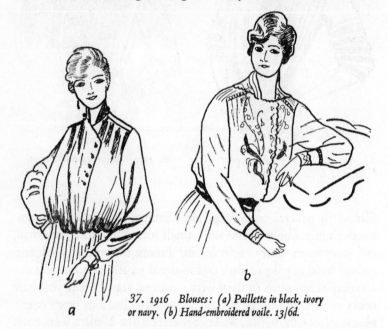

37. 1916 Blouses: (a) Paillette in black, ivory
or navy. (b) Hand-embroidered voile. 13/6d.

1916 long sleeves, wider above and tightening below. In the same year some cape-collars extending over the shoulders, and fichu effects. Pointed cuffs, and a higher-than-natural waistline.

In 1918 the Russian blouse was worn pouched over the belt. It was pleated, with sailor collar or revers, and loose, concealing the shape of the body. In the next year a 'jumper-waistcoat' was an over-the-skirt blouse of satin, georgette, etc. with an embroidered and tasselled border. The coatee blouse of those years had three-quarter sleeves, was of velvet, and fur trimmed. The blouses of 1920 were generally V-necked, with wide, pointed collars, or collarless with a deep crossover or revers. Some with sashes. Some Magyar sleeves.

SHIRTS AND SHIRT-BLOUSES

Generally plainer and worn at first with detachable collars and cuffs and a tie. For sports wear and with plain tailor-mades. Turn-down collars and raglan sleeves in 1915. Loose fitting in 1920. Nearly always front fastening throughout the period. Made of cotton, linen, delaine etc. or 'dressy' ones could be of chiffon or silk, with lace collar.

EXAMPLES

1911 'Ladies Cambric shirt-blouses 1/11½'.

A. & E. Baker, Colchester

1912 'Chic crêpe silk Magyar blouses 8/11 all colours'.

Ibid.

1914 'Smart white silk shirts 5/-'.

Ibid.

1917 'Crêpe de chine blouses from 12/-'.

Ibid.

1919 'Blouses 2/11 to 2 gns. Voiles, Jap silks, crêpe de chine, poplins, delaines, prints, Luviscas, Tricolines 2/11 to 2 gns'.

Walter Hunt, Colchester

JUMPERS

Coming into favour in 1916 the jumper-blouse was generally knitted in silk or wool or was of a material such as stockinette, jersey cloth, silk, crêpe de Chine, etc. It began to replace the blouse and shirt for wear with a skirt or suit. The characteristic was that it pulled on over the head without any fastenings. The jumper-blouse came to below hip level, sometimes with a sash or belt.

38. *1916 Knitted sports coat in cashmere. Black or white. 31/6d.*

39. *1919 Wool crochet V-neck sports jumper and 'pullon' hat, crochet in brushed wool.*

Front buttoning coats of knitting or stockinette etc. were also fashionable, worn with a tie or buckle belt; some with outside patch pockets.

Home knitted and home crocheted jumper-blouses and coats were very common from 1917, and there was also a vogue for a jumper-frock to slip on over the head and also devoid of fastenings.

Generally long sleeves at first, but elbow-length for games and even shorter in 1919 for fashionable day wear, as in the 'jumper-waistcoat', a hip-length, loose garment of satin or georgette, with a deep embroidered hem, from which, as from the short sleeves, tassels dangled.

By 1919 the jumper-blouse was known by its present name of jumper, and the knitted coat was in many respects assimilating the cardigan.

The cardigan, originally a male garment, had been appropriated for ladies' sporting wear: it could also be known as a jersey. (See p. 87.)

EXAMPLES

1912 'Fashionable Sporting Jersey [buttoned down front, with pockets at waist level, long sleeves] 31/6'.

Army & Navy Stores

1915 'Knitted coats from 4/11 [Sale price]'.

A. & E. Baker, Colchester

1919 'Sports coats, silk and woollen jumpers'.

Horwood's, Colchester

1920 'For the Smartest Jumpers – Ardern's Star Sylko.'

Advertisement, The Family Journal

SKIRTS

For wear with blouse or jumper. Followed lines of the costume skirt. Some corselet skirts 1911–13. Tubular, tight and hobble until 1914. Some slit for ease in walking. Decorated by buttons and strapping. Side panels and button-over effects.

Drastic change in 1915. Skirts short, flared or bell-shaped. Belts or leather girdles worn. Fluted effects and hems 8 inches or more off the ground by 1917: side pockets: front panels and laid on yokes: cummerbund-depth belts.

Narrower skirts in 1918 ushered in the 'barrel-line' and emphasised the scarcity of fabrics. Skirts of 1919 and 1920 were longer, plainer and straight. Some with all-round or side pleats.

1918 'Washing skirt in good-wearing white piqué cut with fine gores and with waistband and smart pockets 6/11'.

John Noble Ltd.   Mail Order, Manchester

EVENING DRESSES

Generally one-piece design with tunic or overdress.

SKIRTS

The tunic generally more or less draped, or could be in the form of front and back panels. Skirt to ground until 1915, when it shortened to the ankles. The line in 1911–13 was straight and tubular, with some markedly Empire models. Trains were popular and the skirt or overskirt could be caught up below the knees. In 1912 tight bands above the knees. Waists were generally high throughout the period, dropping in 1920. Barrel lines popular in 1919. Hip drapery in 1915 and 1916, sometimes with crinoline material on the hips between the folds of dress fabric: the pannier effect appears throughout from about 1912. The hem of the skirt becomes wider during the war years, becoming tighter again in 1919, although dance frocks tended to retain a wider skirt. In the same year the overskirt could be composed of three or four deep flounces; the length was now mid-calf. To obviate the tightness of some skirts there were slits up the front, sides or back, about a foot in length. In 1917 and again in 1919 it is known that elastic was sometimes inserted in the hem to combine locomotion with the fashionable peg-top outline.

In 1920 an attempt to reintroduce the hooped crinoline style skirt, ankle length, proved abortive.

TRAINS

Trains were square-ended in 1911, pointed or square in 1912, pointed in 1913 and 1914 and in the latter years sometimes from the waist. In 1915 the square end was again fashionable. During the war the train seems less in evidence, though a popularity of large sashes, with the ends trailing on the ground at the back substitutes for them. In 1920 narrow trains from the back or side, waist or shoulders.

40. 1912 *Evening dress in pink chiffon studded with crystal beads and pink satin bows. Ivory satin underdress caught at feet with narrow crystal insertion. Long stole with tasselled ends.*

41. 1915 *Evening robe of soft satin and ninon. Bodice draped in broad folded belt style. In sky, pink, mauve, grey or black. 49/6d.*

Tunics and overdresses for dance frocks, demi-toilettes, etc.
were generally of a light, diaphanous nature, such as gauze, ninon,
unlined net with bands of velvet or satin. For full dress satin,
brocaded silk, velvet, etc. The war, however, blurred the distinctions, and by 1918 'a demi-toilette is all that is needed in nine
cases out of ten'.

BODICES

Ranged from the elaborately constructed types with bodice,
underbodice and lining, suitably boned, of 1911, to a simple
drapery covering one shoulder only in 1920. Throughout the
period décolletage was deep, with round, square or V necklines.
The V was often of a cross-over type. Fichu draping noticeable in
1911 and 1918. The décolletage extended to the back as well as
the front of the dress, and could be filled in with a chemisette of
some type: in 1916 and 1917 these were popular in a flesh colour
or transparent material. Some high collars in 1915. In 1915 a loose
tunic with armholes open nearly to the hips, the sides connected
by bows or Swiss lacing, worn over a satin underdress. Swathed
corsages in 1918 and 1919. Some coat-bodices, coming below
hips. Short basques, or frills, in 1916.

Bodices were close fitting in 1911, although the drapery tended
to obscure the outlines. By 1916 the introduction of the brassière
had helped to emphasise the shape of the breasts, but by 1919 these
were again played down, bodices becoming looser in 1918, and
even the quite tight lines of 1920 displayed no shape. Backless
dresses were seen in 1920.

> 'Mary, Mary slightly airy
> How do the fashions go?
> Scraped up hair and shoulders bare
> And vertebrae all in a row.'
> *Punch*

SLEEVES

Short, shoulder, or to elbow. Magyar cut very popular. In 1914
floating drapery was fashionable over the upper arms, and again

42. *1918 Evening dress in gold brocade with gold lace apron tunic and square ended train.*

in 1918–19 transparent hanging sleeves, the ends cut into long points before and behind and finished with tassels. 'Handkerchief' sleeves *c.* 1918 floated from the end of short elbow sleeves.

In many cases sleeves are absent and the bodice supported by shoulder straps, sometimes ornamented with jet or jewels.

DECORATION AND TRIMMINGS

Sashes were a very distinctive feature, and belts were also worn. The sash could be tied in a large bow, or trail train-like on the ground. Tassels throughout the period. Embroidery and broderie Anglaise in 1911–12. Bead fringes common in 1914. Much fur trimming from 1912 to 1918. Bead embroidery, gold and silver embroidery, sequins and artificial pearls in draped ropes.

EVENING DRESS MATERIALS

Brocade (sometimes metal embroidered), charmeuse, chiffon, diamante, gauze, georgette (from 1914), lace, metal embroidered brocade, net, ninon, satin, silk, taffeta, tulle, velvet, voile.

Either singly, or generally in combination of two or more.

EXAMPLES

1911   Pink and blue shot and watered silk with pink and blue gauze tunic. Embroidered net and appliqué lace trimmings to bodice, sleeves and hem of tunic. Bodice cross-over V neck with fill-in, elbow sleeves, narrow cord girdle, high waistline. Skirt straight and narrow, the back section overlapping tunic and falling to form a square train.

Gallery of English Costume, Manchester

c. 1911   Yellow satin and silver net and silver lamé. Very narrow skirt and underskirt. Skirt draped from hip with wrap-over back. Low square décolletage, bodice draped, shoulder sleeves and back of bodice of embroidered silver net. Ninety-one inch train of satin and lamé divided at upper end to come over the shoulders and fasten to front of bodice as two pointed ends secured by press studs.

Northampton Museum

1912   'Evening frock of ninon and silk. 7½ gns.
Velvet and ninon evening frock trimmed with skunk 10 gns.'

Advertisement, quoted Cunnington

1917-18   Evening dress of salmon pink satin underdress and brown net overdress
          embroidered with fawn colour solid motifs in chain stitch. Gold cord
          shoulder straps attached to front of bodice by muslin triangular pieces,
          giving a 'look, no visible means of support' effect. Waist rather high;
          gathered. Gold girdle ending in heavy acorns. Unlined.

                                                    Holly Tree Museum, Colchester

1919   'Dance frock of silver lace and rose pink satin $10\frac{1}{2}$ gns.'

                                              Advertisement, quoted Cunnington

1920   'A dinner gown in black charmeuse, with a fish tail train suspended from
          the shoulders behind, and a plaque of jetted beads and diamanté on the
          front of the skirt. This frock clung to the figure, but reached a really decorous
          length on the ankles. . . .'

                                                               Pan, February

'A very charming evening frock for satin and lace. Satin bodice, square cut,
medium deep décolletage, lace sleeves ending above elbow, high waist with sash
and artificial flowers on left hip. Skirt of satin over lace underskirt, the overskirt
draped and caught up to waist on left side, exposing underskirt. Calf length,
narrow at hemline.'

                                     Illustration for paper pattern, December, 1920

FASTENINGS FOR DRESSES

Throughout the decade the primary fastenings were hooks and
eyes or hooks and bars, or hooks and thread loops. Most fastenings
are centre back neck to waist of bodice, and waist to low hips
level for the skirt: occasional centre front or side fastening.

In some cases the opening is mounted with buttons on the
outside of the dress to simulate a buttoned closure.

Bodice linings and skirt linings where present, were separately
fastened, sometimes with 'poppers'.

Occasionally actual buttons, sometimes with loops instead of
button-holes used for fastening, either alone or in combination
with hooks and eyes.

Some skirts are partly detached from bodice at side and back
and secured by 'poppers' or hooks and eyes to bodice.

Patent 'poppers' mounted on heavy satin ribbon were obtainable by the yard and lengths sewn on the edges of the opening.

1912   'Hooks and eyes. Sizes oo to 4
       Black or white per doz pkts. [of 36 pairs each] 9d.
       Plaquet closer or bodice fastener
       Double satin, best spring studs, Black or white 1/1 & 1/3 per yard.'
                                                          Army & Navy Stores

The zip fastener was manufactured in this country from 1919
and was applied to skirts and dresses, but did not gain acceptance
for another ten years or more. It was originally sold as the 'Ready'
fastener.

CLOTHES FOR SPECIAL OCCASIONS

WEDDINGS

1911   'For the ordinary middle-class girl of average means . . . the bridal dress is
       worn as a best evening gown afterwards.'
                                          The Woman's Book, J. C. & E. C. Jack

Wedding dresses followed the lines of gowns of the day. Juliet
caps with veils hanging down behind c. 1910. The war caused
many brides to marry in travelling dresses. In 1916 when a
wedding dress was worn the veil often formed the train.

1915   White silk net over chiffon foundation, with bodice of white velvet and
       bands of white velvet on skirt. Upper part of bodice, shoulders and sleeves
       of silver embroidered net. Purple artificial clematis at bosom.
                                                             London Museum

1920   White satin dress, length just above ankles, tunic falling in long points
       from waist to hem, ending in tassels. V-neck, short wide oversleeves, tight
       under sleeves ending in wide lace cuffs. White embroidery on bodice. White
       stockings and court shoes with pointed tongue. Veil and orange blossom
       wreath worn rather far forward on head.
                                                          Private photograph

MOURNING

Period of mourning considerably lessened as result of the Great
War.

1912   'Black crepe (Courtauld's) showerproof, 3/9–8/6 per yd.'
                                                          Army & Navy Stores

1916 'Mourning orders tastefully and expeditiously executed'.
          J. W. Caley & Co. Ltd. Silk Mercers & Shawlmen, Norwich

COURT DRESSES

The rules quoted in Chapter One still applied. Court dresses followed the fashionable line. Trains from waist or shoulders or neckline of back décolletage. A number of splendid specimens survive from the Coronation Courts of 1911.

WAR WORK

The increasing number of women employed in all occupations during the years 1914–18 greatly loosened many conventions about dress. Although in 1916 it was said that the tailor-made was 'carrying all before it' because 'nowadays most girls are working', many working girls had by then adopted breeches or trousers. Not only the Land Army girls, but also female shipyard workers, window-cleaners, munition workers and stokers were seen in a working garb including these male garments.

In 1916 a Sunlight Soap advertisement showed a picture of a woman worker at Port Sunlight dressed in a 'becoming and workman-like costume'. This was a single-breasted linen coat coming to below the knees with a belt, two patch pockets and a turn-over collar, worn with trousers.

Varieties of mob-caps were the most popular headgear for indoor and outdoor work.

1916 '"Clyde" Munition Coat, an ideal coverall for war workers. Useful also for garage, factory, warehouse, etc. Price 7/6'.
                                                              Advertisement

SPORTS CLOTHES

TENNIS

1912: Princess dress, straight skirt, ankle length, three-quarter sleeves, high neck, in washing fabric. Embroidered by hand on bodice, cuffs, and in a panel ascending the front of the skirt.

43(a). 1916   Ride-astride habit. Knee-length coat over breeches. Boots, round soft felt hat.

43(b). 1914–1918   Girl in industrial war work. Long overall coat and trousers. 'Mob' cap.

1916: White blouse and skirt or dress. Wide turn-down collar and V neck, black scarf or tie; hair held back by pink ribbon.

RIDING

Apron skirts worn over breeches. When dismounted the rider's legs could be seen from the back: some were made to button round to obviate this. For riding astride, divided skirts; or long coats to the ankles over breeches. By 1920 jacket and breeches, with no skirt, were pictured in the fashion magazines, if not actually worn by many in public.

MOTORING

Less protective clothing was needed by passengers in the motors of
the second decade of the century. However leather and fur or
fur-lined motor coats, silk or holland, etc. dustcoats, and veils and
goggles were still worn in open touring cars.

1912   'Motor coats in various new shapes, lined with check cloth or grey and
       white squirrel, in nutria, musquash, etc. from £7. 12. 6. to £45'.
                                                           Army & Navy Stores

       'Smart silk motor scarves 2/11½'.
                                                           Horwood's, Colchester

GOLF, SHOOTING, etc.

Little change from last decade. Cardigans and knitted jerseys for
golf; cardigans for shooting. Norfolk jackets. Skirts some inches
above ground, often leather bound at the hem. Some tweed suits
with belted jackets and worn with mannish collar and tie in 1914.

BICYCLING

Cycling skirts in 1911 with an inverted pleat down the centre of
the back.

SPORTS COATS (see also p. 76)

A general fashion appearing about 1912 was for machine or
hand-knitted 'sports coats'.
     These originally seem to have been of close-fitting cardigan
design, but by 1916–17 were looser, hip length, and with a sash
belt or a buckled belt. Large side pockets and flat collars with
wide lapels, or revers turning back from neck to hem. Some
buttoned, others closed by belt only.
     Apparently for wear over a blouse and skirt, or, it is noted in
1915, made of striped crêpe de Chine and worn with a linen suit
in the summer. These coats were popular during the war years,
and were not confined to athletic activities.
     Increasingly knitted of artificial silk yarn from 1914 when wool

became progressively scarcer and dearer. By 1920 complete 'jersey suits in artificial silk' are advertised.

1912 'Knitted sports coats in white, saxe, blue, navy, grey @ 21/-.'

A. & E. Baker, Colchester

1916 'Artificial silk sports coats 18/11–35/6'.

Ibid.

1918–20 A sports coat knitted in brown and fawn wool and artificial silk. Hip length, body is brown and fawn check effect. Tie belt, cuffs to long close sleeves, pockets, and turn back revers from neck to hem, all in fawn.

Gallery of English Costume, Manchester

OUTDOOR CLOTHES

In the years 1911–14 coats are long, close fitting to give little width: some wrapping over to fasten with a single button at waist level on the left side, with long rolling collars. Some were single or double breasted, front buttoning with deep revers and with or without half belts at the back. Many 'dressy' cloth coats were heavily embroidered and braided on collar and revers, cuffs, and sometimes the upper part of the body. Silk and satin summer coats, braided, embroidered, or trimmed with lace. Winter coats lined or half lined. Tweed and cloth travelling coats, fur lined. Long fur coats with one button at the left waist, or buttoning centre front with long rolling collars or square deep lapels. Some cloak-like mantles with deep collars, or falling in a point at the front, trimmed with deep fringe. Some long, close-fitting, double-breasted knitted wool coats. Coat-like evening wraps gathered in at the back of the knees, and short, hip-length opera cloaks of brocade.

In 1914 a looser, shorter, country coat, single breasted, four buttons, patch pockets, collar with lapels, and cuffs. Short capes and long cloaks slung from the shoulders; for evening wear, long cloaks.

In 1915 a full-back style, all round belts and outside pockets: Raglan short sac, swing back, cross-over draped front, long tight sleeves, fur cuffs and collar or tie.

44. *1912   Coat in black peau de soi trimmed with silk cord, fringe and braid. Long roll collar. Silk lined. £3. 9. 6.*

45. *1912   Coat in dyed musquash. Deep collar with large square revers. Satin lined. £25. 18. 0.*

46. 1916   Coat in seal skin. Very
full flared back. Deep collar and cuffs.

The coats of 1916 were shorter with a military flavour. Three
quarter length, some with capes. Very full skirts, with or without
belts, fur trimmed at collar, which was generally high, cuffs, and
hem. Very full fur coats with high rolling collar, or deep turned-
down collar. Double-breasted sacs in 1917, 6 inches above ground.
Fur collars, cuffs, and border of hems still popular in 1918. Some
cuffs are elbow-length and muff-like. Cape and sailor collars and
V necks. Belts; pockets; yokes or pleats from shoulders. Some
three-quarter-length velvet coats trimmed with fur. Cloaks with
contrasted coloured lining. Long coats assuming barrel shape.

The barrel-shaped coats of 1919 were voluminous all wrapping, with added emphasis to the hips given by large outside pockets. Three-quarter coats with lapels and velvet collars.

The three-quarter length was popular in 1920, waisted, with large collars, standing up, or falling as deep square capes at the back. Also longer, looser coats, some in Raglan style. There was much fur trimming.

Evening cloaks with brocaded tissue lining and big fur collars. Short three-quarter-length fur coats with large flat collars.

1911 'Full length tweed coats, fur lined 49/6, usual price 3 gns.'

A. & E. Baker, Colchester

1913 'Coats in blanket cloth, serge, tweed, 14/11 (sale price)'.

Ibid.

1917 'Winter coats from 21/9.
Seal coney coats £4. 10. to 9 gns. (Sale price)'.

Ibid.

1919 'Cosy blanket coats 35/-, 45/-, 63/- (sale price)'.

Horwood's, Colchester

RAINCOATS

Silk oilskin coats. Cashmere, canton, covert, tweed, etc. water-proofs, single- or double-breasted, mostly full length. The Burberry 'combines the body warming powers of an ulster and the distinctive appearance of a smart overcoat for formal occasions'. Fly-front Raglan styles in 1914. In 1916 the trench coat, full cut, belted, with deep collar and revers, pockets and storm cuffs with wrist-straps or elasticated insets to keep out wind and rain, came to just below the knee. Sometimes worn with a sou' wester hat. Military styles prevailed for the rest of the war.

1912 'Very light weight silk oilskins in mole and yellow. Three qualities at 18/-, 38/- & 56/9.
Cravenette. Covert coating, fly front. 30/9, 32/3, 42/-'.

Army & Navy Stores

1915 'Aquatite showerproofs from 23/9'.

Advertisement

1917 'Trenchcoat for ladies in shades of khaki 21/9–35/6'.

A. & E. Baker, Colchester

47. *1912 Raincoat, long single breasted.*

48. *1916 Raincoat, in proofed twill.*

HAIR

Rather wide, low and puffed out over the ears. Some tendency to backward elongations. By 1914 was somewhat less wide, with parting left of centre popular. Loosely waved with 'bun' or coil at the back. Evening styles tended to be higher on the head. By the end of the decade those women in war work who for convenience or safety cut their hair had begun to popularize the 'bob'.

49. 1920 Marcel waved hair.

MILLINERY

Large hats with wide turned-up brim; high toques; tam o'
shanters and berets in 1911 and 1912, made of beaver, plush,
velvet, straw and tagel straw. Trimmed with satin, silk, ribbon,
tulle and feathers, especially osprey and ostrich. Smaller in 1913,
tending to project backwards worn with a sideways or backwards
tilt. Designs gave a hard line around the brow in 1914, with
many brimless hats and high toques, and hats with turned-up
brims. Artificial flowers, feathers, plumes and wings for trimming, also waxed satin ribbon. Tilted to the right side in 1915,
sailor styles and turbans fashionable: veils. Small close hats
in 1916–17: high crowns and narrow brims, or 'Spanish'

50. 1920 Hats.

type flat straws with wide brims. Some tricornes. Ribbons, especially checked, wings, brocade and metal trimmings. Eye-level veils. Fur trimming popular in 1917. Trimming less evident on the semi-toque shaped hats of 1918; also this year flat wide brims pulled down to eyes. Cloth, knitted wool, velour etc. Crowns larger, scuttle or mushroom-shaped in 1919: pulled well down on head: more trimming. Shapes very varied, as also in 1920, when 'you can wear what you like'; e.g. close-fitting with

51. 1920 Hats.

circular feather band, large brims flat or upturned; berets draped over one ear; scarlet kid tammies. All pulled well down to eyes.
Evening. Bandeaux or forehead bands popular throughout period, with or without feathers or plumes. Juliet caps in 1913, sequined turbans in 1919. Silver bands in 1920.

1913   'Millinery – fine real Tagels 6/11'.

H. S. Horwood, Colchester

1914   'Casino chapeau in black velour plush. Real cross-osprey forms sole decoration 11 gns.'

Barkers, Kensington High Street

1914   'A Speciality: Hats and Bonnets for elderly ladies'.

A. & E. Baker, Colchester

1917   'Recherche Millinery, attractive and refined in style'.

Fred Fish, Ipswich

1920 'Picture hat of straw with fringed edge, trimmed wide ribbon velvet and
      finished velvet berries to match. In fuchsia, copper, royal, seal brown, or
      carnation, 5½ gns.'

                                        Dickens & Jones Ltd. Regent Street

FOOTWEAR

As previously. Brogues with fringed tongues in 1917. Shorter
skirts called for higher lacing boots, some with cloth tops, such
as the side lacing fawn cloth and patent leather 'Russian' boots
of 1915. Cromwell and court shoes with buckles. More coloured
leather, suede and satin for day. Court shoes with cross-gartering
ankle straps or strings. Evening shoes with embroidered heels:
large paste buckles (1919). Boots simulating court shoes and
gaiters. Gaiters and spats.

1914 Glacé kid court shoes, black, 2″ Louis heel, ⅜″ diameter, metal and paste
      rose decorating centre front.

                                                  Northampton Museum

1915 Dri-Ped super leather for soles.
      [A patent treated leather, with a green finish.]

1918 'Good shoes are costly today, take care of those you have, use Wood-Milne
      Rubber Heels'.

                                              Colchester advertisements

STOCKINGS

The most significant event during this decade was the introduction
of artificial silk stockings in 1912. Generally, however, lisle, cotton
wool, etc. stockings as in the previous period, predominated.
Pale coloured silk became fashionable for evening wear in 1913.
Stockings in all colours in 1919, but black usual for day wear.

1912 'Ladies black cotton hose for 1/6 per pair.
      Plain black cashmere for 1/7 per pair.
      White, black, tan and boot-bronze lisle for 1/5 per pair.
      Black silk with lace fronts for 8/6 per pair.'

                                                  Army & Navy Stores

1914   'White lisle hose with woollen feet, especially for tennis 1/11¾ per pair'.

1917   'All wool cashmere hose, slightly imperfect, 1/4¾ per pair'.

1919   'Ladies coloured hose, very smart, exceptional value 1/11½. Also a big lot of Black and Coloured Artificial Silk Hose 2/6 per pair. These are very much below today's prices'.

Advertisements, Colchester traders

ACCESSORIES

GLOVES

Long or short kid, suede, silk, etc. Two, three or four buttons for day. Up to sixteen or twenty for evening in black or white kid. Evening gloves worn very wrinkled in 1914. Washable gloves popular 1918. In 1919 it was remarked that 'the swing of fashion's pendulum seems to be tending once more in favour of gloves for evening wear'. Lined gloves and knitted woollen

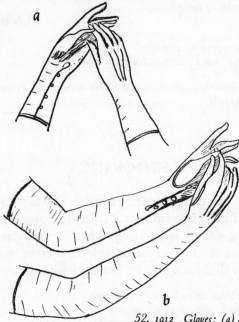

52. 1912 Gloves: (a) Short suede four buttons. 4/3d. (b) Long white kid evening gloves three buttons. 5/6d. and 7/9d.

for winter. Black and white lace mittens. Some gauntlets – embroidered ones fashionable 1918.

1912 '2 button Black French Suede 2/11 per pair.
16 button suede, grey, beaver or pastel, 7/6 per pair'.

Army & Navy Stores

1917 'Canadian Gloves . . . of a thumb and a bag for the fingers. They will be found very comfortable to draw over the hands when walking in the garden on a windy day and also for wearing over kid gloves in very cold weather or when travelling'. [Knitted]

Weldon's Practical Knitter

HANDBAGS

Leather on metal frame, leather handles; chatelaine bags in leather or velvet with hook to suspend from waist belt. Safety underskirt bags on belt to fasten round waist. Dorothy bags. Shoulder purses and bags on long cords. Silver chain bags. Soft bags of textiles, crochet, etc. especially for summer, by 1920. Some with angled sides sloping to top and pointed at bottom.

HANDKERCHIEFS

1916 'Handkerchiefs in fancy boxes 6¾d. to 5/11½ with initials 2¾d. to 6¾d. each.
With fancy borders 2¾d. to 1/3¼ each.
Embroidered and hemstitched 3¾d. to 1/11¾ each.
Khaki for troops 2¾d. to 1/0¾ each'.

Walter Hunt, Colchester

MUFFS, STOLES AND BOAS, etc.

Fashionable throughout period in various furs. Long, wide and flat stoles in 1914. Large barrel or round muffs. Animal-shaped fur stoles from 1917. Muff and stole in sets. Feather necklets and boas.

1912 'Russian sable stoles £39 to £350; muffs £25 to £250.
Fox stole and muff sets – muff displaying tails and mask, £14. 3. 0.
Long feather boa 17/6; 36" necklet with new tassel ends, 11/6'.

Army & Navy Stores

G

53. *1912   Ermine stole and muff. £31. 19. 6.*

1917   'Feather necklets and boas, sale price, 3/11 to 12/11'.

Horwood's, Colchester

1920   'Real fur sets at half-price. Tango wrap with head and four tails. Large fur muff to match with head and three tails. 16/- plus 1/- postage'.

The Leed's Bargain Co.

RUFFLES, COLLARS etc.

Tulle ruffles 1913. Lawn etc. collars and jabots. Tulle scarves for evening 1915 and 1916. Some revival of ruffles in 1920. Silk scarves: gauze and chiffon scarves for evening wear.

UMBRELLAS AND PARASOLS

Length as previous period but are much plainer: some revival of
Japanese paper sunshades. The 'en-tout-cas' for sun or rain.

FANS

Folding, for evening wear. Unfashionable by 1914. Revival of
large ostrich-feather fans in 1919.

JEWELLERY

Much as in previous decade. A certain Oriental influence
apparent in some items. Jewelled anklets from about 1916. Snake
bangles. Eternity rings and diamonds clustering around a central
coloured gem popular during war years. A revival of jet is noted
in the *Daily Mail* in 1915.

MATERIALS

In addition to those previously mentioned the following are
specifically noted. Some are new, some, of course, were also well
known in earlier periods.

Artificial silk (including Courtauld's 'Luvisca' from 1915),
blanket cloth, crepon (a woollen material), drill, duck, gaberdine,
georgette (new 1914), knitted fabrics (including jersey), shantung,
zephyr.

COLOURS

In opening year of decade colours are strong, with no pastel tints.
Examples are: emerald, cerise, saxe-blue, mauve, sulphur yellow,
in 1912 and 1913.

Later, primrose, grey, tan, camel, sky-blue, champagne, putty.

Also purple, navy, brown, pink, and of course black, white
and mauve.

1920-1930

INTRODUCTORY REMARKS

The post-war decade of 1920–30 was one of fashions based upon youth. The war had been the end of many conventions and ideas, and, as far as this country went, had upset the normal balance of the sexes.[1] The deaths of so many young men in Flanders, and a score of lesser battlefields, had produced a psychological glorification of male youth. To quote Willett Cunnington, 'young women sought by every physical means to obliterate their feminine outline and assume that of the immature male'.[2]

From 1921 economic troubles of a seemingly uncontrollable kind prevailed throughout the world, in Britain causing declining exports and rising unemployment. For men contemplating marriage such conditions discouraged thoughts of raising a family, and the anti-maternal schoolboy-shaped girl became his ideal. To appeal to such tastes the girl of the period flattened her breasts and bottom and disguised her waist.

The war and its aftermath had brought disillusionment to young and old alike; the younger generation determined to start a fresh world and gain social dominance in a way that they had never before achieved, whilst the older generations tended to ignore the immediate past and the unpleasant present and to hope for an economic recovery in the near future. From 1924 to 1928 there was indeed a slight but steady improvement with export and employment figures both showing a happier trend, despite the abortive General Strike of 1926.

It was perhaps this small measure of economic improvement,

[1] Newspapers in 1920 spoke of 'A million surplus women'.
[2] *English Women's Clothing in the Present Century.*

allied to the receding memories of the war, that caused the change in fashion which appeared at first in 1925, when women's clothes, especially for evening wear, began to acquire a more feminine line, while still keeping to the idea of extreme youthfulness. Skirts of evening dresses began to acquire flare and flounces, although remaining very short. In 1928 and 1929 the skirts were becoming longer, with eccentric, uneven hems. In this latter year the great world Depression was first felt in America, bringing economic and political disaster to all the world, and unrest and war spread over the globe. By 1930 the post-war youthfulness and its dreams which had so gallantly struggled on for ten years and more were both fading, and the feminine ideal was once again entering into an age of womanliness and maturity, perhaps as a reversionary symbol of comfort, and hope for a continuing future.

Lesser occurrences during the decade were, in 1922, the discovery of the tomb of Tutankhamen, with a consequent affect of Egyptian influence in design, and in 1924 and 1925 the Empire Exhibition at Wembley, adding to the Oriental influences of the deceased Pharaoh and of Bakst.

The cinema also played its part, not so much in affecting the clothes, but in spreading the cult of facial make-up, based upon the faces of the popular stars.

In accepting the importance of Youth during these years one may be apt to overlook the residue of Edwardian, and even Victorian, attitudes that lingered on. Up to the 1930's it was not uncommon to see elderly ladies, especially of the poorer classes, wearing the mantles and bonnets of the 1890's.

Technically the growing importance of artificial silk was allied to an increasing output of ready-to-wear clothes of all kinds. In 1924 the name 'rayon' was adopted in place of 'artificial silk'.

The zip fastener, developed in the United States, appears to have been first used on clothing by the U.S. Navy in 1918. In 1923 this fastener was being employed on rubber boots, and in 1925 it was to be found on leather 'Russian' boots in this country.

A notable feature of the decade was the great increase in the number of knitted garments: jumpers, dresses and two-piece costumes, both home-made and commercially produced.

*54. 1921 Summer day dress of
voile with Magyar sleeves.*

55. 1925 Woollen day dress embroidered single lapel and tie sash belt.

DAY DRESSES

The one-piece design predominated, the separate bodice and skirt version now being mainly represented by blouse or jumper and skirt, or by the jumper suit or by the afternoon silk gown with matching jacket or coatee.

SKIRTS

Waistlines were somewhat lower in 1921, and the skirts longer and wider than in previous years, but by 1923 they were eight inches from the ground for walking and slightly longer for afternoon frocks. Apron tunics and overskirts, some with scalloped hems, or with side points. Centre or side panels; accordian pleats; net insertions for afternoon wear, when fur edging to hem was also fashionable. Tunic effects were narrower in 1924, day dresses had plain straight simple lines and skirts were shortening. Some tunic dresses were in the form of a bodice extended to the knees, opening back or front over a sheath skirt. Single flounced tunics also. The waist line was non-existent, or at the top of the hips, sinking the next year (1925) to low on the hips, often marked by a belt or band. Godets at front or sides or both to give fulness. Hemlines uneven by scalloping etc. or decorated by band of vertical ruching. Skirts of afternoon frocks provided a 'fluttering motion'.

During 1926 and 1927 skirts rose from fourteen to sixteen inches above ground level, in the latter year underskirts ascended

56. 1928 Day dresses: (a) Cashmere stockinette. (b) Silk taffeta. (c) Silk georgette. All 30/-.

to eighteen inches, with hanging over-drapery, some as handkerchiefs from waist. Pleats, flares, scallops, petal effects, panels and
ruffled effects. Afternoon frocks with deep fringe trimming or
lace pieces falling to uneven hem. In 1927 evidence of circular
and bias cuts to produce flare; and pleating, tiering or gathering
on left-hand side. Bows on the hip in afternoon dresses. Seven-
eighths or full-length matching coats.

Left-handed tendency in decoration and construction still
noticeable in 1928, with knee-length skirts, many with yokes.
Afternoon dresses in 1929 showed more flare from midway
between hips and knees, many hip yokes, and uneven hems.
Diagonal flared flounces, gathered panels, often falling below the
hemline, sometimes pointed giving 'handkerchief' effect. The
waist line begins to rise and skirts are slightly longer.

The rising waist line and lengthening skirt continues in 1930,
when the afternoon dress fell to eight inches below the knee;
walking skirts covered the knee. Skirts close fitting around hips,
some circular and in two tiers. Pleats, many one-sided, some cut
into narrow panels. Godets, scalloped or blunt-pointed. Intricate
cutting below thighs to produce flare and fulness.

BODICES

U or V necks, or round or square or boat-shaped throughout
decade. In 1921 some high, close collars, also deep V with vest
or fill-in. Generally round or square neck lines predominated until
about 1927 when the V in varying degrees of depth became the
more fashionable, often with a handkerchief or scarf knotted at
the base in front.

Round necks sometimes with Peter Pan or larger flat round or
pointed collars: some Medici collars still in 1921 and 1922. V
necks with revers, sometimes square ended.

The bodice basically was straight and shapeless, more or less
elaborately decorated. Some cross-over designs; yokes popular in
1927. 1927 and 1928 waist line was becoming more defined; in
1929 a blouse effect is observable, and a more mature shape is
beginning to emerge; breasts are acknowledged, if only by

57. *1929 Day dresses: (a) Art silk crêpe with new hip yoke in navy,
royal, emerald, cocoa. 29/11d. (b) Plain flared skirt. Suede crêpe.*

bosom friends. The later years of the decade see more drapery,
often one-sided; matching coats and coatees; capes and cape back
effects; long open tunics over close-fitting slips.

SLEEVES

Either long and close fitting or none in general. Some Magyar in
1921. Bell-shaped openings 1926 and 1930. Some short to elbow

or above, especially in 1924 and 1925, often with cuffs. Puffed to wrist and then tight, 1926. Cuffs, often decorated with buttons or drapery etc. on long tight sleeves, 1928. Many afternoon and summer sleeveless.

FASTENINGS

Hooks and eyes, press studs or buttons, but the simple slip-on dress with no fasteners increasing in number.

COAT FROCKS

Lose their importance as the decade advances. Made in repps, serge, heavy silk etc. Often wrap-over fastening left side, sometimes button-through centre front. Patch pockets. Square or round necks, some with collars or stole-ends; or deep V with fill-in. From 1923 cut in two parts with waist seam, bodice often pouched on to skirt. Belt covering waist seam in 1924: patent leather belts 1926.

TEAGOWNS, etc.

Merging with the formal afternoon dress and also with the semi-evening dress, thé-dansant frock, etc. Of flimsy materials over silk or satin foundation slip. Ninon, georgette, lace, etc. Some with velvet incorporated: some fur trimmed. Elbow sleeves or sleeveless, or long frilly sleeves (1929) or sleeveless with matching coat. Cross-over bodices, V necks with jabots. Long sashes continuing on ground as trains (1921), Apache scarfs around neck 1924. Skirts often pleated, sometimes elaborate with panniers, vandyked hems, trains, etc.

PATTERNS

On materials were stylized and geometric, or with Oriental undertones in design and colour. In 1922 *Punch* cartoons Russian effects in fashion. Floral patterns more popular after 1927–28.

Stripes and checks, particularly in earlier years. Embroidery and bead embroidery. Geometric patterns showing left handed eccentricity.

EXAMPLES

1921   'Coat-frocks in super botany coating. Design stitched in contrasting shades.'

Horwood, Colchester

'Ready-to-wear cotton frocks from 12/6'.

Advertisement

1923   Elegant black georgette gown, shapeless, with gathered side panels attached at waist only and turned up under hem at bottom of skirt. Sleeves long and slit from elbow to wrist, where they are attached to a jet bead wrist-band. Decorated all over in geometric pattern of black bugles and small round and square composition plaques set in star formation.

London Museum

'Hand-beaded silk stockinette gowns, 2½ gns. upwards'.

A. & E. Baker, Colchester

1926–7   Picture dress in blue/white shot taffeta. low scalloped waist line, plain boat-shaped neck, sleeveless, side and waist seams piped gold cord. Skirt with lower half decorated gold machine-made lace with scalloped hem with gold painted on green silk leaves and padded gold painted berries. Top half of skirt with very large roses of violet shot silk, outlined in gold, over each thigh.

London Museum

1928   Straight, shapeless dress of plaid material. Knee length. Sleeves, wide round turn-down collar and 'shirt-front' effect plastron all of a plain contrasting material. Band low round hips and small pocket above on right side of same plain material. Long tie from front of collar of matching plaid.

Private photograph

'Frock in artificial silk and wool marocain. Crêpe-de-chine vest, deep revers, and pleated skirt. 39/6'.

Harrods Ltd.

SUITS, COSTUMES, COATS AND SKIRTS

COATS

1921 long and straight, pointed lapels, side pockets. Sailor collars; high collars. Some knee-length or three-quarter-length coats; flared basques. Narrow lapels and waistcoats in 1922, some single-breasted coats with link fastening. Also sac style with high collars. Belts worn low in 1923. Coats with flounces on hip, or caught in above hip; low revers, two buttons, 1924. Wrap-over style with waistcoats, or double-breasted three-quarter-length in 1925. Buttons on sleeves or cuffs generally during these years.

1926 long coats worn over complete matching dress; also short or medium coats, some with double-breasted waistcoats of fancy material. Suits with matching colour overcoat of heavier material in 1927: three quarter coats and waistcoats. Link fronts resembling contemporary men's dinner jackets. Coats, short or long, in 1929 fit slightly at waist and flare at hips. Full-length or three-quarter coats in tweed suits, or short tailored jacket bloused over belt and buttoned below it, in 1930. Four-piece ensemble of suit, matching overcoat and jumper.

SKIRTS

Plain or with panel in 1921: straight or fluted: some hip yokes. Pleats, side panels and kilting in 1922, when skirts are eight inches off ground. Feature of 1923 was inverted pleats at sides. Skirts gathered on to petersham band or occasionally supported by braces of costume material. Two piece, wrap-over, and waterfall skirts with drapery on left hip in 1924: ten to twelve inches off ground. Until about 1924 checked or striped skirts with plain coats very fashionable. Wrap-over buttoning down left side in 1925. Skirts on jap silk bodices. Open pleats and knife pleats in 1926 and 1927: skirts rise to fifteen or sixteen inches off ground. Flare and open pleats in 'sports' skirts of 1928. By 1930 longer, thirteen or fourteen inches from ground, with alternate straight and flared panels, or with fulness in centre front. Close fitting at hips. Pleats. Wrap-over with yoke and leather belt.

58. 1925 Suit.

59. 1927   Suit, check tweed, long waisted jacket, low belt

JUMPER SUITS

Consisted of skirt and jumper in cotton, jersey, crêpe, satin, etc. Or stockinette or knitted jumpers and cloth skirt or stockinette skirt. In 1926 the jumper was often attached to the skirt. Pleated skirts popular. Some jumpers with belts; most coming down over hips, but by 1930 they were shorter. A typical suit of 1930 was of light-weight wool mixture knitwear, pleated skirt, long-sleeved jumper with decorative bordered V neck, hip-length sleeveless coat with ribbed hem line to give a close fit.

*61. 1929   Three-piece
suit of cashmere knitwear.*

*60. 1930   Suit tailored in fine worsted lined with
rayon; double breasted with low rolling lapels.*

EXAMPLES

1921 'Ladies spring costumes, indigo blue serge. Perfectly tailored 7 gns.'

Owen Ward, Colchester

c. 1925 Blue wool cloth coat and skirt. Coat loose with gathers over hips.
Turn-down collar with revers extending to bottom edge. The front, at
waist level, is trimmed with natural suede strap, with rosettes and fringed
tassels. Plain suede band on front of cuffs.

London Museum

1926   '(Suits) will vary by hardly an inch in length or breadth from year to year. Some coats are single breasted, others fasten with a double set of buttons, or again, the link may be substituted . . . but on one and all the straight line is to be found. . . . Tweed suits, once supposed only to be worn in the country, have been adopted with whole-hearted fervour by the Parisian, and today you may be seen walking down Bond Street in a tweed suit. . . .'

How to Dress, Lady Angela Forbes, Thornton Butterworth, 1926

1927   'Dainty suits in fashionable single and double-breasted styles. Many with half belts: excellently tailored and good linings. The neat waisted skirts in most cases introduce pleats or a combination of pleats. From 37/6'.

A. J. Lucking & Co. Ltd. Colchester

1929   Advertisement for 'novelty garments' – three-piece suits of charmalain skirt and sleeveless coatee and silk and wool mixture stockinette jumper of contrasting shades.

62. *1921 Silk blouse, coloured and white stripes.*

63. *1923 Muslin blouse with large turn-down collar, and a ratine skirt.*

BLOUSES

Short, tucked in skirt waistband; or longer and worn over skirt. Short blouses with drawstring or elastic at waist. Long styles sometimes with belts, or in form of coats, e.g. 'Mandarin' coats of 1922–24. Long, straight, tunic blouses: often sleeveless and worn over dress or an underblouse.

Blouses mostly front fastening by buttons. Necks usually V or round, with or without collars. Fasten high or with stand-up collars at back 1921–22. Scarf or tie knotted at base of V: scarf collars in 1929.

Long sleeves, bell or bishop popular in 1922: or short sleeves or sleeveless, especially for summer wear.

Yokes of contrasting colours, 1930.

1921 'Cotton georgette blouses and jumpers from 10/11'.
                                              A. & E. Baker, Colchester

1925 'Blouse-jumpers in crêpe-de-chine 55/9'.
                                                           Cunnington

JUMPERS AND KNITWEAR

Although the jumper is any loose-fitting garment reaching to the waist or hips and donned by slipping over the head, as the century progresses the name is increasingly applied to knitted or crocheted wool or silk or man-made fibres. Worn with a matching or contrasting skirt as country, sports and informal day wear; or worn with a two-piece tailored suit in place of a blouse.

The popularity of domestic knitting and crochet during the Great War and the increased production of artificial silk yarn gave an impetus to home-made knitted garments of all types – jumpers, cardigan-jackets and dresses in particular.

Waist-length jumpers and blouse-jumpers, loose, in knitting and crochet or in material, e.g. marocain. Some with belts, or caught in at the sides with ties etc. in plain colours, or bright bold designs for holiday wear; V, round, or square necks; elbow sleeves, or some Magyar sleeves in material (1921–22). Straight, knitted dresses and suits in wool and artificial silk; suits, machine knitted stockinette with long jackets and tie belt, or of wool and artificial silk mixture. Silk sweaters for sports wear. Fair Isle patterns (1923–24). Sleeveless jerseys worn over blouse and skirt: jumper and cardigan worn with matching tweed top coat and

64. 1923 Crêpe de Chine sailor or
middy jumper.

65. 1923 Cross-over jumper with
Magyar sleeves, knitted in Celanese.

skirt as a 'four piece': wool sweaters in place of blouses for country wear (1926–27). In 1928 the fashion journals noted the popularity of jumpers and skirts for morning wear: many with cross-over fronts and one-sided patterns. Longer jumpers in 1928 were followed by longer cardigans in 1929. Short jumpers worn with coat and skirt in 1930, also a sleeveless version in a 'woolly sort of lace' over a dress. Matching cardigans and jumpers – later known as 'twin sets'. Knitted coats and skirts with a tweed-like effect.

H

EXAMPLES

1922   'Crochet stitch jumpers in check design of two colours in Sylko. V neck,
       elbow sleeves. Worn pouched over a crocheted girdle'.

                                                 Pattern in *Woman's Weekly*

c. 1920–22   Crochet dress: very slightly waisted; ankle length; Magyar sleeves to
       elbow; square neck; silk cord draw string at waist. Made in Khaki
       wool with terra cotta and black wool stripes at waist, neck and over
       both shoulders, down back and front, to waist.

                                                 Stranger's Hall Museum, Norwich

1929   'Three piece knitted suit in soft wool: tweed herring-bone pattern, with
       plain colour border, cuffs to jumper and pocket edges of jacket. V neck
       long sleeved jumper and sleeveless coat. Skirt pleated all round.'

                                                 Debenham & Freebody, quoted Cunnington

TROUSERS

Trousers appear in this decade for sport, leisure and evening wear.
The harem skirt of pre-war days did not achieve success. There is
a hybrid garment in Northampton Museum, a sack-like dress of
gold lamé, made up of a single length of material open at the top,
which is elasticated and with cord shoulder straps, and closed at
the skirt hem, with two leg holes in the side-seams. It dates from
about 1912–20.

Pyjamas and Turkish trouser suits of brocade etc. for evening
wear (albeit only in one's own home) are mentioned in 1926.
A black and white check suit of knitted jacket and plus-fours
(loose knickerbockers) was featured at the Drapery Exhibition of
1927, but did not establish a precedent. Man-like trousers with
turnups, and worn with a wide sash with dangling ends were
seen on the tennis court in 1928. Beach pyjamas with wide
trousers and a sleeveless bolero worn over a blouse, and a 'smoking
suit' of jumper, coatee and trousers flared from the knee, all in
crêpe de Chine, are described in 1930.

SKIRTS

Worn with blouse or jumper and in general follow line of costume skirt.

In 1921 were longer and wider than the previous year: some with side panels, some hip-yokes. Suede skirts for wear in the country.

Eight inches from the ground in 1922, but a little longer in the summer: panels and pleats. Checked and striped materials very popular.

Novelty of 1923 – inverted pleats at sides. In 1924 knowledgeable Mr. Punch notes that skirts are ten to twelve inches from the ground and they are getting shorter. In 1925 and 1926 they are still ascending reaching the knee in the latter year: pleats, godets and flare increasing. Front pleats and flares, and straight backs and an average of sixteen to seventeen inches from hem to ground in 1927 and 1928. Fashion was decreeing more length in 1929 but there seems little evidence that, in fact, most day skirts were any longer. But flat pleats gave greater width: flare was kept low down and yokes were popular. In 1930 the skirt was definitely longer, close fitting down to the knee, with yokes, pleats and flare. Fulness was centred at the front. Walking skirts made of alternate straight and flared panels.

1927 'All wool repp and gaberdine dress skirts 8/11. Sale price.'

Piper's Ltd. Colchester

EVENING DRESSES

Evening dresses of the decade were generally characterized by straight skirts with over drapery and many uneven hems, and plain, straight bodices, sleeveless, with deep V décolletage back and front, or with shoulder straps. From 1922 to 1928 one-sided effects were noticeable both in skirts and bodices. Low waist lines and short skirts predominated during the middle years – skirts lengthening and getting fuller and waists rising from 1929. An attempted crinoline revival in 1920–22 did not succeed. Trouser suits and pyjamas in velvet or metal tissues for evening wear were an innovation of this decade and reflected the fashionable Orientalism. Bead embroidery very popular: many short, heavily beaded dresses of 1925–26 survive.

SKIRTS

Long pointed side panels, or petalled or vandyked overskirts; length to top of ankle or to instep, waist line lower than previously (1921). Drapery on one hip, uneven hem line, sashes with bow in front (1922); frilled skirts of taffeta, lace skirts, side draperies and higher waist line in 1923. Slim and flat silhouette, slightly draped in front in 1924; tunics hanging straight from shoulders; side panels; waistless, low hip line; wide hem with puffing: scalloped uneven lace skirts; beaded dance frocks; metal tissue on embroidery side panels (1924). Skirts slanting to one side or cut in points as shorter in front than behind in 1925: some tight to thighs, then fuller; length to just below turn of the knee; open tunics over slip; dance frocks with godet pleats from waist; flowers or bows on left hip; long fringe trimming; uneven and transparent hems (1925 and 1926). Ornaments at centre front below waist; hip yokes, low at back; back or sides longer than front; large bow or bunched drapery on one hip still popular; tiered skirts (1927 and 1928). Longer skirts with suggestion of natural waist line in 1929; short and straight in front, longer and flared behind. In 1930 'long legged look' with higher waist; yokes; frills below hips; upward or downward points at waist in front. Skirts or panels longer, more even hems. Skirts of 'Empire' dresses in two or three tiers: frills. Skirts to ankle for dancing, otherwise touching the ground.

BODICES

Straight and shapeless; low, square or cross-over V or U necklines, with low décolletage or high, oval neck: sleeveless, some diamanté shoulder straps or with long sleeves, wide or wing-like, many transparent. Large armholes. Fur edging to neck and sleeves.

66. *1922   Evening dress of gold embroidered corded taffeta over gold lace underskirt. Pannier effect obtained by wire at hips.*

67. *1927   Evening dress red chiffon velvet and silk fringe. 14 gns.*

68 (a). 1928   *Black chiffon and lace evening dress with underslip.*
68 (b). 1929   *Wedding dress of lace with a tiered skirt.*

Sashes over shoulder tied on hip with ends forming side-train,
or round hips and tied in a bow at side or in front (1921 and
1922). Egyptian and Oriental effects in embroidery, patterns and
colours in 1923 with wide cape-collar or capes from back shoulders: round or square necks or deep Vs with an underslip. Low
décolletage front and back, but in 1924 some dresses higher in
front. Big armholes or deep U openings at sides. Sleeves absent,
but optional in tea-dance frocks. Dinner dresses with small square
train from waist. Bead and thread embroidery; scarves to float
from back; draped sashes; low broad girdle swathing hips (1925).
From 1926 pouching or blousing is evident in some bodices.
Neck lines still with deep V or U at front and back, or high in

front with V décolletage deep at back, or diagonal décolletage. Sleeveless. One sided effects very noticeable in 1927 and 1928 with bow on one hip, or drapery bunched or massed on one side; flared basques in 1928.

In 1929 the dress fits the figure down to the thighs, midway between hips and knees, thence the skirt has more width; deep décolletage at back in some cases reaching to waist, which is now higher. 'Empire dress' in 1930 with short waist, slightly bloused bodice, frilled neck line and tucked shoulder straps giving a draped effect. Or short bloused bodice, pouched more at back than in front, belt at waist level, frills around shoulders and on berthas and fichus; frilled décolletage at back; bows at waist or bottom of décolletage at back.

EXAMPLES

1923   'Tinsel brocade, plain bodice, slightly trained skirt, deep swathed belt and large bow at side. 6 gns.
       Evening gown with Egyptian girdle, the ends hanging down nearly to the ground; train draped to left side'.

                                                    Advertisement, quoted Cunnington

1925–26 Silver lamé evening dress, lined natural silk. Decorated with multi-coloured ribbon rosettes on thighs, bottom, and centre front below waist.

                                                                London Museum

1926   'We have pyjamas and smoking coats presented to us by most of the big dress-makers . . . [of] . . . velvet or tinsel tissue. For those of less advanced ideas the smoking suit is represented by a loosely fitting jacket and skirt, in one or other of these materials, and for the little dinner it is an ideal garment . . . but the Turkish trouser suits are really intended to be worn in the sanctity of one's own room, although full-length coats can at an emergency be slipped over them and worn for more occasions with decorum. Certainly such clothes are in keeping with the shingled heads'.

                                                    How to Dress, Lady Angela Forbes

1927   'Evening and afternoon frocks. Delicate shades in crepe-de-chine, taffeta, satin, and marocain, reduced from 45/- to 15/-'.

                                                                Joys, Colchester

1929   Evening dress of dark blue watered silk over blue georgette and beige crêpe underskirt. The skirt has cross-cut panels draped diagonally from back and each hip to touch the ground: hem generally mid-calf, front section cut into downwards-point, echoed by diamenté V trimming at waist, and low V décolletage and separate V collar joining shoulder straps.

Platt Hall, Manchester

CLOTHES FOR SPECIAL OCCASIONS

COURT DRESSES

Previous rules applied; skirts of fashionable shortness were permitted, but with a train from the shoulders.

WEDDINGS

Long dresses retained their popularity throughout the period, but short skirts and skirts with uneven short-and-long hem lines also appeared. Generally long sleeves. Trains. Short or long veils, the latter sometimes trailing on the ground to substitute for a train. White generally the favourite, but pink, or gold and silver cloths and also coloured linings to the train were acceptable. Pearl and diamenté embroidery. (Fig. 68b)

Juliet caps, or coronet-style headdresses, or plain chaplets of orange blossom.

MATERNITY

Various patent makes of adjustable-size skirts and dresses.

MOURNING

Periods of mourning were substantially shortened and the use of crêpe, even as a trimming, greatly declined. Mauve, violet, etc. more usual than black and white for half mourning.

SPORTS CLOTHES

BATHING

Throughout the decade a tunic and knickers, or a one-piece costume with separate or attached skirt was popular. Length of skirt or knickers varied from knee in 1921 to upper thigh by the last years. One piece 'regulation' costumes with no skirt were also worn. Fashionable from about 1928 'American' style costumes of separate trunks and tops – the tops often of horizontal stripes. One-piece costumes patterned with spots or abstract designs in

70. 1926 Bathing costume, one piece with cross-over bodice trimmed with braid, and concealed short drawers.

69. 1921 Stockinette Canadian style bathing costume. Tunic over knee-length drawers. Rubber cap and ribbon fastened sandals.

the closing years. Tunic and skirted styles generally followed the
fashionable waist line with belts or braid trimming.

GOLF

Tweed skirts, shirts and ties, cardigans or Fair Isle jerseys. Blouses
with sleeveless overblouse of jersey material. Capes with arm slits
(1921), checked wool stockings. From about 1923 cloche hats.

1923 'Crepe rubber soled shoes, recommended for golf, everyday wear, tennis and
      bowls'.

                                   S. Buckingham & Sons, Colchester

TENNIS

'Quaker' style dresses in chintz with white collar and cuffs, or
sponge-cloth with coloured embroidery; paisley pattern jumpers;
blouse and skirt, hair ribbon or cap (1921).

Skirts ten inches from ground in 1924, and just below the knee
in 1925: tennis dress now usually white. Pleated skirts. White
cardigans. 'Lenglen' bandeau (named after the popular Ladies'
Champion) to confine the hair, from about 1924. White stockings
and shoes.

'Helen Wills Peak' (named after another popular Ladies'
Champion), a large eye-shade worn on a band; short pleated
skirts; white trousers with turnups from 1927. Sleeveless white
crêpe de Chine dress with tucked bodice, front of skirt pleated,
two pockets, belt (1930). White stockings and laced or strapped
white shoes.

1921 'White tennis skirts in gaberdine, drill, and piqué. Smart jumpers in voile,
      georgette, pique and drill.'

                                   A. & E. Baker, Colchester

1929 'Tennis frocks in cotton, spun silk, and crepe-de-chine'.

                                                            Ibid.

BICYCLING

Some divided skirts and an attempt to reintroduce knickerbockers.

*71. 1926 Winter sports outfit,
knitted jersey and scarf. Trousers
tucked in boots. Cap and gloves.*

SKATING AND WINTER SPORTS

Long, thigh-length woollen pullover, trousers tucked into thick
socks, boots, woollen gloves and large muffler, peaked cap with
medium height round crown for winter sports (1923).

Skating outfit of short pleated skirt, jumper, boots and cloche
hat (1927).

MOTORING

Leather and imitation leather coats.

1929 'Leatherette motor coats 25/11. Leather motor coats 4 gns.'
                                     Alice Sanders, Colchester

RIDING

The apron-skirted habit, with the back of the skirt cut right away, so as not to catch on the saddle pommels, etc. and covering the legs when mounted: divided skirts or breeches for riding astride. By the middle of the decade breeches and boots, or Jodhpurs were common and the riding habit almost disappeared.

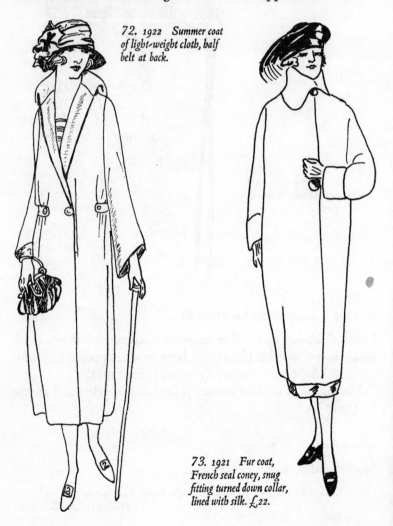

72. 1922 *Summer coat of light-weight cloth, half belt at back.*

73. 1921 *Fur coat, French seal coney, snug fitting turned down collar, lined with silk. £22.*

OUTDOOR CLOTHES

Generally top coats were loose, with big collars, and single-breasted fastening with one button at waist or hip level, often referred to as 'wraps'. Backward-sloping rounded fronts; collars fastening high; long fur coats showing a waist, or short fur wraps. Capes. Suede and leather coats and jerkins for sports. Single-breasted kimono-cut coats. Bolero fronts; side pleats; side belts; cape-sleeves; single-breasted Ulster pouched at waist. Fur collars and cuffs. Imitation fur also used for trimming. Fashionable length to lower calf (1921–22). Some coats full at the hips in 1923. Tubular coats of cloth and of fur with one button on left side; fur collars, cuffs and at hem. Afternoon coats teamed with dresses, e.g. dress and coat lining of same material, or silk coat matching trimming of dress. Summer coats of satin or lace (1924–25). Tailored coats en suite with costumes. Tweed country coats. Macintoshes to fold up and go in pocket or bag. Coloured waterproofs. Length now to knee; fur coats of same length (1926–27). Bell sleeves or sleeves flared over wrists; fur collars and cuffs. Cape coats. Double-breasted Chesterfield and Raglan styles, with belts, in tweeds (1928). Scarf collars tied with long ends at back (1929). Patch pockets, long revers in plain cloth coats; fur trimming as before. Coat lengths varying considerably (1930).

Unfashionable elderly ladies still to be seen in shawls and mantles.

EVENING COATS AND WRAPS

Capes with fur collars: in 1924 cut as full circle, embroidered, and gathered into wide fur collar. Coats, also generally with fur collars, had wide sleeves. Sometimes matched the evening dress; often of brocade. Oriental effects in colouring and decoration: Egyptian motifs prominent 1923–24. Hem line uneven, longer at back, in 1930.

74. 1924 *Paris fashions in wrap-over clutch coats.*

75. 1925 *Long tweed coat, double breasted with long rolling lapels and pockets at low hip level.*

76. 1928 *Face-cloth coat. Collar, cuffs and lining in real fur.*

77. 1925 *Evening cloak, black velvet embroidered with coloured silks and pearls and with large white fur collar.*

EXAMPLES

1921   'Fur coats from 16 gns.'

Horwood's, Colchester

1925   'Hoar-frost velour wrap, three-quarter lined heavy crepe-de-chine. Taste-
       fully trimmed opossum fur. 13 gns.'

Rogers Bros. Colchester

c. 1926-28   Evening coat of chocolate brown crêpe with multi-coloured and gold
             machine embroidered floral motifs. Waist at thigh level with multi-
             coloured fringe to hem level all round. Large, full sleeves gathered into
             deep, brown fur cuffs and with high fur collar. Lined green velvet.

Northampton Museum

1927   'Winter coats. Plain tailored and fur trimmed. Navy, brown, and green.
       1 gn. [Sale Price]'.

Joys, Colchester

'Electric seal-coney coat, collar and cuffs natural skunk, long rolled revers,
fancy lining £12.15.0.'

A. J. Lucking and Co. Ltd., Colchester

1929   'Coats. The new Basket and Flecked Tweeds, trimmed suede or leather
       with scarf and bag to match, 39/11 to 4 gns.'

Alice Sanders, Colchester

'Real leather coats, full length, 59/6'.

Northern Leather Co. Ltd.

HAIR

Increasingly worn short, bobbed, or from 1923–24, shingled with
the hair tapering off evenly into the nape of the neck. In 1924 the
evening coiffure 'must expose the ear'. Hair straight or in flat
waves. A flat wave circling the head and a side parting in 1927;
or shoulder-length and rolled in nape of neck.

The Eton crop, very short, straight, and dressed like a man's,
was favoured by some women from 1925. A writer of 1926 speaks
of hair cut like a 'medieval page'.

From 1928 there was a tendency for hair to be a trifle longer;
by 1930 it was definitely worn longer at the back with clustering

curls, sometimes artificial. In front it was clear of the forehead, or with a forehead curl, and loosely covered the ears.

Long hair in 1921 was dressed over the cheeks at the side, rolled and turned back, and the back hair turned up into a loose chignon with a comb.

Generally long hair was dressed in soft waves, often with a wave coming down over the right forehead, and gathered into a chignon, bun, coil, or plait at the back.

1920 'Marcel's Permanent Curl or Wave. If you cannot call have a Home Outfit.'

Pan

1927 'Permanent Waving, full head £1.10.0.
    Shingling, first time   1.6.
       „   trim   9.
    Bobbing, first time   1.0.
       „   trim   6.'

Beaumonts, Colchester

1928–29 'Haircutting 1/-
    First shingle 5/-
    Permanent Waving, shingled head, from 3 gns.'

Harrods, London

MILLINERY

Small, narrow raised fronts; Breton and mushroom shapes. Some wide brims trimmed all round with ostrich feathers. Cut felt motifs on some brims. Summer hats decorated with bunches of artificial fruit. Pull-on caps with tassel: Tam-o'-shanters. Made of straws, velours, panne, velvet, felt (1921). Oval shape with feather over one shoulder: broad brims in summer: small turned-up brims in winter. Some toques. Wings and feathers, etc. for trimming (1922). Turned up or rolled brims, or brims cut and the cut portions turned up unevenly: holes cut in brim. Hats with wide brims worn tilted forward because of high coat collars. Cloche hats with very narrow brim turned down, or up. Summer hats with domed crowns and wide drooping brims in various straws with swathed trimmings. The 'helmet', a variety of cloche (1923–24).

I

78. *Hats: (a), (b), (c) Summer fashions
for 1923. (d) Suede cloche. 1927. 2/9d.*

Domed crowns; wide brims turned down over eyes: high
crowned cloche hats: large picture hats in summer. Ribbon,
flowers, etc. at left side (1925–26). Lower crowns and shaped to
head in some cases in 1927, but cloche still popular. Drooping
brims, wider at sides, or one side only, or slashed brims. Small
veils to nose. 'Vagabond hats' – with a tall crown, turn down
medium brim, and a scarf tied round and hanging down (1927).

Small felt hats with front of brim turned up, osprey feathers at
right side of brim; helmets with brim turned up in front; hats

with domed crowns and brim turned down at sides or all round; brims arching up in front and down at sides; large picture hats for summer (1928-29).

During these years hats were, in general, worn well on the head and pulled down, in some cases with the brim covering the eyes.

In 1930 a new style, with shallower crown, closely fitting the head, appeared. In this style the hat was made so as to appear slightly tilted backwards, the brim turned up off the face and coming down over the ears. Also turban hats, the crown covered with material leaving long ends which could be tied in a bow or swathed around like a turban.

79. 1929-30 *Typical hats.*

Throughout the period there were crocheted and knitted hats, following the fashionable shapes: caps, and berets. Suede hats for sports wear.

Evening Bandeaux; turbans, with aigrettes in 1922, and covering the hair in 1924; or no headdress at all, especially in the later years.

> 'Bright coloured hats are seldom either attractive or becoming except to the very young. An exception may be made in favour of red . . . .'
>
> Lady Forbes, op. cit.

1921 'The ever fashionable Velours Hat. Real velours from 39/6. Velour finish 27/6'.

Horwood's, Colchester

1925 'Hats made of ottoman silk and georgette 11/9'.

Alice Saunders, Colchester

1927 'Sale. Felt and felt cloth hats, mostly fawns of course, 1/-'.

Joys, Colchester

> 'A really delightful little silk hat with tam crown. May be worn with becoming effect by maids and matrons. Rosebeige, carnation, almond, dark walnut, Sahara, reseda, pansy, beige, Biskra, black and blue, 5/11.'
>
> Joys, Colchester

1929 'Cloche hat in fine bangkok, lined crepe-de-chine; hat band of same crepe-de-chine and matching scarf. In navy and white and black and white'.

Quoted Cunnington

BOOTS AND SHOES

SHOES

Pointed and bulldog toes. Cuban heels most fashionable. Heels $2''-2\frac{1}{2}''$.

(a) Court style with or without buckle; a peaked front popular from 1924 for smart wear.

(b) Bar style with single bar across instep, or wide strap with cut out portions, or two or three bars. Bars often buttoned.

(c) Instep bar with right angled piece running down foot, giving T effect.

(d) Cross straps.

(e) Sandals.

(f) Oxford.

(g) Brogues for sport and country wear.

Made of leather, suede, glacé kid, reptile skins. Combination of leather and suede. Brocade and satin for evenings; also gold or silver kid. Colours were black, brown; bright colours; beige from *c.* 1925; grey. Combination of colours popular late in

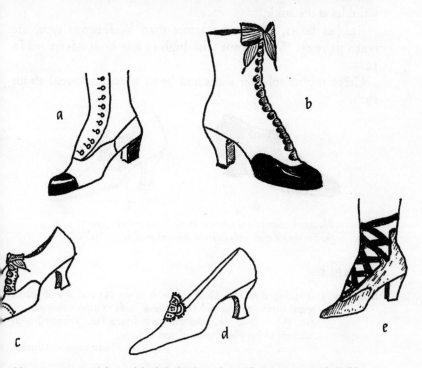

80. 1921 *Boots and shoes: (a) Black glacé button boot with patent toe cap. 50/9d. (b) Lace French kid with patent toe cap and Cuban heel. (c) Antelope lace shoe with Louis heel. 60/-. (d) Antelope or suede court shoe with Louis heel and decorated tab. 45/-. (e) Tango slipper with ribbon ankle lacing and Cuban heel. 60/-.*

decade. Brown and white or black and white for wear with jersey frocks from *c.* 1929 in Oxford styles.

Evening shoes often embroidered and with contrasting heels, often jewelled.

In 1927 'Charleston' sandals, with one bar and low heel.

BOOTS

These were disappearing, except for riding and some sports, by
c. 1922. There was a revival for general wear in the form of
'Russian' boots, knee high, in 1924–26. Russian boots were mostly
without fastenings, but some had a long zip; they fell into
wrinkles at the ankle.

Rubber boots, of Russian rather than Wellington type, are
noted in 1925. Wellingtons with high or low heels advertized in
1929.

Crêpe rubber soles for shoes and boots were introduced about
1921.

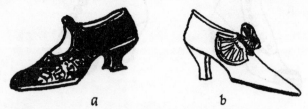

81. 1927   Shoes: (a) One-bar shoe in brown crocodile, from 50/-.
(b) Bronze kid court with elaborate coloured pearl buckle. 52/6d.

EXAMPLES

Early 1920's   Evening shoes. (a) Gold calf with instep bar and tab of green:
green trimming: ivoroid buckle inset with imitation emeralds on
tab. (b) Fuchsia pearlized calf with instep bar. Trimmed with
stitchery and appliqué motif of pink kid.

Northampton Museum

1921   'Glacé Kid walking Boots and Shoes. Brocade and Fancy evening Shoes.'
T. H. Doe, Colchester

1925   'Russian boots, Patent leather 2″ heel, 21/-'.

Craft Shoe Co.

1927   Women's knee-high brown rubber boots with zip fastener.
Northampton Museum

1928   'Lizard skin shoes in grey and fawn, 69/6. Court shoes in best Patent
Leather, hand sewn throughout. Also in pastel shades of Glacé Kid in
Oak, Stone, and Bois de Rose. Sizes and half sizes. 39/6'.

Harrods Ltd.

STOCKINGS

Still mainly black or white in early years, but beiges and flesh colours superseding them as skirts get shorter. Lisle still very popular. Wool and silk and wool mixture for country and sports wear. Silk stockings often had feet and tops of lisle for longer wear.

Some open work designs in fancy motifs in 1921: lacey or embroidered clocks.

In the mass market artificial (art) silk (Rayon) stockings were ousting other types.
Colours in 1924 included tan, beige, flesh, grey, smoke and fawn. In 1928, greys, silvers, fawn, beige, flesh, mushroom, and nude, as well as black and white in some makes. Evening silk stockings of gold, tinsel silver and 'opera pink'.

1923   'Ladies Art silk hose: black and all newest colours, 1/11½.
         Heavy knitted ribbed silk and wool, black, putty, mastic, nigger, 6/11½'.

1925   'Ladies Ladder-proof Art silk stockings 1/11¾'.
                                                    W. Hunt & Sons, Colchester

1928   'Fine quality chiffon lisle stocking with lace clock. All shades of flesh,
         beige, fawns, beavers, greys and nude. Sizes 8½–10, per pair 3/11'.
                                                    Harrods Ltd.

1929   'Hosiery in Pure Silk, Artificial Silk, Silk and Wool, and Lisle thread'.
                                                    A. & E. Baker, Colchester

ACCESSORIES

GLOVES

Still considered a necessary article. Leather, fur, knitted wool, or string for riding and country wear. Some long suede and kid with up to twenty buttons for evening wear and formal occasions. Doeskin and suede for London: buckskin and chamois for country. Some gauntlets. Gloves generally plain, but some with bead trimmings or embroidery. These last frowned upon in some circles. Fewer buttoned gloves – many with elastic inset in wrist. Colours mostly white, greys, browns and fawns, but brighter colours in 1929, when also it was fashionable to team gloves and stockings.

1923   'Ladies all-wool gauntlet gloves 1/11½ per pr.'

W. Hunt & Sons, Colchester

1928   'Ladies fur back gloves 5/11'.

A. J. Lucking & Co. Ltd, Colchester

1928–29   'Camel wool gauntlets 4/11 per pair. English washable doeskin gloves, pull-on model with elastic wrist 5/11 per pair.'

Harrods Ltd

FURS

Wide stoles (1921); necklets and ties; fox very popular, mounted with head and paws as well as tail.

1927   'Natural fox animal ties 21/9'.

A. J. Lucking & Co. Ltd., Colchester

PARASOLS AND UMBRELLAS

En-tout-cas for sun or rain. Chiffon sunshades for Ascot, garden parties, etc. Long umbrellas with crook handles, or straight handles ('militaire'): wooden, plain or gold mounted. From about 1923 'chubby' or 'dumpy' umbrellas and sunshades about two feet long overall; generally with straight handles of wood or composition. Natural colour raffia sunshades embroidered with coloured raffia. Patent collapsible models. Umbrellas generally black or conservative colours: made of silk or cotton or mixture.

1924   Collapsible parasol with telescopic handle and sliding/extending ribs. Covered cream and pink silk: plated metal stick: composition handle and tips to ribs.

London Museum

1928   'Chubby umbrellas from 10/6'.

Harrods Ltd.

FANS

A revival in 1921: large ostrich feather fans in 1923. Generally not fashionable later in decade.

HANDBAGS

Silk or leather. Silk with thin frocks. Initials recommended on leather bags (1926), which were mostly flat envelope shape ('pochette'), or fuller, pouch-shaped on metal frames. Some soft leather, and silk bags on tortoiseshell or composition frames.

Evening bags in brocade, embroidered silk, metal beads, etc. Matching dance frocks in 1921: brightly coloured in 1924.

Large leather 'steamer' bags, twelve to fourteen inches in length.

Some leather bags fitted with zip fasteners from about 1926.

Fashion for matching bags and shoes (1929).

Gold mesh 'vanity bags' for evenings.

c. 1920   Mud coloured crochet artificial silk bag on semi-circular, composition frame, with design of elephants. Press clasp and composition chain handle.
London Museum

c. 1924   Gold and black brocade evening bag, lined pink crêpe de Chine, on composition semi-circular frame with design of stylised lotus flowers and leaves and an Egyptian head, in black, ivory, greens and red. Press clasp and black ribbon handle.
Author's collection

1928–29   'Morocco leather handbag with lightening fastener, mirror and purse, $7\frac{3}{4}$ ins. 21/-. Fine quality lizard pochette. In new Beige shade or grey, 8 ins. 92/6, $9\frac{1}{2}$ ins. 107/6.'
Harrods Ltd.

HANDKERCHIEFS

As previous decade.

BELTS

Generally worn hip level: of leather, self-materials. Metal and composition buckles and clasps.

NECKWEAR, SCARVES, etc.

Scarf or tie knotted at base of V necks. Scarves fastened on shoulders. Batik scarves in eastern colours (1924). Painted scarves (1925). 1925 onwards scarves for sports and country wear. Chiffon squares around neck for evening wear (1926). Squares knotted round neck on one shoulder and draped loosely.

Some white vests, collars and cuffs with tailored dresses. Modesty vests in georgette, etc.

Handkerchiefs displayed in outside breast pocket of suits (1926). Large embroidered Spanish shawls with long fringes for evening wear.

1928–29   'Crepe-de-chine ties. Newest shades and colour tones, 4/6.
Smart "fronting" for Modesty vests. Georgette with daintily trimmed tucks, width 12 inches, 15/11 per yard.'

Harrods Ltd.

BRIDGE COATS, MATINÉE COATS

In plush, velvet, velour, brocade, silk, etc. Some fur trimmed. Generally hip length.

JEWELLERY

Much jewellery as in previous period.

Diamonds and pearls very popular. Long earrings. Gold slave-bangles. 'Barbaric' and Oriental effects, especially after 1923.

Shoulder and corsage brooches; rectangular shape popular from *c.* 1928.

Beads and artificial pearls became very fashionable, especially in waist length or longer strings; but short 'choker' type with tailor-mades.

Crystal in favour, and rings and bracelets made of wood, at close of decade.

Gold and jewelled anklets, also watches, seen on some more advanced legs.

FASTENINGS

For dresses and skirts usually hooks and eyes or bars, or press-studs ('poppers') at the centre back or left side.

Many of the straight, shapeless dresses were designed to slip over the head and had no placket or fastenings. Some dresses and coat frocks were front buttoning.

MATERIALS

Among others the following are noted as popular fabrics during this decade:

Blanket cloth, Celanese (artificial silk), Cellophane (a viscose film; also as 'straw' for hats), chiffon, chiffonette (a cotton fabric), cotton, crêpe de Chine, crêpe marocain, crêpoline (silk and cotton mixture), flannel, foulard, gaberdine, georgette, kasha,[1] lamé, marocain, organdie, piqué, rayon (artificial silk: from 1924), repp, satin, saxony, serge, shantung, sheenore (cotton crêpe), stockinette, suede, taffeta, tweed, velvet, velveteen, Wemble-chine (1925. 'Something quite new: takes the place of crepe-de-chine', Advert: Hunt's, Colchester), wool crêpe, wool cloths.

Leather, fur, fur-fabric and leatherette were all used alone or in combination with textile fabrics.

COLOURS

Black and white will never go out of fashion, either used separately or together...'
Lady Angela Forbes, op. cit.

Also, it appeared, beige, which 'came in' in 1922, would never become unfashionable: it is probably the one colour associated by everyone with the Twenties.

Apart from blues, browns, greens and reds, the following colours or shades are noted:

[1] Woollen material invented by Rodier of Paris.

Almond, apricot, biskra, carnation, cedar, eau de Nil, heather mixtures, ivory, jade, lacquer-red, mastic, mauve, mole-grey, pink, putty, reseda-green, rose-beige, Sahara, sand, tangerine, violet, wine, yellow.

1930‑1940

INTRODUCTORY REMARKS

As the post-war decade and post-war attitudes passed into history, the Thirties opened with a returning ideal of maturity, already apparent in the fashions. The higher waist line, longer skirt and complex cut of women's clothes produced a silhouette more elegant and more natural than the schoolboy and schoolgirl shapes of previous years. The evening dress exploited femininity and sex appeal to a far greater degree than the day costume, and a gulf soon became fixed between the average women's ideal of a 'glamour' dress and her almost uniform-style day attire, which was largely the result of mass-produced clothes and diminishing class distinctions. Intricacy of cut, especially in the cut-on-the-cross skirts, compensated, particularly in evening dresses, for a certain simplicity in the fashions, probably dictated by the Depression.

The cinema now influenced the details and accessories of dress, if not the main designs, and names like Greta Garbo, Madelaine Carroll and, at the end of the decade, Veronica Lake, were associated with styles and hair-dos.

By 1934, it could be written that 'Junoesque forms are fashionable, with round and naturally curved derrières', and in 1935 'breasts no longer apologized for'. In 1937 the fashion journalists declared that 'we've all got to develop waists and hips this winter if we want to wear the fashionable new styles, tight at the waist and flaring out over the hips', and that sex appeal was the prime motive of the Autumn Paris collections.

As the slump years slowly began to pass, the fashions of the Thirties showed distinctly less original inspiration than those of the Twenties, and as warning rumbles emerged from Italy, Spain and Germany there appeared tendencies interpreted by both Mr. Laver and Dr. Cunnington as evidences of prophecy and also wishful thinking.

But as well as prophecy was a degree of retrospection, seen in the later designs with wide skirts, leg o' mutton sleeves and in 1938

'Crinolines or petticoats stiffened with whalebone hoops support the new evening dresses'.

Picture Post, 5th November

Royal occasions in the decade were the marriage of the Duke of Kent to Princess Marina of Greece in 1934, the Silver Jubilee of King George V in 1935 and the Coronation of King George VI and Queen Elizabeth in 1937. All these had a greater or less effect on the fashions of the day, and Marina hats, Jubilee blue, and Royal purple had a place in the smart woman's wardrobe, as had the short double row of pearls favoured by Princess Marina.

Casual clothes, including trousers and shorts for beach wear, were a feature of the decade, as was an increasing American influence, including the spread of American shoes and ready-to-wear clothes in English shops: an influence allied to that of the cinema noted above.

In addition to the more complicated cut and construction of many clothes, compared with the simpler lines of the Twenties, the increasing use of artificial fibres in materials and the introduction of the zip fastener were notable technical features of the period.

Among the evidence of prophecy mentioned earlier were the widening shoulders, becoming padded and square from about 1936, the aggressive tilt assumed by many hats, the lessening hold of French fashions, and, in 1938, the statement by a fashion journal that 'above all, we must cultivate an erect carriage and a perfect balance'. Prophecy pointed to war, the beginning of which marked the end of the Thirties.

Hair, worn longer than in previous years, gradually acquired an up-swept look, and make-up became less garish in effect, with subtler application, darker face powder, and matching nail varnishes and lipsticks.

DAY DRESSES

ONE-PIECE DRESSES

With variations in some cases of tunics, matching coats, boleros and shoulder capes.

Pinafore dresses in 1931 and 1940, worn over a blouse.

Princess line is seen in some models throughout the decade.

Shirt-waist or shirt dresses with front buttoned bodices, collars and revers.

SKIRTS

In 1931, 12 inches from ground, afternoon dresses six inches

82. 1931 Woollen tweed dress with pleated skirt and hip yoke. 15/11d.

83. 1931 Summer dress in rayon. Skirt flares from knee. Hip and shoulder yokes.

84. 1933   (a) Blouse and skirt.   (b) Day dress. Bodice with bolero front effect.   (c) Two-piece of cross-over jumper and skirt.

longer. By 1932, 10–11 inches from the ground. Afternoon dresses a few inches above ankle.

From 1931 to 1934 waists rather high, with the skirt hanging straight, even when bias cut. Some afternoon bias cut skirts moulded the figure. In 1933 yokes formed by V-tucks.

Straight cut, ankle-length skirts, some split up half way to knee (1934).

The waist line fell slightly in 1935, reaching the natural waist level by 1938.

Flared tunics reaching to the knee or below were worn with

85. 1935 Day dress in
soft wool with panelled skirt.

86. 1936 Afternoon dress
with tunic overdress and belt.

K

close-fitting dresses in 1936, as were two-piece tunic-frocks. Hip yokes, up-curved waist line, or waist line in a V or inverted Λ from 1936–37, from which year skirts were becoming fuller, flared, pleated, and tiered. The dirndl, copied from Austrian peasant costume, was a four-piece skirt the waist gathered by elastic thread. A slightly fuller small waisted silhouette appeared in the summer of 1938, and full ballet-type skirts for afternoon frocks. Alternatives were pleated skirts or slim tunics ending above the knee. Day skirt lengths 13–14 inches above the ground, and 'polonaise' apron over-skirt. Fairly wide belts were features of 1937; another similar fashion was a detachable apron and sash in 1939.

Normal waist line in 1939 with many varieties of pleating; 'tiered' skirts with two flounces; some bustle effects achieved by means of tuck, or bows at the back of skirts. Afternoon dresses with short circular skirts. A 'little girl feeling' was alleged to be the effect of wearing a full skirt and a tight bodice finished with a white collar.

The 'shift' dress fell full from the shoulders, gathered in by a sash or wide belt.

The 'petticoat' dress showed an embroidered underskirt.

In 1940 skirts were 16 or 17 inches off the ground, generally straight and slim-fitting, some with pleats or slight flare. Hip line flat and waist line fitted. Some peplums at the hips. Afternoon dresses with corselet waists and tucked or pleated skirts.

BODICES

In 1931 short, wide and with built out shoulders. Some basques. Drapery and folds in afternoon frocks. Some buttoning back, front, or diagonally. Cape collars, shoulder capes and cowl neck lines. Neck line medium, V necks popular, some with a 'fill-in'. Some cross-over bodices with girdle ties (1932). Neck line higher 1933 onwards, although a lower cut, generally a V, with or without collar and revers occur throughout the period. From 1933–36 shoulders were less wide and softer in outline, then widening again.

87. *1936 (a) Silk afternoon dress. Cowl-like neck line with gauging on shoulder.*

(b)   *Afternoon or informal evening dress. Circular yoke with gauging.*

88. *1937 Washing frock in rayon.*
Inverted front skirt pleat. Yoked bodice.
In brown, navy or spotted rayon. 5/6d.

89. *1938 (a) Floral silk summer frock.*
Short puffed sleeves. Bodice gauged at shoulders,
pleating across waist. (b) Summer two-piece
in silk; skirt and bolero.

Neck scarves, bows, jabots, collars, often of organdie (1933–35).
Scarf sometimes attached to the dress.

Square neck lines fashionable 1934–36 and in 1940.

Collarless dresses were popular in 1937–38, but in 1940 collars
are again more in evidence.

As the waist is lowered, the bodice lengthens and in 1934 pleats
and panels were introduced to give roundness to the bust. Some

shoulder yokes and round yoke-collars in 1936, with the breasts emphasized by pockets, buttons, pleats and gathers, or by Λ-pointed skirt panels carried up into the bodice; or blouse-frocks with front fulness in the bodice.

Tunic frocks in 1935 and 1936, some fur edged, some with a flared hem, or flaring from the waist, and circular cut. Tunics could reach to above or below the knee level.

Gauging, particularly at the neck and shoulders, was a feature of 1936 and 1937, and basques also in the latter year.

Draped fronts and shoulder or back yokes in 1937, tight-fitting bodices in 1939, some with vestee fill-ins, and bloused bodices in 1940 were also feature of the later years of the decade, and in 1940 left-hand gathering or swathing at the hips. This year also saw tucking and shirring of bodices.

90. 1939 Wool day dress. Roll collar with fill-in; sleeves raised at shoulder. Fox fur stole.

COATS, JACKETS AND BOLEROS

Teamed with dresses were popular from about 1932. Tunic-length jackets with revers in 1935, short, fitted and with lapels in 1936 and boleros with short or long sleeves for wear with summer dresses.

In 1937 'you must have a matching jacket for your best dress this season' wrote *Woman's Pictorial*, and 'a little bolero coat, such as all smart women are wearing this season' was also featured. Loose, boxey, swagger coats were popular in 1938, sometimes called coatees. They hung straight from the shoulders, unfastened and between waist and hip in length. Box jackets with buttons, and longer fitted jackets, some belted, were in the fashions for 1940.

Boleros, waist length or shorter, were with or without collars or revers, with square cut, or more generally, rounded fronts. They were most popular during the years 1936–38.

· Coats, jackets and boleros could be of the same material to match the dress, or of contrasting material and patterns. In 1940 a vogue for one-piece dresses simulating skirt and jacket.

SLEEVES

Varied from short to long, with some sleeveless afternoon frocks in the earlier years. Long sleeves were generally close fitting throughout the decade, with some bell-shaped in 1936 and again in 1939, in which year looser long sleeves were popular. Some longer puffed sleeves in 1932.

Bishop sleeves were especially to be noted in 1931, 1936–37, and again in 1940.

Sleeves full to the elbow and from elbow to wrist tight fitting were features in 1937.

Short puffed sleeves, up on the shoulders, from 1937 to 1939.

Long or three-quarter close sleeves pushed up in wrinkles below the elbows, 1938–40.

Raglan and Magyar cut sleeves appeared throughout the period.

The shoulders were built out in 1931, becoming less wide in 1933, and beginning to slope in 1934, although they were often padded in 1936. 'Dropped shoulders', attributed to a Victorian influence, are spoken of by a fashion writer in 1937, the centenary of the Great Queen's accession, but the prevailing war-like climate of Europe caused a squaring of shoulders in the following year, and by 1940 grimly square and slightly raised shoulders in day fashions indicated that even if the women of Britain did not know what was to come, they were prepared to resist it.

TWO-PIECE DRESSES

Consisted of tunic-frocks of skirt and a back buttoning tunic-blouse, with a fur border for winter wear. Tunic varying from fingertip length to knee length (1936–37 and 1940). Or jumper-frocks of separate matching skirt and top in the form of a high-buttoned, basqued and belted jacket or buttoned and belted jumper (1937). Or matching skirt and bolero to wear with a contrasting blouse (1938). Or skirt and matching top which was high necked with a small round collar, two breast pockets, button-down front, belt and rounded basques (1940).

COAT FROCKS

Of tweed or coating materials. Plain and tailored. Often button-through at front, or wrap-over and secured by buttons, belt, or buckle at side.

TEAGOWNS, HOUSEGOWNS,
CINEMA FROCKS, etc.

An increasing variety of informal dresses for wear in the home or for 'undress' occasions were to be seen during the decade.

The teagown was merging more with the dinner frock, as a ground or ankle-length gown in materials ranging from georgette to velvet. Shorter versions, generally in silk were 'tea-time' frocks and ensembles of blouse-bodice and separate skirt advertized as 'just right for dancing, supper, and tea dates'. The teagown proper, long and generally figure moulding, still retained, at least in the fashion writer's eyes, its powerful seductiveness.

Housegowns of the later years of the decade featured long full skirts and from illustrations seemed to differ little from dinner dresses of the day.

Cocktail suits or cocktail pyjamas had wide-legged trousers and tunics or coats. Materials were velvet, satin, chiffon, etc. The cocktail frock could be full length, but was not low cut.

The cinema costume of the mid decade was between calf and ankle in length. Its advent indicated the importance now played by the cinema in the entertainment of society.

1936 'The dinner dress and the robe de cinema is ankle length, opened in front
from neck to hem to reveal a foundation of different colour'.
Weldon's Good Taste, April

Housecoats, long, wide skirted, Princess line, with front zip or buttons from neck to hem were a superior type of dressing gown worn at home in the evening, or for breakfasting.

EXAMPLES

1931 'Figured voile frock with very short cuffed sleeves; V neck with white
collar. Hip pockets edged with white: white belt. 19/11'
Joys, Colchester

c. 1932 Day dress: plain navy blue skirt with bodice of floral design on blue
ground; short cape sleeves; collar very deep in front, pleated and scalloped,
becoming very short at the back. Half belt with self-covered buckle of
bodice material and mauve ribbon bow in front.
London Museum

c. 1934 Afternoon dress: lilac shot green chiffon over lilac satin slip. Bodice
gathered up at centre front seam. Flared skirt elaborately cut in overlapping sections and enhanced by floating drapery. Long sleeves with
semi-cape sections over shoulders and extending and tapering down to
centre back waist. Fine quality.
London Museum

1936 'Fashion's not so whole heartedly on the parade-ground as she was last
season [the 1935 Jubilee year with its attendant military parades] . . . If you
want to achieve just the right degree of militarism, study Eleanore Whitney,
of Paramount, in her brown wool two-piece frock, patterned in squares of
tan, with two impressive rows of gold buttons and a semi-stand-up collar
of gold metal cloth.'
Weldon's Good Taste

*91. 1936   Cinema frock of chiffon with very full
pleated sleeves. Diamanté clip at neck. In black, ivory,
violet or silver. 6½ gns.*

*92. 1938   Housecoat. Wrap-over front with
one button.*

93. 1940 Housecoat. Long, full skirted, cross-over bodice.

'Tea gown in crease-resisting velvet . . . unusual sleeves form cape at back and skirt falls to fulness below the knee. In fuchsia, myrtle, wine, black. Price 7½ gns.'

Advertisement, quoted Cunnington

c. 1938   Day dress: red and white floral print rayon. Bodice fastens with three white composition ball buttons in front panel with horizontal gathers over breasts at each side. Small collar and revers. Waist with applied basques at front sides over hips. Calf-length skirt flared with six gored panels. Self-material belt. Waist placket fastening with hook and loops at right side.

Holly Trees Museum, Colchester

1938   'Activity frocks. Wash frocks made in crease-resisting rayon which looks
        like linen. All pastel shades and navy, 9/11.'

                                                                Joy's, Colchester

1940   'Smocks, ideal for town and country and Canteen wear.'

                                                                        Vogue

        'Molyneux and Paquin have designed Collections for the first time in
        London . . .. Jacket dresses of a new type, outwardly suits and shirts;
        actually the shirts stitched to the skirts at hip level [Molyneux].'

                                                                Vogue, October

SUITS, COSTUMES, THREE-PIECE SUITS

Up to about 1936 suits with skirt and jacket of different materials
and colours were popular as well as the conventional all-of-a-kind
suit. Suede jackets and jerkins with cloth or corduroy skirts.
Light jackets and dark skirts in 1933–34. Throughout the decade
suits could be with or without pockets in the jackets.

Three-piece suits of skirt, jacket and long top coat, or skirt,
jacket and cape, or suits with waistcoats – double breasted particularly in 1931–32. Suits with matching hats are noted in 1935.
Long coats or jackets worn with a matching dress.

SKIRTS

Twelve to fourteen inches from the ground on a hip yoke with
pleats or flared panels. Pleats often in groups at back, one side, or
front. Or flared with back box pleats or with inverted pleats
(1931). Front panel cut on cross, the rest cut straight in 1933.
Straight or with slight flare from knee, some pleated and some
slightly split in front (1935). Inverted pleats up to knee level in
front, or shorter at sides (1936). Plain straight pencil skirts, or
pleated, or with slight flare or box pleats. Skirts 14 inches from
ground (1937). Skirts cut on the cross. Check skirt with plain
jacket or vice versa (1938). Straight or flared skirts in 1939. In
1940 straight slim skirts, some with slight flare or with varying
number of pleats. Darts and seams at waist, 16 or 17 inches from
ground.

94. 1933 *Suit with contrasting short, plain jacket and skirt.*

95. 1935 *Suit in linen tweed with short boxey jacket.*

JACKETS

Nipped-in waists, fitted coats with mannish lines. Single breasted with rounded fronts. Double breasted, some with scarf collars. Belts and basques. Pointed lapels (1931–32). Straight coats worn over double-breasted waistcoats (1932). Square box coats hanging straight from shoulders, jackets straight and hanging looser. Some with front cut on cross and the rest straight. Cross-over front fastenings, one-side pockets. Boleros. Sleeves tight and straight, long or three-quarter (1933). Sleeves wide and padded (1931–33). Shoulders sloping and lines softer in 1934: double-breasted styles with large buttons: 'Bowery' suit opening in a deep V over a vest or waistcoat. Fitted jackets: finger-length swinging coats; short and boxey reefers; fitted waist-length jackets with basques. Three-piece suits with long top coat or with matching jumper, coat and skirt (1935).

Three-quarter-length loose 'swagger' coats (1935–36). Fitted hip-length jackets, buttoning high, closed or with revers. Short fitted jackets. Three pieces; three-quarter-length 'jigger' or swagger coats. Single-breasted jackets with rounded fronts (1937–38). Boleros, some flared; three-piece suits with cape instead of top coat (1938).

In 1939 high buttoned single breasted, some with wide lapels, or flat collars; collarless jackets; jackets with wide long revers open to waist, with one button. Square or slightly rounded fronts. Some nipped-in waists. 'Barrel' jackets with three buttons. Wide shoulders.

High buttoned single breasted in 1940: becoming somewhat longer. Wide lapels, or buttoning to neck with small turn-down collar. Shoulders broad and padded. Some bloused effects. Military touches evident in the autumn.

EXAMPLES

1931 'Tailored two-piece suit in flecked tweed, the skirt box-pleated, the bodice with vest and collar of pastel shades; coat finished with fur collar. 7½ gns.'

Advertisement, quoted Cunnington

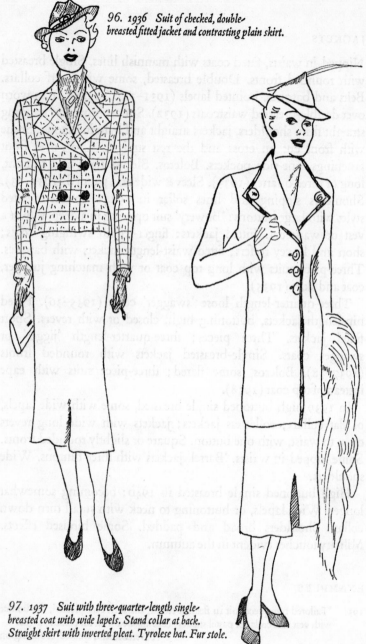

96. 1936   *Suit of checked, double-*
breasted fitted jacket and contrasting plain skirt.

97. 1937   *Suit with three-quarter-length single-*
breasted coat with wide lapels. Stand collar at back.
Straight skirt with inverted pleat. Tyrolese hat. Fur stole.

98. 1940 *Suit with fitted mannish-cut jacket; padded shoulders. Skirt with deep inverted front pleat.*

1934   'Tailored suit in Yorkshire tweed 98/6.'

                          Advertisement, quoted Cunnington

1935   'Three-piece suits in all the newest materials. Fancy cloths and checks. Man tailored tweed costumes with blouse and hat to tone.'

                          Hutton, Colchester

1936   '. . . a tailored jacket worn with a grey skirt is in a new yellow-green called *vert tilleul* . . . for really warm days there is a very charming three-piece suit with narrow skirt and sleeveless jacket both of navy blue woollen, and a blouse of white piqué with draped collar wide bouffant sleeves. The jacket fastens from top to hem with numerous buttons.'

                          Weldon's Good Taste

1937   'Suit in West of England cloth. Link button 42/6.'

A. J. Lucking, Colchester

1938   'Harris tweed tailor-made two-piece, collar with lapel and revers, rounded
fronts, one link button. Straight skirt with inverted pleat. Also in double-
breasted style 3 gns.'

Joy's, Colchester

1940   'Suits. Here are six, all single-breasted, slim in outline (in spite of skirt
pleats), trim-waisted, buttoned high, with jackets ending well below the
hip line. That's the way your suit should look to stay smart for several
seasons. Town suits . . . two fur trimmed. For town or country the three
tweed suits. For those who like suits to go under coats, the jersey one,
beautifully unbulky.'

Vogue

SKIRTS, TROUSERS, SHORTS, ODD JACKETS

SKIRTS

For wear with blouses, jumpers, jerkins or odd jackets: 'morning'
and country.

In general followed the lines of costume skirts. Twelve to
fourteen inches from the ground in 1931, dropping to ten or
eleven the next year. Plain or slightly pleated: hip yokes, some
pointed in front. In 1933–34 skirts are long and straight: straight
or flare from knee. Four-piece skirts: pleats from knee (1936).
Dirndl skirts (1937) cut on cross; short and free swinging; slight
flare; pleats; 13–15 inches from ground (1938). Flared or straight;
pleats (1939). In 1940, 16–17 inches from ground: straight and
slim, but often with flare or pleating; hip yokes. Throughout
the decade skirts for wear with blouses, etc. often had pockets at
hip level or slit side pockets, and belts of self material.

TROUSERS AND SHORTS

Khaki shorts for hiking and bicycling reaching almost to knees;
trousered skirt reaching below knee and with inverted pleats.
Beach trousers of cretonne: grey flannel slacks; pyjama teagowns;
cocktail suits with wide pyjama-legged trousers falling full and

looking like a skirt (1931–34). Dark shorts reaching almost to the knee for 'health and beauty' exercises. Divided skirts; khaki shorts; mannish tailored suits of jacket and trousers in flannel and woollen cloths; cocktail pyjamas; pleated shorts; trousers with zip in side placket (1935–39).

Bifurcated garments for women were still regarded with disapproval by a large number of people and it took the exigencies of the Second War before the majority could accept that the female was after all a creature with two independent legs.

See also 'Sports Clothes' and 'Clothes for Special Occasions'.

99. 1931 *Double-breasted sports coat of blazer cloth. Brass buttons.*

100. 1937 *Short boxey bolero.*

ODD JACKETS

Jackets were worn with skirts and blouses or jumpers or with dresses. On occasion skirts and jackets of differing material and colour were worn as a suit; sometimes dresses had jackets, coatees, boleros or long coats en suite.

Suede jackets or blouse-tops; boleros; double-breasted jackets, or single-breasted with peplum effects for outdoor wear; coolie coats with kimono sleeves (1931–34).

Short, boxey, reefer jackets; basqued jackets with fitted waists;

L

boleros; blazers with patch pockets worn with sports clothes; boleros of fur-cloth; thigh-length boxey single-breasted with a tubular line; very short boleros just covering the breasts (1935–39).

Jacket-dresses, of dress and matching jacket, very fashionable in 1940; lengths from bolero to below the hips. The jacket could also be teamed with skirt or slacks.

EXAMPLES

1931   '. . . skirt and a blouse and a waistcoat and a long silk scarf and a beret and handbag to match; all in the most beautiful tweed.'

Essex County Standard

1935   'Perfect fitting fancy pure wool trousers, finished with button and button holes either side. In navy, brown, or white 59/6.' ['bell-bottom' for beach wear].

Advertisement, Debenham & Freebody
(quoted Cunnington)

1935–36   'Flannel trousers: well tailored and perfect fitting with zipp fastening at side. Navy, grey, or white, from 12/9.'

Army and Navy Stores

1936   'Smartly cut skirt with inverted pleats and hip pockets. Size 40 takes 1½ yards of 54″ material. Pattern in hip sizes 36 to 44 inches.'

Weldon's Good Taste

1938   'Jackets were never more in Fashion's favour than they are this spring. You will see them everywhere, brief and square or long and slim. You slip one over every dress you wear.'

Woman's Pictorial

1940   'Quilted art satin for making up into siren suits and jackets.'

Essex County Standard

BLOUSES, JUMPERS, KNITWEAR

BLOUSES

Short and worn over skirt, belted, short sleeves. Criss-cross patterns accentuating breasts; double-breasted waistcoat effects (1931–32). Cap sleeves: long full sleeves; flat buttoned collar, or turn-down collar with revers; buttoned cuffs; tucked-in or over skirt. Some with belts. Some short over-blouses buttoned at back (1932–34). Softly draped in woollen or jersey material; long or short sleeves; cross-over fronts; or tailored with turn-down collar, buttoned front and wrists, shoulder yoke. Bows at neck; jabots; frills (1935–36).

Wide revers or long pointed collars, or small turn-down or stand-up collars; long sleeves with narrow wrist-bands, or short puffed sleeves; large buttons; sham pockets or flaps. Tunic-blouses, worn over skirt to thigh-length, cowl collars, back buttoned (1937). Tunics with corselet waist, cross-over front and sash; waistcoat-like blouses, some in flannel or suede. Long, loose sleeves with buttoned wrist-bands. Short, puffed sleeves. Blouses tucked in or worn over skirt. Collars with bows or ties, or high at neck, plain or with standing collar with front points turned down (1938–40).

JUMPERS AND KNITWEAR ('WOOLLIES')

Wool more popular than artificial silk. Jumpers with horizontal stripes (1931); with criss-cross pattern to emphasize breasts; contrasting colour edging to neck and hem; wool embroidered floral motifs; V necks; cross-over fronts, loose, turn-down necks. Belted, hip-length jumpers; sweaters buttoning high at the neck; jumpers with wide front opening and silk chemisette. Cardigans with deep V openings, some with pockets. Sleeveless cardigans like waistcoats; no collar but wide lapels, or deep U opening. Scarf collars. Short waists (1932–33).

A novelty of 1933 was a rubberized elastic fabric of silk or velvet made up into evening pullovers.

Jumper suits of skirt and cardigan, some with jumper, handbag and beret knitted en suite. 'Pullovers', 'slip-overs', 'slip-ons', to wear over a blouse or under-jumper. Square or round necks. Decorative stitching, smocking. Longer jumpers with belts and deep ribbing at the waist. Jumpers and cardigans to match. Yokes; scarf collars; draped necklines (1934–36).

Cardigan suits with deep V opening worn with high-necked

102. 1938 *Blouse, yoked shirt type with matching bow at neck.*

101. 1933 *Blouse and skirt. High waisted wrap-over skirt. Three buttons. Yoked blouse with tie neck line.*

jumper or blouse. Cardigans with large decorative buttons. Jumpers with round, square or polo collars. Some cardigans and jumpers with high plain necks or scarf collars. Some sleeves with kick-up at shoulder. Fancy yokes and decorative buttons, some square, on jumpers (1936).

High necks with small turn-down collars; zip fasteners at front in some cases. Fancy yokes (1937).

Ribbed cardigans; knitted suits of coats with collar, revers, and flapped pockets and matching knitted skirts; jumpers with belts; matching jumpers and cardigans (1938–40).

Knitted wool dungaree suits; wool stockinette siren suits (1939–40).

EXAMPLES

1931 'Shantung blouse, with jabot ... 25/9.'

Advertisement, quoted Cunnington

103. 1931   Knitted jumper with geometric patterns.
104. 1935   Woollen jumper. Belt and bag crocheted string.

1932 'A becoming jumper for the Young Matron. The silk chemisette ... gives a softening effect very becoming to the older woman and the long tight sleeves are finished with matching silk cuffs.'

Weldon's Cardigans & Jumpers

1933 'This attractive little coat is the very newest version of the cardigan coat with the very latest fashion features – the short waist length and the convertable fronts. For the home you will allow the revers to fall open, while for the street you will probably prefer to button them up across the fronts and tuck a gay scarf into the neck.'

Bestway Pattern

1936 Smart well-cut blouse ... in white or oyster coloured Tricoline. Pattern in bust sizes 32 to 40 inches. 9d.'

Woman's Pictorial

c. 1937   Beige rayon blouse with brown pattern of small geometric motifs. Bust
36 inches, length back of neck to hem 20 inches, waist 30 inches. Small
pointed turn-down collar, long sleeves ending in cuff with two buttons.
Four buttons from neck in front. Half-belt fastening in front with button
and button-hole. Buttons of clear glass in stylised flower shape. Hooks
and loops at neck and waist level to reinforce buttons. Slightly shaped to
waist by two darts at back.

Author's collection

1939   'Knitting wool in the new autumn shades and khaki.'

Essex County Standard

1940   'All kinds of knits: sweaters, cardigans, woolly shirts, blouses and boleros
. . . Boat-necked short sleeved sweaters in fleecey Shetland wool 14/11 and
matching cardigan 18/11.'

Vogue

EVENING DRESSES

Generally throughout the decade the long skirted evening dress
was slim fitting giving a tall 'long-legged' look. From *c.* 1930 to
c. 1938 the fashionable evening frock had varying degrees of deep
back décolletage, making them in many cases quite backless.

SKIRTS

Cut on the cross. Were sheath-like and figure-fitting to hips,
thighs or knees, from where they flared out, but some wide
'Victorian' skirts for young girls. From 1936 some skirts began to
hang free from the waist and full 'Victorian' effects, drapery, and
panels were in fashion. Some bustle effects by use of sashes and
bows, curved and raised waist lines, and flared tunics over
narrower pleated skirts, and some dresses shorter in front than
behind (1936–37). Calf-length ballet skirts for dancing; wide
'Winterhalter' crinolines with hoops in 1937 and 1938. The
crinoline less full in 1939; also Princess dresses having fitted tops
and puffed shoulder sleeves. Princess, Empire and tubular lines;
some bustle effects; pointed skirt yokes; and drapery at the hip line
were features of 1939–40. In the latter year evening skirts worn with
a jacket or blouse became increasingly popular; some short
dresses also to be seen: more formal gowns with fuller skirts.

105. 1931 *Printed velvet backless evening gown. 3 gns.*

106. 1932 *Cocktail pyjama suit. Very wide full trousers and hip-length tunic. Contrasting material over shoulders, upper arms and bosom; fur around bottom. Long scarf tied in bow on left shoulder and caught by a clasp at centre of neck.*

BODICES

Fashionably with deep back décolletage, in 1931 as a wide V or U to the waist. Other models had pouched backs and shoulder yokes or with a less deep décolletage. V or square cut at the back in 1933. Drapery, capes, cape sleeves and epaulettes or puffed sleeves. Shoulder straps with simulated sleeves formed by drapery at top of bodice. Some front décolletage square, some V. High cowl fronts in 1934; drapery frills edging back opening; generally sleeveless, but long, or short puffed sleeves for dinner gowns. Fulness pleated over bust; shirring between and under the breasts, or wide fronted belts supporting the bust (1935–36).

'The bust line is emphasised on most of the new evening frocks.'

Weldon's Good Taste

Coatees, jackets and boleros worn with backless dresses. Ensembles of skirt, jacket and blouse or vest.

Bodices gathered at centre front and attached to necklace or chain round neck; or bolero-like yokes; V or round necks general (1937), also heart-shaped neckline appearing later in the year:

1937   'At a dress show this week I noticed that all the evening gowns have the becoming new heart-shaped neck line....'

Woman's Pictorial, December

Deep, square décolletage at the back, or backless with a fichu in 1938; also boned, strapless bodices. Dinner dresses with tight drapery and square necks. Halter necks. Heart-shape and V necks, high backs; or sleeveless 'brassière' top curving under breasts and crossing over with a medium V at the back. Sleeveless or with short raised and puffed sleeves, or short leg o' mutton.

Dinner dresses with tight drapery and square or V necks, long tight or fancy sleeves.

High necks, heart- or boat-shaped in 1939. Princess dresses with fitted top and puffed shoulder sleeves. Draped tops with small V. Lace edged neck lines or fichus. Boleros and jackets with peplum basques. For dinner, plain shirt-blouse with short sleeves and a pleated skirt.

By 1940 the war was enforcing a greater informality in all types of dress: instep-length plain dresses with matching jacket for

107. 1933 *Evening dress, black rayon with deep back décolletage, pouched and cowl-like. Belt. 4½ gns. Juliet cap.*

108. 1936 *Evening dress. Front and back view. Slim fitting skirt. Diamanté belt and collar. Sleeveless bodice cut low at back, but with two broad strips of material waist to neck. Two fluted panels below collar at front.*

dinner; dress with or without sleeves; jacket with short or long sleeves. Evening dresses with high round or V necks, slender soft lines, though shoulders, when present, somewhat square and the sleeves raised. Short sleeves; three-quarter sleeves wrinkled up to elbow, bishop sleeves.

Blouse and skirt ensembles. Short-skirted dresses again appearing as cut-down versions of the long-skirted patterns, the bodice similar in both types.

More formal occasions warranted a slightly lower décolletage.

EXAMPLES

c. 1930–31   Evening dress in emerald green machine lace over green crêpe de Chine foundation slip. Ground length. Bodice with basques fluted by insertions of godets (triangular pieces). Shoulder cape similarly fluted attached, curving up to shoulders at front. Skirt hanging straight to mid-calf, where it is fluted in a similar manner to the basques. Belt with diamenté clasp and narrow shoulder straps beaded with green glass beads. Medium décolletage. No fastenings.

Holly Trees Museum, Colchester

1932   'Dinner ensemble in soft silk, skirt figure-fitting to mid-thigh, then flared to ground. Crossover bodice with cape bolero, of which the long ends are swathed round the waist. 8½ gns.'

Advertisement, quoted Cunnington

1936   'Dress of white and gold gauffered satin with a neckband and waistbelt of gold lamé embroidered with coloured stones. The skirt is cut on the cross and two vertical bands are looped from the back of the waist to the neck.'

Weldon's Good Taste

1937   Brown velvet ensemble. Ground-length skirt flared from the knee. Gold lamé blouse or vest, plain with V neck. Long, plain jacket with long sleeves large collar and wide lapels. Brown velvet belt with gold lamé lining and gilt metal clasp.

Stranger's Hall Museum, Norwich

1938   Evening dress, black crêpe de Chine, by Marshall & Snelgrove. Long sleeves puffed at the shoulder. Square neck line, slightly gathered yoke. Fastening self-covered buttons neck to waist at back. Plain long skirt cut on the cross. Optional 'romantic' overskirt of watered rayon with a high shaped and boned waist band, bright cyclamen in colour.

London Museum

109. *1938* (a) *Evening dress with wide full skirt. Low-cut bodice with shoulder straps. Bertha-like shawl set low on shoulders.* (b) *Velvet evening swagger coat. Square shoulders, wide sleeves.* (c) *1939 Wedding dress. Lace yoke, draped neck line.*

c. 1938–39   Evening dress of pale blue silk with arrow-head shaped net insertions
revealing flesh-pink rayon underdress. Bodice back fastening with
net edged bra top and narrow shoulder straps. Matching blue silk
bolero with curved fronts shaped to bust by darts at side sections,
leg o' mutton short sleeves with insertions similar to the dress.

London Museum

1939   Evening dress in brown silk crêpe decorated on bodice with copper-
coloured sequins applied in leaf-shaped motifs around neck, down fronts
and radiating out to the hips at waist level. Two strips of similar sequin
motifs continue down both sides centre front to hem. Similar decoration to
short, padded and square cap sleeves.

V neck fastening centre front with hooks and loops continuing through
waist to thigh level by a zip added later. Bodice and skirt cut straight at
back. Front skirt side panels ruched on to back and to the two front centre
panels, which are gored and bias cut. Skirt flares from knee. Waist line
rather low.

Holly Trees Museum, Colchester

1940   Dinner dress with green skirt and bolero, midnight blue top and orange
scarf around the waist.

Pattern for full, bouffant skirted evening dress with short puffed sleeves,
heart-shaped neckline and swathed girdle tied in a bow in front. Deep
V décolletage at back. Waist rises in front to point between breasts: sides of
bodice gauged under them.

Vogue

CLOTHES FOR SPECIAL OCCASIONS

WEDDINGS

1931   'Long sheathed lace gown . . . of . . . trailing white satin with long tight
mousquetaire sleeves and . . . a little tricorne hat with yards and yards of veil
sweeping behind you . . . after you take off your veil slip into a little bolero
jacket with elbow sleeves banded in white fox or ermine which will make
a perfect evening ensemble.'

Essex County Standard

Generally throughout the decade ankle- or ground-length
dresses were worn with veils and wreaths or chaplets of orange
blossom.

1939   'Gowned in embossed satin flowers on white silk, veil and orange blossom
and white satin shoes.'

Essex County Standard

MOURNING

Full mourning with black veils was customary with the Royal Family (see accounts of the funeral of His late Majesty, King George V, in 1936).

Among private individuals the custom was greatly diminished, and the rules which had begun to be disregarded during the Great War were further eroded. However, such advertisements as the following still appeared.

1933   'Mourning and semi-mourning wear.'

Hutton's, Colchester

MATERNITY

A great many varieties of garments from simple three-quarter-length, full smocks to complicated constructions of dresses and skirts.

1937   'Maternity Frocks from 25/-.'

Advertisement *Restcots*

1940   'Patent woollen maternity dress 69/6.' [With a loose front panel over a skirt open up the centre front and secured by tape ties.]

Dubarry advertisement, *Vogue*

COURT DRESS

New Instructions, 1937.

'Ladies attending Their Majesties' Courts must wear long evening dresses with Court trains suspended from the shoulders, white veils with ostrich feathers will be worn on the head.

'The train, which should not exceed two yards in length, must not extend more than eighteen inches from the heel of the wearer when standing.

'Three small white feathers mounted as a Prince of Wales Plume, the centre feather a little higher than the two side ones to be worn slightly on the left side of the head, with the tulle veil of similar colour attached to the base of the feathers.

'The veil should not be longer than forty-five inches.

'Coloured feathers are inadmissible, but in cases of deep mourning Black feathers may be worn.

'Gloves must be worn.

'There are no restrictions with regard to the colour of the dresses or gloves for either debutantes or those who have already been presented.

'Bouquets and fans are optional.'

Lord Chamberlain's Office

AIR RAIDS AND WAR WORK

Dungarees and trousers. Steel helmets for air raid wardens, ambulance drivers, etc. Smocks or long buttoned overalls for canteen workers. One-piece 'siren' suits with elasticated wrists and ankles, some with attached hoods or cowls, to put on during night air raids.

The issue of gas-masks to all civilians necessitated some form of carrying bag or satchel. In late 1938 employees of a Colchester cinema were pictured wearing white canvas shoulder satchels to hold their gas masks.

1939   'Don't forget warm clothing for emergency use.'

1940   'Quilted art satin at 3/11 per yard for making up into siren suits and jackets.'

Essex County Standard

'Shield your brain from blast with a Webflex anti-concussion bandeau.'

Advertisement, *Punch*

SPORTS CLOTHES

GOLF

Suede tops or jerkins, tweed skirts; dresses, pullovers, jumpers; trousers and checked shirts. Crocheted caps; small skull caps.

TENNIS

Sleeveless, collarless dresses with short skirts; divided skirts. Belted silk dresses, collar and revers (1931–33). Helen Jacobs was pictured in 1933 in America, wearing white shorts with a short-sleeved shirt and turned-down ankle socks. Shorts more common by 1936, but skirts or dresses also. By 1939 circular, flared or sun-ray pleated 'little girl' skirts with tight pants underneath were more popular than shorts.

110. 1935 Golf outfit. Skirt and plain shirt blouse with sleeveless cardigan knitted with decorative front panel.

111. 1931 Tennis dress with cross-over bodice; skirt with front panel.

WINTER SPORTS

1931 Full trousers tucked into wool socks; ankle boots; belted jacket with pockets and large buttons; wool cap, scarf, and gloves.

Fashion photograph

1937 Trousers as above, 'windcheaters' tight at waist; ski-cap with vizor; wool gloves and scarf.

Illustration to magazine story

MOTORING

Nothing distinctive, but in 1933 a 'motoring three-piece suit' of skirt, cardigan and long coat was advertised. Long leather coats, and up to about 1938, crash dust-coats also were advertised.

CYCLING AND HIKING

Shorts or skirt, shirt, beret.

112. 1936 *Bathing costumes: (a) With short overskirt. (b) Without skirt.*

SWIMMING

Suits with divided skirts or wide legs or skirts with pants beneath; shoulder straps. Or two-piece of bra and shorts. Fancy rubber caps (1935). Many bathing dresses backless. Machine-knitted wool was a favourite fabric. By 1940 silk lastex (stretch) yarn, one-piece or bra and pants version. Towelling or shantung wraps. Raffia sandals.

CRUISING WEAR, PLAYSUITS, RESORT CLOTHES

Trousers, beach pyjamas of cretonne etc. (1931). Flannel slacks; divided skirts; backless linen dresses with matching coatees;

113. *1939 Beach wear: (a) Cotton dungarees and short-sleeved blouse. (b) Bathing dress with bra top and flared skirt over concealed pants. (c) Bell-bottom trousers, long sleeved shirt and head scarf. (d) and (e) Play suits.*

front button-through dresses worn over shorts and worn un-buttoned from the waist down; playsuits of shorts joined on to bodice or separate shirt, shorts and wrap-over skirts (1935–37).

Cork or wood 'beach jewelry'.

Cotton evening dresses.

OUTDOOR CLOTHES

Overcoats were, in general, long, mostly straight, but shortening by 1937–38. In 1931 long coats with fitted high waists, collars

M

high at the back and revers, or no collars at all. Raglan and Magyar sleeves popular, also buttoned cuffs. Fur trimming less fashionable.

1931 'The new furless fashions are very charming because collarless necklines are jaunty, scarves are very flattering and . . . the collars of our dresses . . . show over our coats.'

Essex County Standard, March

Masculine, flattened shoulders, and some collarless coats feature in 1932. Some detachable scarf collars. Long coats cut straight with no flare. Also appearing were seven-eighth's-length coats and three-quarter-length 'swagger' coats, hanging loose and full from shoulder to hem. Fitted or swagger styles persisted side by side. Some fitted coats collarless in 1933; with 'highwayman' cape collars in 1934. Bows or scarves at the neck; revers; fur collar during 1933–35. Short swagger coats in 1934; coats of all lengths – hip, finger-tip, seven-eighths, full (1934–36). Pagoda, Raglan, bishop sleeves. Wrap-over coats (1935). 'Military' style long coats in 1935 inspired by Jubilee Review. Also shorter coats slightly flared; fur collars and revers; bibs, jabots and flowers worn at the neck.

In 1936 'Fashion's not so whole-heartedly on the parade-ground as she was last season . . . .' *(Weldon's Good Taste)* but squarish shoulders and wide revers on swagger coats and three-quarter-length coats. Some coats with belts; some swinging from the waist. Indian lamb collars popular.

Box coats or jackets, three-quarter or hip-length hanging full and loose in 1937–38, either double-breasted or single-breasted. Also coats with a pleat in the back above the waist and an inverted pleat below or with a straight front and flared back. Plain and straight coats with zip fastener or buttons from neck to waist; or flared coats with one button at the waist. Square shoulders; wide, fitted, dolman or bishop sleeves.

From about 1937–38 edge-to-edge coats, with buttons and loops or a tie at the waist and possibly a hook and eye at waist and neck were worn in the spring and summer. Sometimes these edge-to-edge coats matched or contrasted with a dress.

In 1939 coats with epaulette shoulders revived the military look,

114. 1930-31 Outdoor coat, waisted, long lines, very large fur collar and cuffs.

115. 1936 Outdoor coats, single button fastening, large fur collars.

this time with a more sinister air. Some were straight with built-up shoulders, wide revers and pockets. Some coats with back fulness, some with fitted waist and circular skirt, some with full skirt gathered on to a waist band, or flared and pleated. Loose swinging 'swagger' coats of all lengths. Princess line reefer coats. Some three-quarter-length capes.

The 'martial air' persisted in 1940 with high shoulders; short revers; pockets, some slanted; belts. Double-breasted and single-breasted styles. Also loose coats with inverted pleat at back from shoulders. Wrap coats with tie belts; coats with attached hoods.

FUR COATS

Fur jerkins and jackets as well as long coats. Suede coats and jerkins. Mink, musquash, mole, Persian lamb, fox, baby seal, skunk, pony skin, squirrel. Imitation fur fabrics.

1939   'Rising prices in the fur market will undoubtedly reflect in higher prices this winter.'

Advertisement, *Essex County Standard*

EVENING COATS AND WRAPS

Long or three-quarter-length, some trimmed with monkey fur. Long fur wraps and fur jackets and boleros. Three-quarter-length velvet with wide sleeves, hanging full from shoulders and fastened at neck and trimmed with artificial gardenias (1937). Long coats with fitted waists and large swirling skirts; full elbow sleeves (1938).

Short wraps, or scarves, or shawls were worn with those dresses that had full flare from the knee.

RAINCOATS AND MACINTOSHES

Of artificial silk, gaberdine, leatherette and rubber-proofed fabrics. Double-breasted or single-breasted. Belted or without belts. Some trench-coat styles.

116. 1938 Spring edge-to-edge coat. Secured by the belt. Lining matching dress worn with coat.

117. 1939 Tweed swagger coat with pleated back, vertical pockets.

EXAMPLES

1931 'All wool faced cloth coats trimmed fur collar and cuffs 25/-
Leatherette macintoshes   5/-
Art silk macintoshes   12/6
Gaberdine raincoats   20/-'
Advertisement of sale, Whale's, Colchester

1933 'Indiana Macs 4/11½. Stitched storm collar; rubber lined. Single-breasted style. Saxe, putty, fawn, brown, green, navy.'
Lucking's, Colchester

1935 'Tweed coats with hat to match 2½ guineas.'
Hutton's, Colchester

'Cloth coat trimmed with opossum 84/-. Mink marmot coat 19 guineas.'
Gardiners, Ipswich

1936 'Spring coat in plain coating. Single-breasted wrap-over secured by buckled belt. Small standing collar and wide revers. Square shoulders, bishop sleeves. Small triangular patch pocket on right hip. Revers, pocket and wrist bands decorated with lines of stitching.'
Weldon's Good Taste

1937 'Swagger coat of British moleskin fur with cravat 10 guineas.
Full length coat of café-dyed ermine 98 guineas.'
Advertisement, quoted Cunnington

1940 'Harris tweed country coat to just below knee. Double-breasted, large collar and lapels. Belt. Turn-back cuffs. Six buttons and one button on each cuff.
'Double-breasted coat with shoulder yoke, wide lapels, flare to skirt and slit pockets. 4½ guineas'
Advertisements, *Vogue*

HAIR

During this period the hair was generally brushed back, with or without a parting and turned or curled up in the nape of the neck. Hair was mostly well-waved.

The 'Greta Garbo' style of 1932 was swept behind the ears and curled loosely on the neck.

By 1934 hair was higher on top of the head and the nape of the neck was exposed in 1935.

Centre parting, sleek on top and curls framing the face in 1936; or 'page boy bob' – chin length and turned in at the bottom. By 1937 upward styles are being noted in America; by 1938 shoulder-length curls piled on top of head, swept up from the sides and nape of the neck; or braided hair with a 'screwed-up' look.

In 1939–40 swept back from the face, with short side curls, or a revival of the chignon and snood for the back hair: or the 'Veronica Lake' hair-do, loose and shoulder length, turned under or over.

1935   'Permanent Waving, whole head, £1.1.0.'

1940   'Jamal Machineless Permanent Waving.
       No electricity or wires used. Whole head 25/- Eugene waving 21/-'
                                    Advertisements, *Essex County Standard*

MILLINERY

The hats of the Thirties did not, as in the previous decade, obscure the eyes, although the fashions in the first years were for drooping brims and draped hoods or for shallow hats tipped forward or to one side.

By 1933 all shapes worn at all angles were popular – high, narrow and fez-like worn forward; berets; pill-boxes; small Breton sailors; long, narrow and boat shaped or, in summer, large and wide.

Some fur toques and Tyrolese hats, tricornes and tailored felts in 1934, worn over one eye or pushed back. Berets and sailor hats remained popular, and the pill-box was favoured by Princess Marina, who in that year married the Duke of Kent. She also favoured picture hats for state occasions, and thus both types received added impetus in Fashion's race.

Flat hats with fairly high brims, halo berets worn far back, hats with brims rolled up in front (1935).

Crowns were becoming higher in 1936, some pointed, and brims narrower. Berets less popular.

Hats off the face in 1937; tall turbans or pill-boxes. Large flat hats, brims turned up or down for summer. Juliet caps, round, segmented, and worn with or without a veil.

Halo hats, worn well back with the brim framing the face; sailors; saucer-like hats; Homburg-type with front brim turned down: all worn tilted (1938). Also the 'vagabond' hat revived a name of the Twenties; but this time it was a slouched felt hat, worn over one eye and possibly with the side brim tilted up. Scarves or handkerchiefs tied over the head began to be seen at the seaside.

In 1939 hoods and snoods to cover the back of the hair; tiny hats with veils; jersey turbans with scarf attached; caps; and flat

118. 1938   Typical spring hats.

berets with a band at the back. Shallow sailors, skull caps with a flat crown, tilted forward; shirred snoods; foulard 'sponge-bag' caps; head scarves tied turban or 'mammy' style (the head covered and the ends brought round the front and tied in a bow over the forehead) in 1940.

Veils appeared occasionally during the decade, nose length or tied under chin. In 1935 coloured veils floating behind in the summer.

Trimmings of ribbon loops and bows, flowers or feathers. Some top trimming *c.* 1933. Feathers often in form of a single quill stuck in the hat at a jaunty angle. Fur trimming popular 1938–40.

Knitted and crocheted hats and caps, often with matching ties or scarves, were prevalent during the early years of the decade, and revived in 1940.

For evenings the hair was usually unadorned, but some flowers, ribbons and tulle veils decorated with sequins. Turbans for cocktail parties in the second half of the period.

1931   'Dainty straw hat. Trimmed chenille flowers. Bound edge. Very becoming shape 12/11'

'Velour hat trimmed with self-coloured ribbon. Specially suitable for the dignified woman requiring a young style. 12/11'

1935   'Berets and velvet Tams. Also Marina hats. From 2/11–12/11'

1938   'Hats in fur felt. Rolled brim cut in fancy design and trimmed with straw motifs. Azure, nigger, or any shade to order 16/-'

Advertisements, *Essex County Standard*

BOOTS AND SHOES

SHOES

A trend towards darker colours and rounded toes is evident. Evening shoes however continue with a pointed toe. Heels generally high, but in mid-decade some low heels for town and afternoon wear, as well as low or high evening sandals.

Some mixtures of colours and materials: two-colour 'co-respondent' shoes. Slashed uppers and multiple straps, open cut-outs (1932–34). Court styles, T-straps, bars, Oxfords and Ghillies (i.e. with eyelets or loops in separate tags, not all in one piece of leather) all popular.

Between 1931 and 1935 a rigid-soled moccasin type of sandal or light shoe was in fashion. Peep-toes for evening sandals (1935).

Wedge heels were popularized by the Italian designer and shoemaker Ferragamo from 1936 onwards.

From 1937 shoes became 'clumsy' looking in cut with blocked 'barge' toes.

For evening and cocktail wear some peep-toes. From 1937 to 1939 there was an increasing importation of American shoes with a wider range of fittings.

Heels became lower, wedges more popular and the clumsy look increased in 1940. Sling-back and peep-toe models in favour.

BOOTS

Bootees of suède from 1937–38. A large variety by autumn of 1940; mostly in suède but some of leather: low or medium heels. Ankle height most common, generally with turn-over top. Unlined or lined with sheepskin. Leather or more usually crêpe rubber soles. Laces. Some calf-high boots with zip. Rubber Wellington boots and zip fastened 'fashion' boots all through decade.

GAITERS

In fabric worn by the less fashionable; and smart ones of zip-fastened rubber attached to heelless galoshes.

BOOT AND SHOE MATERIALS

Calf, kid, reptile, suède, textile materials from jute to satin.
Rubber for galoshes and Wellington boots.

COLOURS

In 1934 ecru, neutral beige, greenish grey, sometimes in combination with brighter hues. Black, white, browns, dark blues, mustard, strawberry; a little green. Gold and silver for evenings.

EXAMPLES

1931   'Brown glacé kid and umber lizard one-bar shoe 25/9.
        Glacé court trimmed lizard 29/9
        Crepe sole sandals from 1/11'

1933   'Real lizard courts 18/9
        Evening shoes with $2\frac{3}{4}''$ heels. Court and Opera court [cut with the quarters separate from the vamp, at forepart, and sloping down to the sole] in silver kid, silk, satin, and crepe de chine 20/-'

1935   'Tie shoes in dark brown glacé with walnut kid insertions 21/-
       Shoes in linen/calf mixtures 16/9'
       'Ladies gaiters, 1/-, 1/6, 2/- per pair'

Advertisements, Essex County Standard

Late 1930's   Evening shoes, sandal cut, of gold brocade with ankle strap and
       trimming of gold kid. 3-inch Spanish heel. Made by Barretts.

Northampton Museum

*119. 1938 Shoes: (a) Court. Black, brown or white crêpe de Chine. 12/9d. (b) Evening
sandal. Black, white, silver or gold kid. 21/9d. and 35/9d. (c) Black glacé walking shoe with
tie-over instep.*

STOCKINGS

As with shoes the colours of stockings tended to be darker. Wool,
lisle, cotton, rayon and silk and combinations of these. Some
short stockings, just below the knee, with elastic yarn tops (*c.*
1935).

Some dark coloured ribbed sports stockings, also short ankle
socks.

In 1940 rumour reached these shores from the United States of a
miraculous new material for hosiery – nylon.

1931   'Lisle and cotton hose 1/-, 2/-, 2/6 per pair
       Silk and wool 8¾d. 1/6, 2/-, 2/6 per pair
       Art silk 1/-, 1/6, 2/- per pair
       Pure silk 2/6 per pair
       Art silk lined wool 1/6, 2/-, 2/6 per pair'

1933   'Pure silk hose 1/11¾'

1940   'Rayon and silk 2/-, & 2/11
       Pure silk 3/11, 4/11, 5/11
       Golf socks in fawn, brown, navy'

Advertisements, *Essex County Standard*

ACCESSORIES

GLOVES

These were of considerable importance both for day and evening wear throughout the decade, gauntlet styles being popular for day wear.

Long gloves for evenings.

1933   'Tan cape gloves, fleece lined 5/11½.'

1938   'White lamb's wool gloves with coloured cape palms from 8/11'

Advertisements, *Essex County Standard*

FURS

Extremely popular, especially fox mounted with paws and mask as stoles. Fur capes and fur trimming.

MUFFS

Appeared spasmodically.

PARASOLS AND UMBRELLAS

As in previous decade. Few parasols, but they were noted among the fashionable in 1939 in lace and organdie to match summer dresses.

Umbrellas in brighter colours with macintoshes to match (1937).

WALKING STICKS

Painted in black and white stripes for use in the black-out were one of many early war-time 'gimmicks' – so were luminous buttons for wear on the lapel.

SCARVES, JABOTS, FICHUS, etc.

Were not so popular.

HANDBAGS

To the middle of the decade mostly medium or small size flat pochettes. From about 1936 they got larger and the variety increased. In 1940 many shapes, boxey or pouch-like, mostly on frames with single or double handles; some with compartments for the gas-mask. Clasp or zip fastenings.

COATEES, BOLEROS, CAPES

For evening wear. Lace or material.

BELTS

Of self material, leather, etc. Wide belts with large square buckles (1936–37).

JEWELLERY

Diamenté ornaments for hats. Clips replacing brooches to a certain extent.

Princess Marina led fashion with a double row of pearls close round the neck.

Glass jewellery from Czechoslovakia.

Old-fashioned pieces, large earrings, amber (1937). Lapel clips and other ornaments; jewellery centred at throat (1938–40).

FASTENINGS

For skirts and dresses generally left side-waist. Press-studs ('poppers') became more popular than hooks and eyes, although a hook and eye was often used at the top of skirt plackets.

Zip fasteners for skirts and dresses began to make headway during this decade.

MATERIALS

Generally as in the previous period. Various brands of rayons were extensively advertised.

The economic depression led to attempts to introduce woollen and cotton materials for evening dresses; from 1934 Princess Marina greatly helped by setting a fashion for cotton frocks.

Lace and tulle for evening wear. From 1937 silk jersey was a favourite fabric.

COLOURS

The usual palette of blues, browns, greens and reds, with, of course, black and white and grey.

More pastel and quiet shades in the beginning of the decade – strong colours by the end.

Beige, fawn, ivory, lettuce green, lilac, pale citron, yellow, pink, putty, sky blue (1930–32).

'The new colour – ash-grey' (1933).

'The newest shades are Margaret Rose, Duchess and Marina Green, Jubilee Blue and Ivory' (1935).

'Trimmings in vivid colours' (1936).

In 1937 – Coronation Year – a vogue for Royal purples and crimsons. Also tartans and pink-black checks.

Colour contrasts and vivid colours (1937–39); a bright cylamen was very popular around 1939.

PATTERNS

Floral, particularly in earlier years. Stripes and checks. Checked or flecked tweeds for tailored dress materials. In mid-decade polka dots, especially in navy and white, very popular.

1940-1950

INTRODUCTORY REMARKS

The whole of the 1940's was overshadowed by the Second World War and its aftermath to a degree that had never before been experienced.

The thoughts, ideas and resources of the entire world were concentrated in an unprecedented manner upon the pursuit of the war in the first five years, and in the attempted reconstruction and rehabilitation of the ravaged nations during the second half of the decade.

'Fashion' throughout the decade fought its own battle – that of Designers and Desire against Austerity and Actuality: Choice versus Coupons and Controls.

Unlike the days of the Great War of 1914–18, all clothes were subject to control both in respect of the amount that could be bought – rationing was introduced in June 1941, and continued for the next ten years – and to the quantity and type of material that could be used in their manufacture.[1] Purchase tax added a financial deterrent to these direct embargoes.

The circumstances of the war which touched on all aspects of a woman's life and which, in the vast majority of cases, involved women in full- or part-time war work to a greater or less extent, combined with the controls imposed, reduced the average woman's wardrobe to a uniform utility: a fashionable un-fashionableness is evidenced by the lack of new designs and modes in those clothes that were mass-produced during the war years, and by the uninhibited way in which old 'best' and 'party'

[1] Between 1940 and 1945 the world production of man-made fibres (mostly rayon) fell by almost a half, and of cotton by a third.

dresses were worn either in their original state or refurbished year by year.

'Utility' clothes were introduced in 1942. Standard patterns for suits, dresses and top coats were produced by a committee of designers and the made-up garments were sold at controlled prices. In general the designs, if uninspired, were good and the materials used were satisfactory in quality, but the cutting and making up was aimed at utilizing the minimum of cloth: hems and seams were skimpy, all inessential refinements were omitted.

All Utility clothes carried a label bearing the mark of a double crescent: ₵₵ 41

The effect of the Utility scheme was at first to introduce a style which was almost a uniform for civilians, although with experience and ingenuity manufacturers achieved, in due course, individualities in their garments which relieved the unfamiliar and unwished for monotony.

True fashion, the deep and unuttered desire of women for femininity and freedom of choice within the contemporary ethos, expressed itself in make-up, colour, and those accessories which could be contrived uncontrolled and coupon-free. For export the fashion journals showed some designs from the studios of native and exiled French couturieres, and for those with coupons and cash to spare, American designs were being introduced and familiarized by the cinema and magazines. Dresses of American origin with calf- or ankle-length skirts and accentuated waists and hips, foreshadowing the lines of the 1950's, were shown in *Vogue* in 1942.

The decade falls into two parts – the first, when all the forces mentioned above were in control, was ending in 1945, as the war was brought to an uneasy end. 'Fashion is going feminine' said *Vogue* in March of that year, and spoke of 'the coup-de-grâce to the over-stuffed shoulder', smaller waists, and fulness in skirts. Although the end of the war did not see a return to freedom for fashion, indeed the controls became for a time more stringent, the reaction among the majority of women was for anti-uniforms, longer skirts and curves. The traditional materials began to re-appear, if largely confined to the export market, and they were being joined in 1946 by the new synthetics and plastics. French feminine reaction to war-time austerity was crystalized in 1947 by Christian Dior's 'New Look', in which shoulders sloped, waists, hips and breasts were emphasized and skirts were lengthened dramatically, the hem line being at calf level, with a bouffant fullness. In this country, however, the 'New Look' was in the main modified and the older styles seem to have been preferred by the majority. By late 1948 skirts, though still long, were in many cases also very tight-fitting, and Fashion seemed undecided in its direction – bewildered as it was by the coupons, controls and costs.

By 1949, a year during which a large variety of garments was released from the rationing of clothes coupons, and financial limitations and non-availability of materials on the home market became the principal restrictive factors, Fashion began to define itself once again. The skirt length for day time settled at about thirteen inches from the ground, and a workable compromise between extreme flare and skimpy slimness emerged. Waists, though small, ceased to be so emphasized and hip padding was replaced by large pockets.

Trousers, forced upon many women during the war years, now came to be accepted by choice and not by dictation.

As mentioned previously new synthetic materials appeared in the after-war years, at first notably nylon. First produced in Britain in 1941, the new yarn was available for war materials only. With peace and the run-down of the Forces, one popular source of nylon material for the home dressmaker was ex-R.A.F. parachutes. Sold free of coupons these provided a supply of white or coloured eleven-foot-long triangular panels, 'ideal for making blouses, lingerie, kiddies' wear, curtains, etc.'

Nylon stockings, which in 1940 were being produced on a national scale in the United States, originally arrived over here with the American troops stationed in England from 1942, and were first seen on the lucky legs of girls who had acquired a 'Dough-Boy friend'.

In 1949 enough yarn to make fifty million pairs of nylon stockings was produced by British Nylon Spinners.

During the years of war and austerity, 'Make-do and mend' had become a patriotic and popular slogan, assiduously fostered by Authority, which had among other devices, inserted a series of advertisements in the press featuring the activities of 'Mrs. Sew-and-Sew'. This somewhat inane know-all, offspring of the Board of Trade, detailed to our besieged countrywomen shifts and strategems for repairing and caring for their clothes. Natural ingenuity supplemented this official advice and some of the versatility displayed is noted in the section 'Wartime Expedients'.

As in all areas of rationing and shortage, the 'spiv' and the Black Market catered for certain types of individual, but as *Vogue* so rightly stated in 1941, 'Ingenuity, within the spirit of the regulations, is legitimate . . . but it is cheating to try to beat the game. No clothes out of curtaining. No coupons from outside the family circle . . .' And to the credit of the vast majority of English-women this principle guided their search for Fashion, or acceptance of non-fashion, through the lean years of the Forties.

DAY DRESSES

Day dresses were simple and tailored. The afternoon dress, when worn, was more feminine and softer in outline. Belts were almost universal.

The pinafore dress appeared throughout the decade.

By 1949 the shirt dress was known as a shirt-waist or shirt-waister.

The sheath dress of 1950 was straight, plain, sleeveless, with a low-cut square neckline back and front.

SKIRTS

In 1941 a skimpy silhouette. Skirts eighteen inches from the ground, straight with kick pleats in the back; pleats in front or all round; some moderate flares. Shirring at front waist. Hip drapery in afternoon dresses. Tucks at waist: pockets or sham pockets at hip level (1942–43). Waists more emphasized in 1944:

some bustle effects such as frills, flounces, peplums, at the back. Dirndls. Slightly longer in 1945, and slimmer, but some front fulness or flare with drapery at the hips from the autumn. In 1946 length to slightly below the knee, narrow with hip-level pockets. Small waists, hips with some side gathering. Waistlines brought up in a curve or point. Inverted pleats in front: some unpressed pleats.

'New Look' in 1947 – eleven or twelve inches from the ground, very full: hip padding. Old styles lengthened by bands at bottom or inserted. Dirndls. Some narrow skirts with hobble effects. If not 'New Look', length about fourteen inches from ground.

In 1948 some skirts very full, some tight-fitting. Hip panniers: side pockets. Some wrap-round models. Unpressed pleats; loose gathers; flares.

Designs still very full or else slim in 1949. Twelve and a half to thirteen inches from ground. Waists still small, but large pockets replacing hip padding. Hip drapery, apron overskirts, flying loose panels.

By spring 1950 the length was fourteen inches from ground level, but by winter it had shortened to sixteen in some cases. Skirts now almost all basically straight and tight. Tiers, tunic-overskirts, peplums, flying panels. Pockets, belts. In 1949 and 1950 an oblique line was often seen in cut and drapery of over-skirts, etc.

BODICES

In 1941 with shoulder yokes in many cases, or with shirring or gathers at shoulders or neck line. V, round or square neck lines, rather high. Some small turn-down collars. Shirt dresses, the bodice cut as a shirt with collar and revers, waist belt or band, front button fastening.

Some fly-front fastening bodices. Jacket-dresses, with matching jacket or bolero, or bolero, skirt and blouse. Men's suitings used for tailored jacket-dresses.

In some dresses the shoulders were now slightly sloping. Some collarless, or very small collars in 1941–43. Some shirring or

*120. 1941 Afternoon dress, bodice gathered into
shoulder yoke. Skirt flared at front.*

gathering at bust, often horizontally. Dresses with different colour
or pattern backs and fronts: or bodice different from skirt, giving
blouse and skirt effect. Jumper-frocks with overblouse or tunic.
Shirt dresses less evident.

Bloused, swathed and gathered effects in 1944–45. Shoulder
yokes with small gathers or tucks. Pinafore dresses. Cross-over

exercises of hand, when novices fix Dacca ... a different colour ...

121. 1941   *Day dresses showing bolero effect. (a) Overbodice attached front waist and opening behind. (b) Mock bolero fronts applied to bodice. Breton sailor hats.*

122. 1942 *Afternoon dress.*
Gauging at shoulder yoke and top of
front skirt panel. Turban hat.

*123. 1945 Simple summer day dresses. Short sleeves, accentuated shoulders.
Upswept hair style.*

bodices. Horizontal gathering or pleating at centre front. Cowl
necklines.

Bust line accentuated and shoulders more rounded in 1946;
basques; peplums cut in one with bodice: tucks from bust to
hips: one sided drapery effects (1947). A longer body line was
aimed at. Girdles and belts. 'New Look' with narrower shoulders
and padded bosom (1947–48).

Flared basques on jacket-dresses. Breast interest with drapery,
pockets, decoration. Turn-down collars; collarless dresses with
wide revers. Mostly V or round neck lines: some heart-shaped,
square or cowl (1948–49): square neck lines with the bodice
front fastening offset to button down from one corner.

Deep bib-yokes: shoulder yokes: dickies or modesty-vests with
deep V necks: dropped shoulders; pleats and tucks. Some
bloused bodices. Small turn-down collars: some wide neck lines,
some deep 'portrait' or 'horseshoe' (1950).

124. 1946 *Day dress of two
different materials. Dolman sleeves.
An 'austerity' conversion from an
old dress.*

125. 1947 *Day dresses: (a)
Cross-over bodice with pleated
front panel to skirt. (b) Button-
through shirt waist. Upswept hair
styles.*

126. 1948 'New Look'. Navy and white spun rayon.
Long skirt with swathed waist line and accentuated bust
line.

127. 1949 Afternoon
dress with neck line looped
with gathers over bust.
Pleated front panel to skirt.
Hat with small eye veil.

SLEEVES

Basically simple. Long and tight, or short or three-quarter. Long
sleeves wrinkled up to elbow. Some raised at shoulder; some
Bishop (1941). Few cuffs. From about 1946 sleeves fuller and
more elaborate in some cases. Pushed up Kimono sleeves in 1948.
Cuffs reappear and are plentiful by 1949.

129. 1950 Afternoon dress. Horseshoe neckline. Close fitting off the forehead hat.

128. 1950 Afternoon dress. Blue, brown, gold or red patterned material. Box cluster pleats in skirt. Hip pockets.

In 1950 Magyar, dolman and kimono cut. Cuffs; slits at wrist with long sleeves.

THE COAT-FROCK OR COAT-DRESS

Of suitings, coatings, corduroy, etc. In 1941, with front-through buttoning, back half-belt and yoke. Inset vertical pockets. In 1950 in heavy wool jersey, button-through front, belt, pockets at front hip level; or in flannel or moss-crêpe with a diagonal wrapover, buttoned through, 'a complete costume in itself when the weather is still warm ... slips easily under a coat later' (*Vogue*).

TEAGOWNS, HOUSECOATS, COCKTAIL DRESSES

THE TEAGOWN

In 1941 is depicted as long skirted and with long sleeves cut from a variety of soft materials. However, the growing habit of taking tea in the kitchen, on the roof, or in the air-raid shelter inhibited the wearing of a teagown by the majority of women for this meal.

HOUSECOATS

Were generally of warm material, wool, and in some cases hand-knitted. They were a convenient and easy garment to change into from the clothes worn for various kinds of war work. Ground length, long or short sleeves, some puffed or bishop style, buttoned or zipped to the waist or to the hem in front. Many had shoulder yokes, some were Princess style, some had belts, sashes and pockets.

In 1949 long, loose, tent-like versions with full, wide sleeves, and of calf or ankle length, could also be worn as evening coats or dressing-gowns.

In more glamorous fabrics the housecoat could be worn 'for dining at home or leisure hours', as could the leisure gown or housegown, cut on the same lines of easy fitting bodice with a long and full skirt, but without the front closure.

These garments replaced for informal evening wear the teagown of the earlier periods.

THE COCKTAIL DRESS

As such did not figure prominently in war time. In 1949 'cocktail or short dinner dress of taffeta or tie-silk. V neckline framed with a stiff double collar'. Sleeveless, but collar wide and covering arm-holes, plain bodice with belt; calf-length, straight, fairly full skirt with some drapery at left hip (*Vogue*).

'For cocktails or informal evenings' in 1950 – slim-line with long sleeves, very wide, stiff collar and cross-over revers, two loose flying panels over skirt, one in front and one behind (*Vogue*).

EXAMPLES

1941   'Your last season's dresses, coats, etc. made to look new'.
                                Dressmaker's advertisement, West Mersea, Essex

         'Leisure gown in printed crepe. Lovely clear designs on grounds of Chartreuse, Saxe, Rose, Leaf Green, Gold and Fuchsia. 69/6'
                                                Advertisement, *Vogue*, April

c. 1942–43   Day dress in green rayon crêpe printed with a pink and blue floral pattern. Flared skirt, the front in pleats sewn from waist to hip level, skimpy at the back. Half sleeves, shaped and padded shoulders; sweetheart neck line caught at sides with bows of dress material. Self belt. Utility label.
                                                            London Museum

1943   'Two-tone frock, blouse and skirt effect. [with a check top and plain skirt] Fine woollen material. 60/- 11 coupons'

         'Jumper-style frock [with over blouse or tunic effect descending to the hips] with smart pleated skirt in black heavy quality satin backed rayon. 70/3. 7 coupons'
                                                            Joy's, Colchester

(Woollen materials cost more coupons than rayon, etc.)

1945   'Button through rayon dress, shoulder yokes, patch pockets. [Square padded shoulders. Knee length] In grey only. 30/- 7 coupons'
                                                                    Ibid.

1947   '5 coupon Frock in gay and charming floral design with Dirndl waist. £1.8.7.'
                                                                    Ibid.

1948   Day dress in small green, black and grey check woollen. Skirt gathered onto waistband, with very skimpy hem and seams. Plain bodice. Low stand collar with pointed revers in front, fastened at back with four buttons at neck. Short sleeves gathered into arm-holes. Small cuffs. Brass zip fastener in left side waist placket.
                                                            London Museum

1949　　'Print dress with fashionable square neckline and side button fastening.
(July)　　Trim waist defined by effective gauging. £1.13.4.'

Joy's, Colchester

1950　　'Classic shirt waist dress .... Traditional collar and buttoning in front;
(summer)　back bodice is tucked to yoke depth. Forearm-length loose cuffed
　　　　　sleeves and a full gathered skirt.'

Vogue

SUITS, COSTUMES

SKIRTS

In 1941 eighteen inches from the ground. Straight; kick pleats in hem; all-round knife pleats; inverted pleats front and back. Some gores; some centre front panels (1942–45).

Slightly longer in 1946. Wider and about fourteen inches from the ground in 1947: some circular gored; pleats. 'New Look' twelve inches from the ground. Pleats, bustles, flares and wrap-over models in 1948, but still some straight and narrow. Town suits fashionable eleven inches from the ground, country wear fourteen.

Slim skirts in 1949, some with overskirts at back. Pleats, groups of pleats at sides; some gores. Thirteen inches from the ground.

Also straight and slim in 1950, some with short slit in back hem. Some pleats, including sunray pleating. Some one-sided effects at hip. Fourteen to sixteen inches from ground.

JACKETS

In 1941 generally long hip length, three to seven buttons, single breasted. Fronts cut square or very slightly rounded. Small collar and lapels. Patch and slanting pockets popular. Shoulders slightly sloped but still padded and square.

Some 'military' touches in belts, breast pockets, etc. (1942). Utility models with three buttons, single breasted, high necks, small collar and plain sleeves and pockets.

Just over hips (1943). High cut, square fronts, wider lapels. Some three-quarter sleeves; some bolero jackets.

130. 1942 Suits: (a) Scotch tweed. Short wide revers, fancy pockets, set-in belt effect. Gored skirt. (b) Jacket dress. Complete dress with high neck, with cutaway curved fronted matching jacket.

131. 1946   Tweed suit, high wide revers,   132. 1947   Three-piece suit. Matching
set-in belt.   jacket and swagger coat with contrasting skirt.
*   Coat worn cape-wise over shoulders.*

Jackets shorter (1944), some with waistcoat fronts.

Winter suits with longer jackets (1945). Short, wide lapels.

'Long look' in 1946 and 1947. Large pockets. Hip padding.
Some double-breasted with a dozen buttons. Also short, closely-
fitting jackets. Waists were emphasized; less padding at shoulders;
Raglan and kimono sleeves of various lengths.

Fitted or boxey types in 1948. Finger-tip length. Flare basques.
Less padding at shoulders. More rounded fronts to be seen.
Waists emphasized.

High fastening; some with small round turn-down collars,
some turn-down and pointed, some with small revers. Straight
fitting or with flared basques. Waisted (1949).

In 1950 the classic jacket with stepped collar and revers, single
or double breasted; or straight, loose and boxey coats; or bloused

and belted; or very short bolero type. Deep, wide horseshoe neck lines with plain collars and 'dickies' or fill-ins. Some sailor collars.

Some jackets were basqued, the basques cut to jut out backwards. Waist and hip interest. Shoulders slightly dropped and rounded. Kimono sleeves popular.

Cardigan suits had a collarless, high buttoned, single-breasted jacket.

In 1941 costumes are noted as being made from men's suitings – possibly the transference of so many men into khaki or blue caused a temporary glut. Top coats were sometimes en suite with a two-piece suit.

133. 1949 Two suits, nipped-in waists, long straight skirts.

134. 1950 Suit with pleated basque to jacket. Three-quarter sleeves, full wide skirt.

o

EXAMPLES

1942   'For town, country, and every season – the classic suit in mixture tweeds of
       brown/blue, brown/pink, blue/fuchsia. Hips 36"–42" 18 coupons 14 gns.'
                                                                          Harrods

1945   'Smart suit in Barrathea cloth for the smaller figure. Coat has the new
       fastening with one button at waist and the skirt is pleated front and back.
       £7.18.7. 18 coupons.'

                                                                    Joy's, Colchester

1950   'Three piece tweed suits; skirt, jacket and top coat. Suit £8.5.0. Coat
       £8.8.3.'

                                          Advertisement, *Essex County Standard*

135. 1943   Dual purpose blouse for day or evening wear.
'Utility' design.

136. 1943   Blouse,
in wool with stiffened
collar and cuffs.
'Utility' design.

137. 1945 Blouses.

BLOUSES, JUMPERS AND KNITWEAR

Blouses and jumpers worn with a separate skirt became increasingly popular as the war years went by.

BLOUSES

High, round necks, short sleeves. Shoulder yokes. Small turn-down collars. Short sleeves; long sleeves. Shirts with buttoned cuffs and pointed turn-down collars (1941). Long belted Russian blouses; basqued blouses to wear outside or inside the skirt. Short sleeves, long full sleeves with wrist-band; or short sleeves (1942).

Pouched over top of skirt. Some waistcoat fronts. Fancy shirt styles. Afternoon blouses, pleated, with high necks, frilled collars and jabots (1943).

Collarless: cowl necks; shirts with full sleeves. White blouses with black skirts very popular (1944). Frills and jabots in 1946; neck bows, 1947. Sleeveless waistcoat-blouses.

Long belted overblouses: sleeveless waistcoat-blouses, long or short sleeves; kimono, Raglan, Bishop; sleeveless blouses. Vertical or horizontal tucks at front; yokes. Collars high, or long pointed turned-down; stand collars; wide boat-shaped neck lines (1949–50).

JUMPERS AND KNITWEAR

Knitting at home or when on air raid duties, etc. was extremely popular and widespread during the war years. Old garments were often re-knitted. Patchwork using scraps of different coloured wools left over from easier days saved coupons.

Twin-sets of short-sleeved plain jumpers and matching long-sleeved cardigans.

Striped jerseys, some in lisle; plain bodied jumpers with striped yokes. Waistcoats. Lacey blouses and jumpers in open stitch. Lumber-jacket styles with high necks buttoning down to a buttoned waistband, same with the buttoned closure down the left side from the shoulder. 'Sloppy Joes', a loose coat. Very short boleros or 'hug-me-tights', knitted woollen skirts, dresses and suits. Shoulders padded (1941–43).

The 'Victory jumper' of 1942 was decorated with vertical columns of Vs in a contrasting colour.

Cardigans could be buttoned high to the neck, or with a small V-opening or open to below the bust, then buttoned to the waist.

From about 1945 Fair Isle patterns. Boleros and short boxey jackets. Bows at neck. Sleeves, or front and back of different colours; Magyar sleeves (1946–47).

Cardigans longer in 1949; evening jumpers with deep square décolletage. Knitted dresses with pleated skirts. Knitted suits. Twin sets. Dolman and kimono sleeves. Some raised shoulders (1949–50).

SKIRTS AND TROUSERS

SKIRTS

The separate skirt worn with blouse or jumper was always popular and became more and more usual from about 1943. From 1944 black skirts with white blouses were much worn.

Following the lines generally of the costume skirt, the separate skirt was 18 inches from the ground in 1941, dropping to 11 or 12 inches in 1947–48 and rising again by the winter of 1950 to 16 inches from the ground.

Dirndl skirts, with pockets, cut straight, or on the cross or gored, from about 1945. Many of these were home-made from old curtains, etc.

Generally straight and slim fitting. Waist lines built up in curves or points (1946). Becoming wider and fuller from 1947. Some full with linings. Straight again by the end of 1949, but some full. Large pockets at front hip level or full skirts (1949–50).

TROUSERS

Increasingly popular for work and to put on at night when roused by air-raids.

Divided skirts, knee length and pleated, were advertized for cycling and sport in 1941, as were three-pieces, of corduroy shirt and alternative skirt or slacks.

Trouser suits, and flared tunics worn over slacks.

House-slacks from old, long, evening dress skirts.

During the war years trousers were generally wide and easy fitting.

From about 1947 the American blue jeans began to be worn by the young, and by older women for holiday wear.

In 1949 tapered trousers, ending just below the knee.

In 1950 fairly narrow, ankle or calf length.

Shorts to mid-thigh.

'Separates' indicated skirt or slacks and blouse, jumper, jerkin, etc.

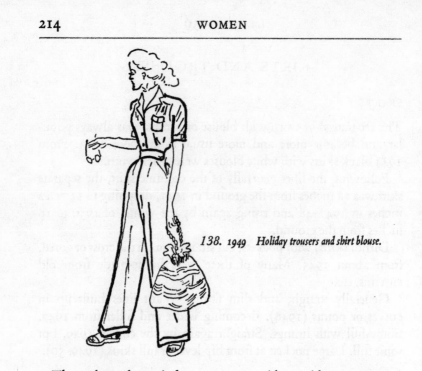

138. 1949   Holiday trousers and shirt blouse.

Throughout the period trousers were with or without turn-ups.
A war-time fashion of wearing trousers with high-heeled shoes
and dangling earrings was frowned on in some quarters.

EVENING DRESSES

During the war years evening dresses of all sorts became of less
significance to most people; when worn, the evening blouse and
separate skirt was a favourite version, and many pre-war frocks
continued to give good service throughout the decade. By 1943
long skirted dresses were seldom seen at public occasions, but
were still worn to some private parties.

The ground-length, formal evening dress with wide or slim
skirt, hip drapery or peplums, fitted bodice, sometimes shirred
across front, with moderate square or V or high round neck line;
short puffed sleeves, or long plain sleeves. Some bodices draped
and gathered over shoulders, or square-cut top with shoulder straps.
Some bare backs or partly bared midriffs.

139. 1942   Evening dress. Bias cut corselet skirt.

Dinner dresses long or short with long or short sleeves. Some with short skirts for day wear and additional long skirt for evening. By 1945 long dresses for dinner again predominating in fashionable circles.

Evening blouses very popular, some with Bishop sleeves.

1941   'Some are cloudy chiffon, starred with sequins; others very trim in tie silk. There are blouses in satin, organdie, lamé, lace, worn with the same simple style of short or long skirt.'

Vogue

Evening jumpers knitted with wool incorporating metal threads (1945).

Some worn with a slim skirt slit up to the knee for dancing (1944).

Heart-shape neck lines about 1945: cap sleeves. Attempts in 1946 to revive pre-war models, with modifications. Bows, peplums, pleats and folds in skirts, as well as pointed yokes and corselet waists. The 'tulip' skirt with four curved, overlapping sections, two above the others.

The skirts were either wide or tight, fitted close to the hips. Bodices shirred down the centre to the waist, cap sleeves, some deep arm-holes. V-necks: off-the-shoulder models; boned, strapless tops.

In 1947 irregular hem lines instep length or about three inches above in front and longer at the back: wide flounced skirts. Drapery at hip; bustles; draped folds at hip level. Dinner dresses with basqued jackets of contrasting colours.

Cowl tops; off-one-shoulder models; straps or halter necks; boned, strapless tops.

Ground, ballet or ankle length in 1948, still with bustle effects and hip drapery. Tight-fitting bodices, high, or round, square, or V neck lines; or very low strapless tops exposing top half of breasts, or wide low collars around the décolletage, or swathed or fichu effect tops. Dinner coat-dress, wide skirt, low neck with large collar, buttons all down front. Separate long skirts and basqued jacket-bodices (1949).

Ball dresses with very wide flared or bouffant skirts, diaphanous shoulder covering with sequins, brilliants or decorative

140. 1947 *Evening dresses: (a) Black crêpe dinner dress
with gold taffeta bow at knee, short puff sleeves. £15. 1. 11.
(b) Ballet length cocktail dress of taffeta. Drapery bunched
on left hip, deep square neckline. £17. 6s.*

embroidery. Fitted strapless bodices; draped and swathed bodices (1949–50).

Some calf-length dresses with diaphanous floor-length over-skirts. Strapless and halter neck lines; tops leaving one shoulder bare. Large collars.

Calf-length dinner dresses, slim and straight.

Strapless dresses with boned, low-cut bodices, of calf or floor length, flared and full; or calf length tight over thighs, then pleated and flared. The full, floor-length dress was still correct for formal and ballroom wear.

Evening blouses and separate skirts still in fashion (1950).

CLOTHES FOR SPECIAL OCCASIONS

WEDDINGS

Many couples were married in uniform or ordinary day clothes.

Wedding dresses were often borrowed, and passed around among members of the family.

Suits were popular wear for brides (c. 1947–48).

When worn, the white wedding dress was of traditional form. In 1941 some trains; long sleeves, sometimes of small gigot design, or short and puffed. Wide or slim skirts. Square or heart-shaped neck lines. Veils; orange blossom or white feather head-dresses. Some short veils, just below the shoulder.

1949   'Lovely fabrics for the Bride.

Ivory velvet	27/6 per yard
Ivory broche satin	15/11 ,, ,,
Ivory crêpe	9/11 ,, ,,
Parchment satin	16/9 ,, ,,
White Organdie	5/6 ,, ,,
Ivory Rayon Taffeta	12/6 ,, ,,

All two coupons per yard, 36"'

Advertisement, *Essex County Standard*

MOURNING

For funerals a black suit was very popular. Light coloured stockings were acceptable.

141(a). 1950 *Evening dress in gold brocade. Front of bodice cut in one with full wide skirt in princess style.*

141(b). 1950 *Evening dress. Long waisted, very full skirt, strapless boned bodice.*

141(c). 1940–41 *Wedding dress of moiré silk. Heart-shaped neckline. Veil and feather headdress.*

MATERNITY

Suits with loose smock-like jackets, pleated skirts with adjustable underskirt.

Smocks. Loose over blouses with full-length pleats from shoulder yoke; skirts, adjustable, hanging from shoulder straps. Dresses with front fulness controlled by external ties at waist.

1945 'Well cut maternity dress in soft wool. Easily adjusted and useful for ordinary wear after. 38"–42" hips. £3.1.0. 11 coupons.'

Joy's, Colchester

AIR RAIDS AND WAR WORK

Despite the example of Winston Churchill and his 'rompers', the siren-suit was by no means in universal wear. Woollies, top coats, fur coats over day clothes or underclothes or nightwear were all to be seen in the shelters. Many people at the height of the bombing only partially undressed, or remained fully clothed at night – others made no difference in their usual habits.

Trousers were widely worn for war work in industry, the public services, etc. many of which latter provided uniform or part uniform for employees and volunteers.

Hair was confined in net snoods or by turban-tied head scarves by women factory workers.

Fibre helmets for air raids were advertised: black or khaki or 'painted in your favourite colour' for an extra charge.

The Ministry of Agriculture urged people to spend their holidays doing farm work and an outfit was recommended by *Vogue* consisting of dungarees or slacks, shirt or sweater, woollen socks, thick shoes and a headscarf.

The civilian gas mask issued in a square, cardboard box with a string to go over the shoulder soon called for a daintier container: an example, in the Hollytrees Museum, Colchester, is made of imitation snakeskin, circular and reinforced at the bottom, widening to a flattened top with a flap secured by a press-stud, and a matching shoulder strap.

142. 1941 Siren-suit or shelter suit. 'A necessary addition these days to every wardrobe.'

WARTIME EXPEDIENTS

Mention has been made of the shifts to which the vast majority of women were put during the period of war and post-war scarcity: some of the expedients resorted to showed individual ingenuity; some were publicized in newspapers and magazines and were more widespread.

Much pre-war clothing was retained and used often with more or less alteration and redecoration: e.g. a pre-war, low-cut, long evening dress would have the skirt cut short and be worn by day over a blouse as a pinafore dress.

Old or surplus curtains were re-formed into dirndl skirts.

143. 1942 Wartime conversion of edge-to-edge coat into bolero suit.

An old dress would have inserted in the centre-front two full-length, narrow panels of a contrasting material and be made to button through.

Two coarse knitted dishclothes could be transformed into a jumper.

Old top coats were cut up and remade into skirt and bolero ensembles.

Patchwork skirts and blouses made from odd scraps; or two or more left-over remnants made into a waistcoat.

Old, long evening dresses could be converted into slacks and old beach pyjamas were suggested as the basis for a new full-length evening dress.

Old cotton frocks were converted into overalls and aprons.

Odd jackets were popular, worn over dresses, as were sleeveless jerkins of various materials.

Short, sleeveless dresses could be worn pinafore fashion over a blouse by day, or alone in the evenings.

Patchwork knitting from odd left-overs of wool and old woollies unravelled and re-knitted to a new pattern were the devices of keen knitters.

In addition to the multitude of home-contrived and home-adapted garments many shops offered a repair and remodelling service to their customers.

SPORTS CLOTHES

There was generally less opportunity for sports or sports wear during the war years, except in the Services, which provided their own designs of appropriate garments, and manufacturers turned their production over to Government contracts. The post-war years of rationing kept the demand for sports wear down; people expended their coupons on more essential clothes. Many pre-war bathing dresses and tennis frocks lingered on.

Traditional forms of dress for tennis, golf, etc. survived, however, and by 1950 hints of brief nylon dresses worn with lace edged and exiguous panties were causing eyebrows in tennis circles to be raised as high as the skirts themselves were eventually to be.

CYCLING

In 1941 the 'trouser skirt' – wide, knee-length divided skirt.

GOLF

Shower-proof poplin skirts and wind-cheaters with elasticated waistband, full-length zip, turn-down collar. Some reversible in two colours. Tweed skirts and jumpers or jersey-jackets with belts.

In 1949 tweed dress with shoulder yoke and inverted pleats each side of the back panel of the bodice.

144. 1941   Sports wear: (a) Shirt and shorts all-in-one tennis dress. (b) Golf outfit. Hip stitched pleats. Cloth jerkin, back or side closing. Cut-away back golf gloves.

TENNIS

All-in-one shirt and shorts dresses, with button-on skirt to go over the shorts. Wide shorts with shirts.
White flannel skirts. White woollies.

RIDING

Jacket with patch pockets and no flaps; close-cut narrow breeches (1941).
Jodhpurs, with pronounced wings, shirt or high-necked jersey, tweed jacket (1947).

SWIMMING

One-piece costumes of woven elasticated fabric. Flared skirts over pants and brassière tops (1941). Two-piece costumes. Very revealing two-pieces (bikinis) from (1947). One-piece costumes, strapless, with boned brassière tops, some with overskirts. Two-piece suits of elasticated fabric.

BEACH WEAR

Playsuits of blouse and slacks. One-piece playsuits of shirt and shorts with separate overskirt. Pyjamas (1941). Dresses with 'sun-tops', deep brassière-shaped décolletage with button-on straps to be removed for sun-bathing, and matching jackets (1949). Shorts and sun-tops with deep décolletage. 'Separates' of sailor blouses and shorts. Sleeveless sun-dresses with frill at top of bodice and shoulder straps (1950).

WINTER SPORTS

Horizontally striped knitted jumper over shirt with pointed collar turned down over round neck of jumper; woollen gloves; dark, loose trousers tucked into woollen socks; wedge heel shoes (1949).

P

145. 1941 *Coat, slim fitting with belt and bloused effect. Crescent-shaped pockets. Robin Hood hat.*

146. 1941 *Coat in camel cloth. High neck, small stand collar, tie belt, wide skirt, pleated back. Dolman sleeves. 7½ gns.*

OUTDOOR CLOTHES

Coats with tie belts and full skirts. Some back pleats. Square shoulders, large collars and revers giving a masculine look to upper half. Double or single breasted. Some pockets. Detachable hoods. Dolman sleeves. Swagger coats and three-quarter-length coats (1941). Wrap-round and tie-belted coats, skirts a little less full; about two inches below the knee. Short boxey coats. Cloth coats in style of trench coats. Fitted waists; shoulder yokes; flared or straight skirts. Some quilted linings: some belted, some not: pockets (1942–44). New style in 1944: full, belted, very large collar, knee length.

Edge-to-edge coats with a dropped shoulder line in some cases continued in favour especially in spring and summer. Most coat sleeves were plain, fairly close fitting.

Shoulders rounded and with yokes; double-breasted; belts. Short coats, swing backs; flares; some waisted coats.

Much wider and bigger sleeves also in 1946. Yokes, big armholes, swing backs or waisted, some with belts. Dolman and Bishop sleeves: shoulders rather raised. Some fur collars. Length just below bend of the knee. A fashion at this time for wearing the coat cloak-like over the shoulders, the arms hanging loose.

Seven-eighths and three-quarter, swing back and swagger coats. Long coats with tight waists and full backs and skirts, or narrow fitting (1947–48).

Fitting tops and full skirts. Large collars with revers, or collars with jutting-forward points, or shawl collars. Shoulders slightly padded. Pockets, some very large. Loose coats with back pleats. Very bulky tent-like loose coats. The short coat, hip-length, straight cut or flared (1949).

In 1950 bulky 'tents' hanging loosely, or sometimes belted; some flared; some with centre-back pleats. Narrower, fitted models, or straight cut with easy waists. Large sleeves; large collars; pockets, some very large. Some fur trimming to collars and cuffs. Short coats, some lined with fur or fur-fabric, and 'pyramid' line swing back outdoor jackets.

147. 1941 *Camel fitted coat. 'Military' appearance. Shoulder padding. Pillbox hat, wedge shoes. Typical upswept front hair.*

148. 1946 *Double-breasted tailored coat. Breton sailor hat. Shoulder-length hair style.*

149. 1949   Loose fitting coat with fur cuffs.

150. 1949   Swagger back tent coat. Large curved collar. Pockets and cuffs.

Shoulders more sloping (1950). Mostly coats were single-breasted, but some double-breasted, generally among the fitted models.

In the winter of 1950 *Vogue* was speaking of the emergence of a 'barrel' line, but its impact was small in that year.

FUR COATS

Full-length, three-quarter and short, in Indian lamb, moleskin, Persian lamb, mink. Shoulders square. Collars. Some belts.

In 1946 loose backs, no collars, long revers. Bishop sleeves. Roll collars. Fur capes for evening wear.

RAINPROOFS

Trench coats; belted double-breasted and belted single-breasted macintoshes. Capes with hoods and inside pockets. Rubber proofed raincoats. From 1946 nylon, rubber or oil proofed. Patch pockets, belts, large collars. Some matching hoods. Trench coat style still popular. All-weather coats of proofed gaberdine, corduroy, etc. some with matching hoods (1950). Lightweight synthetics and plastics beginning to appear in last years of decade.

EXAMPLES

1941   'Tweed coats of outstanding quality. Man-tailored in swagger or belted styles.'

1943   'Women's top coats, 79/6, 15 coupons.'

1945   'Jigger coats [Thigh or three-quarter length, edge-to-edge, square shoulders] for casual wear during spring and summer £4.13.0. 12 coupons.'

Advertisements, *Essex County Standard*

151. 1945 Short boxey coat with large patch pockets.

1946-47   Brown beaver lamb full-length coat. Lined brown rayon. Collarless.
          Fastening edge-to-edge with silk covered hooks and eyes at neck and
          waist. Voluminous Bishop sleeves. Two vertical slit pockets inset at hip
          level. Square shoulders.

                                                          Author's collection

1949   'Swagger coat, brown and fawn diagonal tweed, £8.0.5.'
          'Café-coloured Canadian Squirrel. Deep collar at back with tie in front,
          bishop sleeves on wrist band, full back, wrap over.'

                                           Advertisements, *Essex County Standard*

HAIR

In 1941 short, sometimes only three inches long, a fashion stated
to be favoured by many popular film stars.

> 'Over here girls in the services, the offices and the factories are finding that it lies
> meekly under caps and coifs.'
>
>   *Vogue*

Upswept at the sides and side-swept at the back: brushed up and
curled on top. Or sleek and curled over the ears and in the nape
of the neck.

Later, in 1942 and 1943, the hair was again worn longer, either
brushed up from the back, a style more favoured when 'dressed up',
or falling with long rolling curls over ears and neck.

The 'Veronica Lake' hair-do had a side parting, the hair
brushed over and hanging free, shoulder length.

Upswept styles also in 1944 to 1946; some braids; or long to
shoulder; or with curled rolls at back. A 'sculptured look' was
aimed at in 1945. Swept back with the hair piled on top, or in a
bun on top in 1947, or long into the neck with a chignon.

In 1948 hair could be worn short or, comparatively, long;
straight or waved. Some fringes and chignons.

By autumn the 'new short hair-do' or 'short bob cut', many
with a straight cut fringe or bang in front.

Short and dressed close to the head (1949-50). Sometimes
irregularly cut and brushed forward from the crown of the head –
the 'urchin' cut.

MILLINERY

Some forward, but mostly backward tilts in 1941. Large brims; some high crowns. Pointed crowns and slouch brims. Turbans. Berets of same material as blouses. Headscarves. Cloches cut high in front and down at the back.

Crocheted and knitted caps and hats. Snoods and scarves. Leather hats. High crowned turbans; pill boxes; sailors; berets, and berets with peaks. Generally forward tilt (1942–44). High turbans; headscarves in bizarre designs and colours; skull caps. High crowns, some pointed. 'Fisher girl' – sou'wester type, turned-back brims, worn on back of head (1945).

Hats not elaborately trimmed during years 1941–45. Some veils, feathers, ribbon or fur. A hatless fashion arose and was adopted by many, though, being unrationed, the hat always proved an outlet for otherwise frustrated indulgence.

'No coupons. We have a good selection of Hats. Prices from 12/11.'
Joy's, Colchester

Trimming increased from about 1945, and hats were again becoming more popular from 1947.

In 1946 hats with brims, turned up or down, were worn with a backward tilt, coming over the ears. Also straw bonnets, forward-perched toques, and still headscarves.

Hats tilted sideways with large wide brims, or small up-turned brims in 1947, in which year were many experimental shapes, including caps draped to cover the back of the head and neck. Sideways or forward tilts in 1948, with a modified version of a cloche hat re-appearing. The sailor shape remained popular.

Trimming of veils, ribbons, feathers, flowers and fur.

By 1949 definite head fitting, off the face lines, including a cloche with a turned-up front brim. Also large straw cartwheels for summer.

Small close-fitting hats coming down over the ears in 1950; 'helmet' and bonnet shapes.

Large picture hats for summer wear; some small, round hats,

and pill boxes by the winter. Hats were now generally worn straight, with little or no tilt.

Square headscarves tied under the chin were practical and popular.

Evening wear: not general, but little round caps; veils; flowers; feathers; ribbon; hats of tulle, ribbon and sequins (1941–44) are noted in the fashion magazines: also little, flat pill boxes with veils in 1949 and 1950.

1942 'Turban of smocked nappa [fine, soft, kid], in black, with royal [blue] jersey swathe. Also other colours. 5 gns.'

Harrods

1945 'Selection of attractive felt hats 29/8 and 12/3.'

1947 'Hats. Charming Bretonne style. Can be worn on or off the face. In felt trimmed petersham and small felt flowers. Blue, Nigger, Navy, Wine, Red, Grey, Tan and Black. 26/11.'

1949 'Shallow off-the-face hat. Small turn-back brim. Decorated with two feathers in a cockade. Wool felt 17/6.'

Joy's, Colchester

SHOES AND BOOTS

SHOES

Generally from 1941 to 1947 shoes were sensible and sturdy with round or square toes, often walled. Flat heels or wedges, often of uncovered cork. Tie fastenings; crêpe soles; very thick built-up 'platform' soles; Oxfords, ghillies, brogues and moccasin styles. Suede shoes with elastic inserts at each side.

Plain or sling-back court with a high heel for leisure wear: peep-toes from 1945 (the extreme tip of the toe-piece cut away, straight or in an arc to expose the big toe); or high-cut with elasticated front under a tab, or with a bow.

Sandals, including wedges and platform soles, many of multicolour suede remnants. Raffia sandals with cork soles and heels.

Leather, like other commodities, was controlled, and five clothing coupons were needed for a pair of shoes. Utility models were available. Leather substitutes such as rubber and strong fabrics were sometimes used.

There was a brief vogue in 1943–44 for wooden clog-like soles for shoes and sandals, with leather or suede, or both, for uppers. The wooden soles and heels of these shoes had rubber heel-pieces, and three rubber pieces on the sole, one at the toe and one at each side. A refinement was a cut through the sole, under the ball of the foot, with a leather hinge to give some flexibility.

From 1947 a revival of fashion and quality in shoes. Toes began to become narrower and heels were higher. The wedge, platform sole, peep-toe and sling-back continued until about the end of our period. Ankle straps and instep straps. Afternoon and evening shoes of interlaced strips of leather.

Traditional low-heeled walking shoes.

BOOTS

For winter as in previous section. Rubber Wellington boots.

MATERIALS

Calf, suede, crocodile, textiles and, towards the end of the decade, plastics.

COLOURS

As in clothes generally, an important morale booster. Combination of two and sometimes three colours, e.g. nigger, tan and green. Coloured piping and other trimmings.

Black, browns, tan, navy, wine, greens, yellows. Suede shoes were especially colourful and popular.

EXAMPLES

1941   'Court shoes in calf and suede. Medium heels 47/6.'
        'Suede shoes 29/9. Fleece lined leather 37/6.'
        'High leather shoe, wine, blue, green or black uppers; blue, wine or red
        wedge and platform sole; zip side fastening. 49/6.'
                                                    Advertisements, *Vogue*

152. 1941 Shoes: (a) Court with top decorated with studs. 39/6d. (b) 'Dutchboy'.
Walled platform sole. 49/6. (c) Thick crêpe rubber sole with wedge. (d) High front lace shoe.

1943 'In co-operation with the Government Rubber Controller we are now
      equipped to repair your Wellingtons.'

1945 '"Peeper", or white buckskin shoe with red calf underlay at toe [giving a
      cut-away effect].'

1950 'Grey suede court with reversed collar and platform wedge 49/1.'
      'Black suede with patent ankle strap and platform wedge 48/11.'
      'Cross-strap peep toe with forepart platform and Spanish heel. 49/11.'
                                        Advertisements, *Essex County Standard*

STOCKINGS

The production of silk stockings was banned in 1941.

1941 'The substitutes fall into three classes. There will be rayon stockings. There

will be cotton stockings. Both marvellously like silk. And later look for
stockings that don't imitate silk at all . . . in entirely new weaves, and,
perhaps, gay colours.'

Vogue, January

To rayon and cotton was added wool – home-made versions
in all three materials could be produced by keen knitters.

Knee-length socks and ankle socks appeared from about 1941
as a substitute for stockings; and in many cases, especially in
summer, no stockings or socks were worn at all. Sometimes leg
make-up was applied as a deception or attraction.

Nylon stockings were produced here from December 1946.
Silk re-appeared, and in 1948 were selling at 23/- a pair (and
three coupons).

ACCESSORIES

Colourful scarves, handkerchiefs, etc.; couponless net and tulle
aprons for afternoon or evening wear over an old dress; bows,
jabots and collars to brighten faded favourites of pre-war days.

GLOVES

Worn less during war years. Two coupons per pair. Crocheted
backs and skin palms; leather, wool, etc. and some in coloured
felt. In 1950 long kid evening gloves again.

FURS, MUFFS

Stoles as before, but not as popular as in previous decade. Some
long fur stoles from 1948 for evening wear. Fur trimming in 1950,
also large muffs among the fashionable.

UMBRELLAS

As previously.

SCARVES, JABOTS, COLLARS

Printed silk or rayon scarves, some with regimental badges as motifs.

Long scarves or stoles from 1949–50.

A fashion in 1944 for wearing a scarf round the neck, the end brought down and tucked through a belt; or a square scarf draped and tied at the back or side of the neck.

A few lace or linen collars, frills, etc.

HANDBAGS

In 1941 oblong pochettes, medium size; bags on frames with strap handle, generally oblong; pouches, medium and large, with strap handles.

From 1942 to 1946 plain bags with long straps to hang from the shoulder were very popular, including an issue to the Women's Services. From 1946 still seen but less fashionable.

In 1946 large framed bags with single or double strap handles, often wedge-shaped with sloping sides.

Pouches in a variety of shapes with handles. Square, box-like framed bags. Some pochettes (1949–50).

Handbags mostly in leather. Some materials such as felt and tweed during war. Plastic appearing at end of decade.

BELTS

Remained popular. In 1949–50 some very wide ones, often elasticated.

JEWELLERY

Large bracelets (1941–42). 'Gold' necklets and chains in 1945–46. Shorter hair styles encouraged the wearing of earrings.

Heavy, close-fitting necklaces; multiple short rows of pearls (1949–50).

MATERIALS

All controlled during most of the decade. Utility fabrics from 1942.

Rayon, rayon crêpe, soft woollens, lisle-thread, some silks and satins, cotton, tweed for coats and suits, flannel.

From 1946 the choice gradually became larger and the traditional materials returned to be joined by nylon and the other new synthetics.

COLOURS

Contrasts in 1941, grey/red, yellow/brown or black, navy or black/red.

Strong colours became popular amidst the encircling gloom; 'colours are gay', said *Vogue* in 1942. Emerald green, orange, reds, coral, blues. Pastel shades for summer.

Purples and blues in 1946.

In 1950 browns, greens, reds, purple, grey, beige; red/black, green/black mixtures.

Black and white popular throughout.

PATTERNS

Floral, geometrics, stripes, plaids and checks, all of medium size, getting larger towards the end of the decade. Some abstract and 'primitive' designs from about 1946. Large polka dots in 1950, placed asymmetrically in many cases.

SECTION TWO

MEN

1900-1925

INTRODUCTORY REMARKS

In confining the half century of men's clothes to two chapters the authors were influenced by the slower change in male fashions and the continuance of styles for decades at a time which would, if dealt with *in extenso*, have resulted either in a repetitive catalogue of but slightly differing detail or a mere record of 'no change'.

A. A. Whife, technical editor of the *Tailor and Cutter*, has recorded that the lounge jacket has remained unaltered in its construction, although not in its minutiae, since its origin some hundred years ago,[1] and very much the same tale can be told of the majority of men's wear.

Perhaps the greatest single event to influence the Englishman's costume during the first quarter of the present century was the Great War of 1914–18 and its aftermath. The relaxing of social convention and the economic upheaval that it caused did much to loosen the rigid bonds hitherto confining male attire. But not all the changes of the period are so attributable. The rise of sports and games among all classes, the week-end habit, including the general adoption of the Saturday half-day, and an erosion of the rules of Victorian society were evident influences before 1914. In 1902, for instance, the Vicar of Marlow appealed to visitors, 'please do not permit the matter of dress to keep you away [from Church], come in your flannels and boating dress'. And recording fashions at the seaside in the same year the *Tailor and Cutter* speaks of early morning garments 'loose, unconventional, and summer-like', but notes also that after breakfast these have given place to 'the conventional lounge or morning coat'.

[1] See 'Men's Dress 1890–1914', in *La Belle Epoche*, The Costume Society, 1968.

Q

The war in South Africa, in progress when the century opened, was responsible for some ephemeral effects: 'Khaki coloured neckties will be much in demand out of compliment to the "Absent Minded Beggar"', wrote the *Tailor and Cutter* in 1900 – and possibly for two more permanent ones, the wearing of the handkerchief tucked inside the jacket sleeve, and the use of wrist watches in place of the pocket variety. Both these habits seem to have been popularized by campaigners returned from the veldt.

King Edward VII, both as Prince of Wales and as King, had led the way in a number of innovations; in 1900 it was noted that on occasions he was wearing a lounge suit instead of a frock coat, and in 1908 the *Tailor and Cutter* spoke of his habit of leaving the bottom button of his waistcoat undone, a fashion which has persisted, but of which the King was probably not the originator. Even so, however, the royal approval of the habit no doubt ensured its popularity.

Transatlantic influences were also at work before 1914 in lounge suits with broad shoulders, and an easy deep cut to the armhole, together with peg-top trousers; that is, with wide thighs and knees, thence tapering to the bottom of the legs. Although associated with the American influence, the peg-top trousers were of French origin, and had appeared previously in this country during the nineteenth century. These American styles were noted, perhaps rather disapprovingly, in 1912 as being 'a trifle extreme to what English gentlemen have adopted previously'. About this year also trousers with waistbands were 'very popular . . . especially with flannels that are to be worn without suspenders [braces]'. Pleating into the waistband, said to be the invention of a French tailor, was introduced at this time.

By 1915, due to the war, 'considerable disturbance has taken place in connection with the supply of garments for general wear', and many tailors were glad to take in repairs and cleaning jobs to keep their businesses going. In Hyde Park, still the show ground of male sartorial elegance, 'the lounge jacket appears to be an easy first favourite . . . quite seventy five per cent of those seen wearing this comfortable though plebeian garment'.

(The frock coat, the basic style of the nineteenth century, had become increasingly *démodé*, except for most formal occasions, since 1900, and the morning coat, with its sloping cut-back fronts and the lounge jacket had replaced it. By 1921 the *Tailor and Cutter* described it as 'dead as the Dodo', although it lingered on, especially overseas, for formal wear by politicians, etc. for some time afterwards.)

In 1918 suggestions were made for a 'Standard Suit', and the Director of Wool Textile Production stated that 'a suit of thoroughly sound wearing qualities could be produced on the market at the fixed price of 57/6'. This does not appear to have got far off the ground; nevertheless demobilized soldiers were issued with a civilian suit, presumably to Government specification, and shops advertised 'British Standard Clothing'.

At the end of the war the *Tailor and Cutter* spoke of 'a costume of dull drab monotony'. The silk hat had almost disappeared. The morning coat was confined to politicians, doctors, stockbrokers, young men-about-town, superior shop assistants, and for wear at weddings and funerals, for which purpose it was often hired. For everyday wear by most men its place had been taken by the lounge suit, and, in increasing numbers, by the tweed 'sports coat' worn with flannel trousers.

Into this depressing post-war scene various attempts were made to inject some colour and interest. Not least among the apostles of more colourful dress was the Prince of Wales (H.R.H. The Duke of Windsor). The Prince, a favourite among all classes, did much by his example to popularize such features as Fair Isle sweaters, suede shoes and the dinner jacket, including a midnight-blue version, in place of the more formal evening tail coat, etc.

A noticeable decrease in the weights of cloths used is a feature of the period under review.

Two features of the Twenties ran concurrently with the rising skirts and exposed legs of the women – 'plus fours' and 'Oxford bags'. Both of these appear as an endeavour by the male sex to counter the exposure of female limbs by disclaiming their own legs. The first, a variation of the old knickerbockers, pouched and sagged well below the knees, and the latter garments were trousers of exaggerated fulness, reaching, it was reported in 1925, a width of thirty-two inches in the leg. The former gained wide acceptance, but the Oxford bags were restricted to a smaller public. Nonetheless, their effect was to introduce generally wider trouser legs than had previously been fashionable.

But despite these, and other, novelties, some of which left a permanent mark on male dress, it was said in 1925 by the *Tailor and Cutter* that 'there is a wave of shabbiness sweeping over the country . . . due to a revolution in social conditions'. These conditions were to change even more in the next two decades with the great economic Depression, and the war of 1939, and the effects of the revolution became even more evident in all aspects of the social scene.

DAY CLOTHES

THE FROCK COAT

For formal wear, and more often by elderly men. Mostly double breasted, generally three buttons each side, sometimes only two. Two extra button-holes in each lapel above the line of buttons. Button stand (a separate strip of cloth sewn on the fore part of the coat to carry the buttons and/or button-holes. It lessened horizontal creasing round the buttons) and waist seam. Lapels, medium-high or rolling to waist, silk covered to the edge of the button-holes. Two pockets in back pleats opening into the centre back vent of the coat. Sometimes a ticket pocket in the waist seam. Sometimes inside and/or outside breast pocket. Two hip buttons at top of vent at centre back.

Sleeves generally with plain round cuff, but could have a slit and buttons.

The edges of the coat fronts and lapels and also the round cuffs were often decorated with flat braid.

The full length was about 41 inches and the twentieth-century frock coat was fashionably somewhat longer-waisted than that of the later 1890's. Generally worn open.

Waistcoats worn with the frock coat were generally double

153. 1902 Frock coat. Button stand. Double-breasted waistcoat. High single collar. Silk top hat. Striped trousers.

breasted, though a single-breasted style was sometimes worn. Mostly with lapels, sometimes with a collar. Waistcoats were of a light colour or could match the coat.

The trousers were either matching the coat, or grey striped or of a small black and white check (sponge-bag or dogs tooth).

The frock coat was almost universally black, but some grey or blue-grey; materials were vicunas, worsteds, cheviots.

The silk hat was the correct wear with a frock coat.

EXAMPLES

c. 1909   Fine black cloth double-breasted frock coat with centre back vent and pleats. Silk facings to lapels extending to button-holes. Three buttons each side and two extra button-holes above in each lapel. Two buttons back waist at head of pleats. Sleeves with plain cuffs each with three buttons but no slit. Silk basket buttons. Two pockets in back pleats. Lined silk with striped sateen sleeve linings. Coat-hanger (a loop of cloth) sewn in at collar. Length: back collar base to hem, 41 inches; back collar base to waist seam (the 'fashion waist') 18½ inches. Width: from centre back seam to arm-hole (the 'style width') 7½ inches; between back buttons (the 'back-breadth') 3¼ inches. Waistcoat and trousers of matching cloth. Waistcoat double breasted; three silk buttons each side; four pockets. Lined, striped sateen with waist adjusting strap and buckle at back. Buckle gilt and stamped, *Solide Paris.*

Trousers cut for braces, not very high at back waist. Two side seams. One hip pocket. Width at knee 19 inches, at bottoms 17 inches. Tailor's name on label and buttons.

Christchurch Museum, Ipswich

1912   'Frock coat and waistcoat. Fashionable vicunas, fancy worsteds, mixed cheviots and diagonals, £4.3.0.–£5.7.6.'

Army and Navy Stores

(In the 1970's it is interesting to note that these prices had remained unchanged for twelve years, and that by 1916–17 the lowest charge had been increased by only one shilling.)

THE MORNING COAT

At the beginning of the century was either a coat to be worn with striped or sponge-bag trousers and a differing waistcoat, or was a complete suit with matching coat, waistcoat and trousers. The latter, often in check tweeds, was the 'morning coat suit'. The morning coat was at this time replacing the frock coat in fashionable esteem. Almost always single breasted, it had three or four buttons and fairly high lapels. By 1902 the 'new rolling lapel' was cut lower. Fronts were cut sloping away from the waist. Length about 36 inches, the tails coming to the bend of the knee. Back vent and pleats with two hip buttons at top of pleats. Pockets in pleats; sometimes one or more inside breast pockets and ticket pocket. Occasionally an outside breast pocket.

By about 1906, one-button link and two-button versions were seen; later the one-button style became the accepted form. There was often silk ribbon or flat braid applied to fronts and cuffs.

As time went on the cut-away swept farther back, narrowing the tails, and braiding was going out of fashion. Right-angled step collars and broad lapels, as worn in double-breasted coats, became popular, and tails tended to become shorter. Both these last features were noted in the *Tailor and Cutter* in 1923.

Sometimes outside flap pockets at hip level; these were generally seen in morning coat suits.

After the war, the morning coat was restricted to formal occasions, especially weddings.

Waistcoats for the morning coat were correctly single breasted, but double-breasted ones were also worn. Generally no collar, but these sometimes appeared. The waistcoat matched the coat or was of a lighter colour.

Trousers were generally of striped cashmere.

In the morning coat suit all these garments matched in material and colour.

Correct wear with the morning coat was the silk hat, but a bowler or Homburg could be worn with the morning coat suit.

Materials for the morning coat: vicunas, worsteds, meltons,

154. 1906 Morning coat. Single-breasted waistcoat. Striped trousers, single linen collar. Handkerchief in breast pocket. Silk top hat.

155. 1906 Morning coat suit in check tweed. Pockets at hip, single-breasted waistcoat. Bowler hat.

diagonals, cheviots, serges. Black or iron-grey. Morning coat suits in homespuns, tweeds, cheviots and fancy worsteds: checks, greys, etc.

EXAMPLES

c. 1910   Iron grey herringbone tweed morning coat. Single breasted, with centre back vent and pleats. V notch to collar/lapels. Two buttons: flower button-hole left lapel: two buttons at head of back pleats. Sleeves with slit and two buttons at cuff. Silk basket buttons. Lined black Italian cloth with striped sateen sleeve linings. Lining at chest quilted. Two pockets in back pleats and two inside breast and one inside ticket pocket. Coat-hanger and tailor's label inside collar. Fronts cut to slope away moderately from level of top button.
Length collar base to hem $37\frac{1}{2}$ inches. Fashion waist $18\frac{1}{2}$ inches. Depth of skirt (waist seam to hem) 19 inches. Style width $7\frac{1}{2}$ inches. Back breadth $3\frac{1}{2}$ inches. Original waistcoat and trousers missing.
Author's collection (and still worn to weddings)

1912   'Morning coat and waistcoat. Fashionable vicunas in different weights. Fancy worsteds in various shades, meltons, diagonals, etc. £3.13.6.–£5.1.0. Homespun etc. morning coat suits from £4.4.0.'
Army and Navy Stores

1922   Morning coat in black diagonal weave cloth. Lined black silk and cotton mixture. Sleeves lined with black and white check sateen. One link button. Cuffs with slit and three buttons. Centre back vent and two pleats, button at head of each pleat. All buttons black composition. One inside breast pocket and ticket pocket. Two pockets in back pleats, one outside breast pocket. Lining quilted below and behind arm-holes. Lapels rolling to button, step to collar, flower button-hole in left lapel. Fronts cut well away to back. Length, back collar base to hem 35 inches. Fashion waist 18 inches. Back breadth $4\frac{3}{4}$ inches. Style width 8 inches. Single-breasted waistcoat, five black composition buttons, strap and blacked brass oblong buckle stamped PARIS at the back. Four pockets. Back of black silk and cotton mixture. Lined black and white check sateen. V neck with three pearl buttons each side of opening for two white slips, 12 inches long average width 2 inches, of piqué, with three button-holes in each. Length of waistcoat 18 inches in front, V opening 10 inches. Trousers of black worsted with fine white stripes at 7/16 inch intervals. Cut for braces, back rising three inches. Fly front opening with five buttons and metal hook and bar, white plated, stamped CATCH-ON. Black and white sateen lining at the waist. Two pockets in side seams. Adjusting strap at back waist with black oblong buckle stamped BRITISH.
Tailor's labels dated 1922. Trouser buttons bearing tailor's name also.
Holly Trees Museum, Colchester

156. 1909 Morning coat suit. Hip pockets, single-breasted waistcoat. Wing collar.

THE LOUNGE JACKET

Now generally replacing the frock coat and the morning coat. In 1902 the *Tailor and Cutter* spoke of 'the conventional lounge' and that in the summer a dark grey flannel with narrow stripes was a favourite; and that the older style with a whole back (no centre seam) was going out in favour of a longer jacket with a centre-back vent.

157. 1906 Tweed lounge suit. Short lapels; cuffs; crease in trousers. Double linen collar. Bowler hat.

Generally rather high neck and short lapels, with sharp points to the double-breasted styles. Single breasted with three or four buttons or double breasted, mostly with six buttons. Sleeves with slits at cuff and buttons. Two flapped pockets at hip level, ticket pocket above right-hand one, and outside breast pocket. Single-breasted fronts generally curved away at bottom, but sometimes cut straight. Jackets were cut rather long.

Although a lower, rolling lapel was mentioned in 1902, it was

158. 1906 Tweed lounge suit with an unusually large number of buttons on waistcoat. Bow tie. Homburg hat.

159. 1906 Double-breasted reefer. Wideawake hat.

160. 1909 *Single-breasted reefer. Button cuffs.*
Ticket pocket. Homburg hat.

some years before it really became popular. In 1912 the *Tailor and Cutter* spoke of 'Yankee styles' with low rolling lapels and 'narrow collars' with wide shoulders and fancy finish to the cuffs. In the same year some outside hip pockets were finished with a welt instead of flaps, and outside breast pockets were less usual. One- and two-button single-breasted jackets, some with wide sharply pointed lapels of the double-breasted type. Fashion waist at this time was $18\frac{1}{2}$ inches, about an inch below the natural waist. Four buttons (two each side) double-breasted jackets, some in flannel with patch pockets.

In 1915 the lounge jacket

'is cut a little shorter . . . and without a centre vent. In many instances back cut whole without a seam at all. Practically all have out [outside] breast pockets and may have an outside ticket pocket also. Single breasted coats greatly predominate. Right angle step collar and lapel, although a few have double-breasted pointed lapels. Three buttons; three button cuffs'.

Tailor and Cutter

In 1918 single breasted generally; two, three or four buttons, with or without a back vent. Shaping to the figure by taking cuts out of the foreparts from the top of the side pockets to the breast. Double-breasted styles with four buttons. The post-war length of the jacket was markedly less than pre-war fashion.

There was very often a flower button-hole in the left lapel of single-breasted jackets, and one in each lapel of double-breasted ones. In 1918 a 'somewhat novel feature is . . . the two button-holes in the lapel'.

Over the years the distinction between a double-breasted lounge, especially when cut with a whole back, and the older 'reefer' had tended to become blurred, and the double-breasted style was less popular than the single-breasted jacket. In 1923, however, the *Tailor and Cutter* predicted 'an early revival of the double-breasted lounge or reefer' and quoted as an example a navy-blue suit, six buttons, medium wide rolling lapels, three outside pockets, two-button cuffs and a centre vent at the back. This was worn with a white waistcoat. In the same year 'a stylish lounge suit' consisted of black jacket, white waistcoat and check trousers.

At the end of the first quarter-century, single-breasted jackets

161. 1912   Long, double-breasted reefer.
Trousers with permanent turnups. Straw
'boater'.

162. 1916   Single-breasted lounge
suit. Ticket pocket. Turnups. Watch
strap to waistcoat pocket.

163. 1921   Single-breasted lounge
suit. Fancy tweed. Trousers with plain
bottoms. Shoes and spats.

*164. 1925 Single-breasted
lounge suit. 1 button. Jetted pockets.*

*165. 1925 Double-breasted lounge or reefer. Striped
soft collar matching shirt. Bowler hat.*

had one, two or, probably most popular, three buttons. The slopes and angles of lapels were very varying. Three outside pockets usual. Double-breasted jackets with two, four or six buttons.

Mostly flaps to outside hip level pockets, but occasionally with a jetted finish and no flap.

Double-breasted lapels sometimes seen on single-breasted jackets.

Materials: serge, homespun, tweeds, cheviots, worsteds, striped flannel, Saxonys.

Colours: navy blue, greys, browns, black. Checks and stripes. Generally in dark tones.

1915 'Medium grey is undoubtedly the correct shade in well-dressed circles.'
Tailor and Cutter

Waistcoats and trousers generally matched the jacket but in the earlier years of the century fancy and light-colour waistcoats were popular. With the black jacket and waistcoat grey striped cashmere trousers were usually worn.

The Reefer

Usually double breasted with up to eight buttons; sometimes single breasted with four buttons. Always cut square in front. Generally made without a back seam. Worn buttoned up. It became less fashionable than in the nineteenth century and tended to merge with the double-breasted lounge.

EXAMPLES

1901 'Lounge suits in homespuns, tweeds, cheviots and fancy worsteds. £4.4.0. to £5.10.0.'
Army and Navy Stores

1906 'Ready made, wholesale prices. Lounge suits 18/3 to 21/-.'
Wallace and Linnell, Kettering

1911 Lounge jacket of grey tweed with white stripe. Single-breasted jacket with long skirt and fronts cut in pronounced curve. Two buttons, two flap pockets at hip. Two breast and a ticket pocket inside. Vent at back. Line of stitching round cuff: three buttons. Waistcoat missing; trousers matching jacket.
London Museum

R

1917   'Tweed suits 35/6–50/-
          Serge suits 39/6–50/-'.

                                        Advertisement, *Essex County Standard*

1918   'Lounge suits, lined Italian cloth £4.4.0. and £4.18.6.'
                                                    Army and Navy Stores

c. 1922   Brown tweed lounge suit, single-breasted jacket, two buttons; slight flare
            to skirt; three outside pockets. Cuff with two buttons. Waistcoat and
            trousers to match.
                                                            London Museum

1925   'Single breasted lounge suits. One, two, or three buttons, from £6.8.6.'
                                                    Army and Navy Stores

ODD JACKETS

'Sports' jackets to wear with flannel trousers became more and
more popular; also worn with matching trousers or knickerbockers. Nearly always single breasted.

The Norfolk jacket in tweeds with box pleats at front and back,
and a belt or belted waistband. Sometimes with a yoke. Large
patch pockets, often of the bellows type. Sometimes with stand-up
Prussian collar.

In 1902 tweed jackets with half-belts at the back: a type
persisting throughout this quarter-century. Like the Norfolk,
these sometimes had shoulder yokes and the belt going all round.

In 1904–05 the riding lounge, 'a popular sporting jacket',
single breasted, high necked with four buttons, centre back vent
and flared skirt.

Summer coats of alpaca, etc. for indoor and outdoor wear.

Indoor jackets of light materials, or of unlined serge, including
'library' jackets for clergymen. Such jackets were often worn at
the office in place of the suit jacket.

In 1901 were advertised lounge coats in kid – 'Scandinavian
leather clothing' – for indoor wear in cold weather, as well as for
sport and travel.

166. 1906 *Norfolk jacket. Yoked
and pleated with bellows pockets, self
belt, strapped cuffs. Knickerbockers.
Golf stockings with fancy turn-over
tops. Tweed cap.*

167. 1921 *Sports jacket, half belt at back.
Patch pockets, centre vent. Flannel trousers.
Black and white 'co-respondent' shoes.*

EXAMPLES

1901 'Men's odd coats from 3/11 to 6/11.'

Advertisement, *Jersey Evening Post*

1914 'For real comfort in the warm weather wear a sports coat and flannel
trousers.'

Frank Page, Colchester

1922 'Sports lounge model. Two styles of jacket. Slit back, three buttons and
patch pockets, or without slit at back, and two hand pockets.'

Harrods

DAY WAISTCOATS

At the opening of the century were often conspicuous both in
cut and design. In summer light-coloured linen, holland and
canvas were favourite materials. For winter wear fancy cloth and
knitted styles. But increasingly of the same material as the rest
of the suit, or, in the case of the frock and morning coats worn
with striped trousers, matching the coat. Both single- and double-
breasted waistcoats were worn. The latter was strictly only the
correct wear with a frock coat, but it was often seen with morning
coats and lounge suits.

Single breasted. Cut rather high with a V opening. Collarless, or
with a step collar and lapels or a continuous rolling collar. A few
cut very high to the neck with a small turn-down collar. Occasionally a deep U-shape opening.

Generally four pockets; in the earlier years sometimes three
(two bottom, one top left) only. Usually five buttons, sometimes
four or six. Sometimes an extra, vertical button-hole for the watch
chain to pass through.

The foreparts (fronts) were at the beginning of the period cut
rather square with short points meeting in an obtuse angled V.
Later the frontal slope increased, the points lengthened and the
gap was of an acute angle. Similarly the neck was cut lower, and
collarless models were more fashionable.

From about 1908 the bottom button was often left unfastened.

Double breasted. Generally with collar and lapels. Some cut high
and some with lower rolling lapels. Usually four or five pairs of
buttons, the overlapping front sometimes sloping acutely from
top to bottom. Three or four pockets. Almost straight around
the bottom of the fronts, with a blunt point in the centre.

The double-breasted waistcoat declined in favour, but the
Tailor and Cutter noted a slight revival in 1923.

Generally. Waistcoat foreparts were, as already mentioned, made
to match the suit or of fancy or light-coloured material. Lining of
Italian cloth or sateen. The back generally was of the lining
material. Some with flannel backs and linings for winter wear.

A back strap and buckle adjusted the fit at the waist in most cases. Buckles were of metal, oblong in shape.

DAY TROUSERS

In 1900 the legs tending to be narrow, worn with or without a crease. Some trousers of lounge suits had turnups at the bottom, but this was by no means general. Knee width 18 or 19 inches, bottoms 17 inches.

When without turnups the trousers 'broke' over the boot or shoe at the front. With turnups they were somewhat shorter, ending at about the top of the shoe.

From about 1910, width was generally 19 inches at the knee and 16 inches at the bottom, although a somewhat wider cut is noted for trousers with a morning coat in 1912.

In 1912 there was a return in some instances, via America, of the French 'peg-top' trouser, wider at the thigh and knee, and

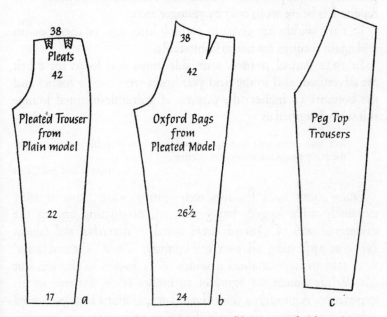

168. *Trousers:* (a) 1925 *Basic pleated trousers.* (b) 1925 *Oxford bags.* (c) 1912 *Peg-top trousers.*

tapering from the knee to a narrow bottom. At first described by
the *Tailor and Cutter* as 'patronised by certain classes of English-
men'; a change of attitude is seen in that magazine's assertion later
in the year that it is 'a style of trousers greatly favoured by all classes
today'.

In the same year pleating into the waistband is said to have been
introduced. Waistbands were becoming increasingly popular,

> 'and are usually advocated where a close fit at the waist is ordered, especially
> in flannels that are to be worn without suspenders [braces]'.
>
> 1912 *Tailor and Cutter*

In the same year, for trousers worn with Norfolk jackets, a two-
inch turnup was fashionable, and raised side seams were popular.
For 'a smart tweed lounge suit' trousers were noted with 'permanent pressed-up bottoms and well creased up the fronts'.

In 1915 widths of 19 inches and 20 inches knee, 16 and 17
inch bottoms, and also, for lounge suits, 18 and $15\frac{1}{2}$ inches, but
generally they appear to have been on the wider side. Turnups were
reported as being worn only by younger men.

In 1918 widths are given as 19 inch knee and 16 inch bottom
and again turnups are not so fashionable.

In 1922 flannel trousers with side-straps and loops for a belt
are advertised, and in the next year knees were cut 19 inches and
the bottoms 16 inches: the trousers of a double-breasted lounge
suit were described as

> 'cut with permanent turn-up bottoms, a fashion that still prevails, despite
> the many prognostications of its decline'.
>
> 1923 *Tailor and Cutter*

From about 1924 the legs were getting wider, and in 1925
extremely wide legged, baggy trousers, originating among the
undergraduates of Oxford, were noted in the *Illustrated London
News* as appearing all over the country. These 'Oxford bags'
were said to have attained a width of 32 inches in the leg, but
Mr. Whife quotes the figure of 24 inches as the extreme in his
experience. Although a short-lived fancy, Oxford bags pioneered
a definite movement away from the 16- or 17-inch trouser bottom.

As the width increased, the legs also tended to become longer.

THE PSYCHOLOGY OF FASHION.

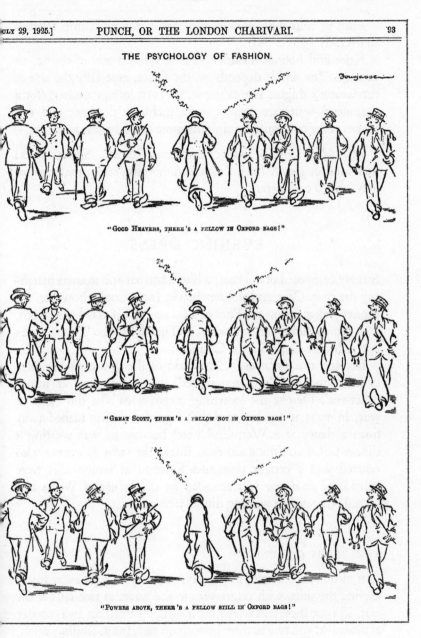

"Good Heavens, there's a fellow in Oxford bags!"

"Great Scott, there's a fellow not in Oxford bags!"

"Powers above, there's a fellow still in Oxford bags!"

169. 1925 Oxford bags. Drawing by Fougasse. By permission of 'Punch'.

Built-in belts with buckles were appearing on flannel trousers
in the early 1920's.

Knee and bottom measurements of trousers are, of course, an
average. The width depends on the figure, especially the size of
the wearer's thighs. For example, in 1912 lounge trousers 'for a
corpulent' figure are quoted as 22 inches at the knee and $17\frac{1}{2}$
inches at the bottoms as against the more usual 19 and 16 inches.

Materials: Lounge suits: matching jackets. Sports coats:
matching or grey flannel. Frock and morning coats: matching or
grey-striped cashmere.

EVENING DRESS

Strictly composed of tail coat, white waistcoat and trousers matching the coat. Coat and trousers black. Increasingly, however, the
dinner jacket cut on the lines of a lounge jacket was being worn.
The dinner jacket was known as a 'Tuxedo' in the United States
and a 'Monte Carlo' on the Continent.

In 1909 the *Tailor and Cutter* said of the dinner jacket (also
called at this time 'the dress jacket') that it was worn at 'minor
functions'. Despite the loosening conventions after the 1914–18
war, in 1923 it was reported that a gentleman was turned away
from a dance at a West End hotel because he was wearing a
dinner jacket and not a tail coat. But in the same year it was also
noticed that a certain unnamed function at which tails were
considered *de rigueur* was attended by the Prince of Wales and
several other people wearing dinner jackets.

THE DRESS COAT

Cut as double breasted, but always worn open. Cut-away fronts
leaving the skirt, with centre vent to the waist, as two tails at the
rear. In 1900 these tails were knee length, the front cut away square
at the waist, and two or three buttons on each front. Rolling lapels,
silk covered, with step to the collar. The sleeves could end plain

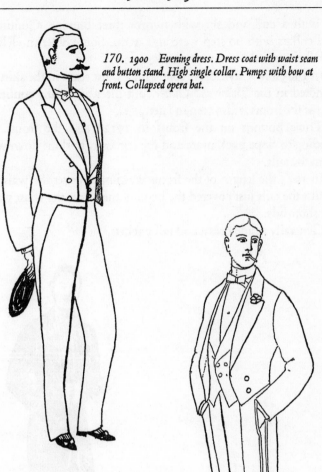

170. 1900 *Evening dress. Dress coat with waist seam and button stand. High single collar. Pumps with bow at front. Collapsed opera hat.*

171. 1916 *Dress coat with double-breasted waistcoat, with long points and three buttons arranged in triangle.*

or with a cuff and slit with two or three buttons. Continuous roll collars with no step were also worn. Some older models had silk facings to the button-hole edges only.

In 1905 a new style dress coat with a waist seam in the skirt only is noted in the *Tailor and Cutter*, but the waist seam continuing across the fronts is also seen in later years.

Three buttons on the fronts in 1912; also the fronts were tending to slope back more and the cut away to slope downwards from the tails.

In 1923 the length of the fronts was just to cover the waistcoat, whilst the tails just covered the bend of the knee: the waist was on the short side.

Generally inside breast and tail pockets.

172. 1921   Evening dress. 13 gns.

173. *1912 Dinner jacket. High single*
collar. From £1. 15. 6, ready made.

174. *1921   Dinner jacket suit. £11. 10.*

THE DINNER JACKET

Cut as a single-breasted lounge, but not intended to be buttoned. Later on, a link button was used and the jacket was sometimes worn fastened. In 1900 with a collar stepped to silk-faced lapels and square cut fronts, or roll collar and rounded fronts. Two outside pockets at hip level, welted or flapped. Occasionally two, generally one button; often a link. Some with cuffs on the sleeves.

In 1909 with a very low continuous roll collar or with collar stepped to wide, pointed, double-breasted lapels. In 1910 a model described with one button, four-button slit cuffs and a ten-inch centre back vent.

175. 1925 *Double-breasted dinner jacket. Jetted pockets.*

At first cut long, the dinner jacket shortened as did the lounge, so that by 1922 it just comfortably covered the seat of the trousers.

In 1925 both roll collars and pointed lapels were worn, and by this year an outside breast pocket had appeared.

In 1921 or 1922 the King of Spain appeared at Deauville wearing a double-breasted dinner jacket. In this country the double-breasted style was later popularized by Mr. Jack Buchanan, a favourite musical comedy star of the day, and received its accolade at the hands of the Prince of Wales.

Materials for both dress coats and dinner jackets were vicuna, angola, hopsack, twilled worsted, etc. Colour, black. Buttons, silk covered, later of black composition materials or of bone.

EVENING DRESS WAISTCOATS

For the tail coat, generally white, but occasionally black. Later the white waistcoat became accepted as correct wear. Straight cut across the front, single or double breasted. By 1912 it was cut to give short points at the front in both versions. In 1925 pointed fronts to single-breasted, and straight cut double-breasted styles were seen. Roll collar and continuous lapels, or sometimes collarless. Two pockets. Three or four buttons, single breasted, four or six if double. In some cases double-breasted styles were cut with the fronts sharply sloping, with fairly long points, and with three buttons only, arranged as an inverted triangle.

The front opening was generally in the form of a deep U or V.

With the dinner jacket a black waistcoat or a white one, cut as for the tail coat. Though white waistcoats are portrayed up to 1925, the black version was by then accepted as more correct.

In 1909 the *Tailor and Cutter* wrote that the 'really up to date vest is now made with a V opening, and wider revers in the peaked style', although the U shape with a roll collar is also mentioned.

Materials for evening waistcoats: black, to match the coat; white, marcella or piqué.

EVENING DRESS TROUSERS

Of material matching the coat. Always without turnups. Usually decorated down outside seams of legs with one or two rows of black braid. Followed the styles and widths of day trousers generally.

SMOKING JACKETS

For informal home wear. Single or double breasted. Of serge, vicuna, silk, velvet, etc. Trimmed with cord and frogging; or with silk facings, sometimes quilted, to lapels and cuffs; or with both. Generally black, some of navy blue. In 1921 brown and claret are also advertised.

Worn with day trousers or evening trousers or sometimes as a smoking suit with matching, easy cut trousers secured by a girdle at the waist, like pyjama trousers.

176. 1916 Smoking jacket. Double breasted. Quilted silk collar and cuffs. Braid frogging to pockets and fastenings.

EXAMPLES

1905   'Navy blue or black serge jacket faced plain silk and frogs 39/6.
Trousers to match 25/9.'

1912   'Evening Dress. Best elastic twill or soft woven material. [Coat, waistcoat
and trousers] £5.5.0. to £7.7.0.'
'Dinner jacket, lined silk and silk roll or step collar £3.12.6. to £4.17.6.
Black dinner jacket, ready made, lined black silk 48/6.'

1921   'Dress suit from £13.13.0.
Dinner jacket suit, one link button, from £12.12.0.
Smoking jackets in blue, brown, claret or black velveteen, trimmed with
cord and frogs £5.5.6.'

Army and Navy Stores

KNITWEAR

SWEATERS

Long sleeved jerseys worn for sports, etc. Generally a roll or polo
collar (a close fitting turn-over round neck).

1902   'Early morning on the way to the morning dip youths in garments loose . . .
sweaters, flannel trousers and canvas shoes.'

Dress at the Seaside, Tailor and Cutter

In 1912 also figured with a low turn-down, pointed collar.
Later with V neck.
Usually white, sometimes navy or grey, later various colours.
After the war becoming known, in its V neck style, as a 'pull-
over'. This style, when white, often had a band at the neck and
sometimes at the hem, of club colours.

WAISTCOATS

Fancy knitted waistcoats were popular before the war and were
also seen afterwards.

1912   'Knitted waistcoats, made up from own material, lined flannel, cloth back
and edges £1.1.0.'

Army and Navy Stores

CARDIGANS

These began about 1890 as short, knitted, close-fitting jackets. Some had a roll collar. If without sleeves they were known as cardigan vests. A longer, knitted version was the coat-sweater, collarless, and with two pockets at hip level in some cases.

In 1919 advertisement for knitted silk coats with four pockets, in yellow, blue, brown, navy and pearl grey.

PULLOVERS

From the early 1920's. Replaced waistcoats for wear with a sports jacket. Sleeved or sleeveless, V neck in most cases, shorter than the sweater. Colourful Fair Isle patterns were extremely popular.

NECKWEAR

COLLARS

In 1900 tall starched white linen collars, up to about 3 inches high, were the accepted norm. As the years passed, the height decreased and soft unstarched versions became more and more acceptable. Coloured collars, at first only seen on collar-attached flannel sports shirts, were appearing by 1909.[1]

Both single and double (stand-fall) stiff collars were worn, but the double collar in most cases superseded the single, except in its winged variety. The wing collar was a single stand collar with the front points turned over downwards. Single collars only were worn with evening dress, and by the end of the quarter century the winged collar was the accepted standard.

By 1912 the tallest single collar was $2\frac{1}{2}$ inches, and the average double collar $1\frac{1}{2}$ inches only and these sizes persisted for many years.

Celluloid collars which were 'waterproof and will clean with a sponge' were worn by the unfashionable and economically minded.

[1] Both separate and attached soft collars were worn across the Atlantic from the end of the nineteenth century.

TIES

Various kinds.

1900   'During the past year the necktie has presented no features that call for any
     special comment. No striking designs or colours were introduced.'
                                                  Tailor and Cutter

The most popular types were:

The bow tie. Of medium size and with square corners. In 1895
it had been decreed that it should only be worn with a soft-fronted
shirt and a single stand-up collar with the points slightly turned
down. Later it was only to be worn with a wing collar.

The four-in-hand. A long tie tied in the manner now universally
used, i.e. with the edges of the tie running horizontally at the top
and bottom of the knot. Square or pointed ends.

The Ascot. A long tie or scarf, with wide square or pointed ends,
twisted or tied once in front and the ends overlapped at an angle
and held by a tie-(or scarf)pin.

The sailor's knot. A long tie tied in a reef-knot so that the edges ran
vertically at the knot, the ends hanging down on each side, or
tucked inside the waistcoat V. Two popular styles were the Derby,
square ended, and the Lombard, with pointed ends.

The four-in-hand style eventually became the normal fashion
for tying a long tie, and by the post-war years the sailor's knot
died out and the Ascot became confined to the morning coat for
formal occasions.

For evening wear a white bow tie was worn with the tail (or
dress) coat. At first either a black or a white one was acceptable
with a dinner jacket, but by the 1914–18 war the black tie was
considered correct. The materials were cambric or piqué for
white bows, and silk or satin for black. The satin tie was rarely
seen in post-war years.

Materials for day ties: silks, satin, poplin, knitted silk. Later,
rayon. In 1922 rubber-lined to prevent creasing.

Colours: black, self colours, spots, printed and woven designs.

s

Khaki, scarlet and blue and white popular in opening years of the century, inspired by the Boer War.

School, regimental and club colours in diagonal stripes were introduced towards the end of the nineteenth century and were considerably added to after the Great War. Worn with sports clothes and lounge suits.

Made-up ties, with the knot ready tied and fastening round the neck with a buckle or patent fastener were obtainable, but were generally considered not the thing.

EXAMPLES

1903 'Peri-Lustre Crochet or Purse Knitting makes beautiful Derby Ties.'

Advertisement

1912 'Four-in-hand ties, plain coloured or spot silk 1/3 & 2/9.'

1921 'Foulard ties, silk ties, poplin ties. Black, self colours and fancy designs 4/6 to 8/6.'

1925 'Regimental Ties 7/6.'

All Army and Navy Stores

CLOTHES FOR SPECIAL OCCASIONS

WEDDINGS

In 1900 the frock coat was the correct formal dress, worn with a light-coloured waistcoat, and this lingered on for some years, being worn by some older men who were wedding guests during the 1920's.

The 1914–18 war relaxed the standards and both the frock coat and the morning coat were often replaced by a lounge suit or, of course, service uniform.

Post war, the normal formal dress for the bridegroom and male guests was morning coat, striped trousers, black or light-coloured waistcoat, bow or long tie with a wing collar, and silk hat. White spats could be worn, and gloves and walking stick were often carried. Waistcoats were sometimes double breasted.

Less formal dress was a lounge suit, sometimes a black coat and striped trousers.

FUNERALS AND MOURNING

For funerals, at the beginning of the century the dress was frock coat, dark trousers, black waistcoat, silk hat with black cloth band, and black gloves and tie.

Black ties and black crêpe armbands were worn with dark suits for mourning. Private mourning was observed for those fallen in the South African War: in January, 1900, the *Tailor and Cutter* wrote in an article on neckties

> 'On account of the mourning into which . . . people have been plunged the manufacturers are again producing the white cambric bow with a narrow black border and black embroidery in the corners.'

The following year was marked by public mourning on the death of Queen Victoria and a decade later King Edward VII was mourned almost as much.

From the time of the Great War onwards the practice of wearing private and public mourning declined greatly, and although the frock coat or morning coat was often worn at funerals, the curtailed periods of mourning were usually marked simply by a black tie or armband. An unfashionable habit was to wear a diamond-shaped black patch on the sleeve in place of the armband.

1912 'Mourning bands for hats 1½″ to 6″ wide, 6d. to 1/3 each.'

Army and Navy Stores

PUBLIC DANCING AND DINING

A dress suit. White cotton gloves when dancing.

A dinner jacket was often allowed in a hotel grill room, if not in the restaurant. (See under Evening Dress.)

COURT WEAR

Velvet court dress, old or new style. Old style was a black single-breasted velvet frock with fronts cut sloping back from the waist;

seven steel buttons but the coat actually closed by a hook and eye at the breast; black silk 'flash' or wig-bag at back of the stand collar. The new style was also a black velvet coat, but of the cut-away tailed style, worn open.

With both styles black velvet breeches, white or black waistcoat, white silk stockings, black shoes, cocked hat, sword, white gloves and white bow tie (with the new style) or ruffles (with the old style) were worn. Button and buckles of cut steel.

Alternatively: cloth dress, with a cloth coat of mulberry, claret or green with matching breeches, and white waistcoat. Gold embroidery on coat collar, cuffs and pocket flaps. Hat, stockings etc. as above. Buttons and buckles gilt.

During the war years and after, a simplified Court dress of black cloth breeches and black evening dress coat was allowed.

In all cases trousers could be worn instead of breeches when attending levées.

THE GREAT WAR (1914–18)

Men's clothes, unlike women's, were not greatly affected by the Great War. No drastic re-dressing for unaccustomed jobs, or modifications of fashion to cope with extraordinary conditions were required of the men, except, of course, those who joined one of the Services, into which it is not our brief to follow them. However certain effects were felt: goods became scarcer, prices higher.

Although on 22nd August 1914 one Colchester tailor claimed to 'supply every requirement without any advance in price', nine months later in the same town, 'everyone knows that wool is dearer than ever'.

By 1918 British cloth was scarce, and inferior foreign material was being imported. In the same year 'silk lining is now very expensive' and Italian cloth or twill were the most common materials used.

Standard suits, and clothing for demobilized soldiers have been mentioned.

At the end of the war it was inevitable that many ex-officers were glad to make use of their uniform trench coats and 'British warms' on return to civilian life. The British warm, a short, double-breasted coat cut on easy lines and generally of melton cloth, was officially known as a 'drab pea-jacket', and had taken the place of the standard officer's great-coat in 1918.

The Government also, finding itself overstocked with military garments, put vast quantities on to the market, and advertisements for ex-Service clothing abounded in the early 1920's. Many working men wore army jackets, trousers, boots, etc. in factories, on building sites, and anywhere else when strong practical clothing was a necessity.

SPORTS CLOTHES

FOOTBALL

Knitted wool jersey or cotton shirt; shorts to the knee; stockings; boots.

CRICKET

Cream or white flannel trousers and shirt. Belt, scarf or tie round waist. White canvas or buckskin boots. White sweater with club colours at neck and waist. Club cap and blazer, or plain navy blue or black blazer with or without pocket badge.

TENNIS

Trousers and shirt as above, tie, flannel coat or blazer. Or tennis suits of white or striped flannel with white shirt and tie. The latter outfit was discarded after the war, as was the tie in most cases. Sometimes a Panama straw hat or a 'boater' was worn. White sweaters. White canvas shoes with rubber soles.

177. 1921 *Tennis: white flannel trousers and shirt. Tie, which by now was becoming unfashionable.*

178. 1916 *Golf and cycling suit in tweed, patch pockets; baggy knickerbockers. From £2. 5s.*

CYCLING

In 1900 Norfolk jacket and knickerbockers (see below). As the bicycle declined from its high peak in the 1890's and was overtaken by the motor car less attention was paid to special clothing except by real enthusiasts who, in the after-war period, began to take to shorts. Otherwise trousers with bicycle clips became the norm.

GOLF

Sports jacket (including Norfolk jacket) or scarlet flannel jacket, and knickerbockers (see below) and stockings (1905).

Jacket and breeches and stockings (1919).

Norfolk jacket or sports jacket, baggy knickerbockers or trousers (1920).

Plus-fours (see below), trousers; jacket and pullover, or pull-over alone. Pullovers often Fair Isle and with pockets (1925).

Headgear: small, close-fitting peaked cloth caps, gradually replaced by the more familiar type with a fuller crown. Soft felt hats.

SHOOTING

Tweed jacket with or without leather gun pads at shoulders, and large 'game' pockets: breeches, knickerbockers or plus-fours (see below). Stockings, boots and short gaiters. Tweed helmet-shaped hat with peaks fore and aft, often with ear flaps that tied up over the top (the 'deerstalker'), or felt or tweed cap or hat.

In 1901 'Scandinavian leather clothing' of kid.

HUNTING

In 1906 novices were advised to wear black or dark grey frock coat; cloth breeches; black jack-boots (fairly heavy riding boots with high plain tops); silk top hat or bowler hat. After a minimum of two seasons they could graduate to a scarlet coat and white breeches and top boots (i.e. black boots with brown leather tops).

Red or black frock coat; buckskin breeches; top boots; silk hat (1925).

'Ratcatcher', named after King Edward VII's reported remark to Lord Harris, who once attended Ascot in a tweed suit – 'Morning Harris, going ratting?' – riding jacket, cloth breeches, cloth cap or soft felt hat.

179. 1900 Shooting suit, tweed.
Gaiters over trousers. Bowler hat.

180. 1912 Riding clothes. Breeches
with flaring wings. Coat with flare to
skirt. Hunting stock. Bowler hat.

181. 1901 *Swimming costume.*

182. 1925 *Holiday dress of flannel jacket, blue or brown, and grey flannel trousers with lapped side seams. Panama straw hat.*

SEASIDE WEAR

Before breakfast, flannels, shirt, sweater or blazer. Later in the day, lounge suit or morning coat. Flannel suits, often grey with a white stripe, were very fashionable (1902).

White flannel trousers, shirt, tie, blazer, Panama straw or felt hat (1920).

For bathing and swimming, either drawers, plain navy blue or horizontally striped, or costumes in similar designs. Navy blue and white striped costumes with half sleeves were advertised in 1912.

In 1916 sleeveless navy blue costumes with short legs and plain round necks were shown, and this type persisted for some years, the arm-holes getting deeper. In the 1920's two-piece costumes were also seen. Most swimming trunks and costumes were made of cotton.

MOTORING

In 1900 described as 'a passing craze' and indulged in clad in a double-breasted reefer jacket buttoned high with a small turn-down collar, wind cuffs with straps, trousers, yachting cap and gloves.

Also worn were leather coats and helmets, fur-lined coats and twill holland, or silk dust coats. Dust coats and leather motor coats were advertised in the 1920's.

KNICKERBOCKERS AND PLUS-FOURS

Knickerbockers, a type of loose knee-breeches fastening with a band buckled or buttoned below the knee, became a favourite country and sporting garment from the 1860's, worn with woollen stockings. In the years immediately preceding the Great War they became baggier and wider at the knee, before being caught in by the band. They were popular with golfers, and in 1920 the term 'plus-fours' was applied to a wide style pouching well over at the knee. The name originated either from the cutting instructions to the tailor to make them four inches longer, or in allusion to the golfing terms describing a player's handicap. Plus-fours reached absurd proportions in some cases, pouching voluminously over the calf.

1923   'Baggy knickers are preferred by many to trousers, and these are cut very full and long, pouching at the knee.'

Tailor and Cutter

Later in the year the magazine refers to 'plus-four knickers'.

1925   'Our new Knicker-suit in "plus-four" style but without the extreme looseness of last year's fashion £5.7.6.'

Rogers Bros., Colchester

OUTDOOR CLOTHES

CHESTERFIELD

(Or 'Chester') was probably the most popular style of overcoat. It was single or (less usually) double breasted; if single, then often fly-fronted. Slightly waisted with a back vent, and long to the calf, or in the form of a knee-length sac. Two hip-level pockets and mostly with an outside breast pocket and also a ticket pocket over the right hip pocket. Generally with a velvet collar, often with silk faced lapels also.

In 1909 a loose, single-breasted sac style, with or without a fly-front, was fashionable.

In 1915 it had centre seam and vent and a fitting waist; and in 1918 the *Tailor and Cutter* declared 'fly front Chesterfield the correct wear in well dressed circles', and stated that the 'length usually extends to the knee. Flap pockets on the hips are now the invariable finish, with a ticket pocket on left and sometimes an out [outside] breast pocket with a welt'. Occasionally the Chesterfield appeared with no sleeves, but a shoulder cape.

The Chesterfield retained its popularity after the First War, subtly modifying various features: for instance, in 1923 it was double breasted, with a velvet collar, four buttons and three pockets outside. Some overcoats had fitted waists and shaping

183. 1900   Three varieties of Chesterfield overcoats.

darts at the breast, double breasted with six buttons, three pockets and low rolling lapels.

TOP FROCK

Worn for a few years at the beginning of the century. This was cut on the lines of the frock coat, but longer; generally double breasted. Intended to be worn without an undercoat.

ULSTER

A less fashionable garment and often worn when travelling.

184. 1909 *Short fly-fronted Chesterfield.*

185. 1902 *Caped travelling Ulster.*

Generally heavier than the town overcoat, and looser, but with a belt or half-belt. Sometimes with a cape or hood. Single breasted or double. The 'Scarborough' Ulster had a shoulder cape but no sleeves. Very often patch pockets at hip level. No outside breast pocket in many cases.

COVERT COAT

Short, about three inches longer than a lounge jacket, fly fronted, single breasted, with two side vents and four outside pockets. Sometimes with Raglan sleeves.

RAGLAN OVERCOAT

Had appeared at the end of the 1890's; it was long and full in the back. Fly fronted, with vertical pockets and slits in the side seams so that the trouser pockets could be reached. Made of waterproof material and worn as a raincoat.

INVERNESS CAPE

A coat with a cape-like front composed of two 'wings' taking the place of sleeves and covering the arms.

In addition to the above there appeared, during the period, a host of named varieties of overcoat, some confined to one maker's or tailor's trade name, others indicating a general style: basically they all conformed in principle to one or other of the above categories.

Fur-lined and fur overcoats for motoring and travelling.

MACINTOSHES

And raincoats of rubber, cotton, tweed, paramatta, etc. Trench coats with belts and added shoulder protection in the form of a double-yoke were popular during the war and were carried by demobilized officers into civilian use afterwards.

Belted macintoshes and light-weight models to roll and carry in the pocket, etc. appeared in large numbers after the war.

186. 1902 *Single-breasted Ulster.*

187. 1912 *Unlined rainproof coat.*

OVERCOAT MATERIALS

Cheviots, tweeds, worsteds, meltons, vicuna, coating cloth. Alpaca and silk Chesterfields for summer wear (pre-war). Mostly in black, greys and blues, but also coloured and checked Ulsters.

EXAMPLES

1905–06 'Overcoats [ready made, wholesale prices], 11/9 to 25/6.'
Wallace and Linnell Ltd.

'Fur-lined coats; black beaver cloth, calf-length, double breasted, three outside pockets.
Lined hamster, collar and cuffs genet, £6.15.0.
Lined and collar and cuffs in sable £100.0.0.'
Army and Navy Stores

c. 1910 Single-breasted Chesterfield overcoat of fancy black cashmere woven with a faint self-colour stripe. Fly front and four silk basket buttons. One flower button-hole in left lapel. Two flapped outside pockets at hip level with flapped ticket pocket over right-hand one. Two inside breast pockets. Lined black silk, which continues on to front of lapels to form facing to edge of button-holes. Sleeves lined white striped black satin. Pockets of Italian cloth.
Length 45 inches. Chest 40–42 inches. Style width 7½ inches. Waist 18 inches from base of collar. Vent in centre back seam 16½ inches long.
Author's collection

1911 'Men's overcoats from 16/3.'
Owen Ward Ltd., Colchester

1912 'Weatherall Burberry. Combines the body-warming power of an ulster with the distinctive appearance of a smart overcoat for formal occasions.'
Advertisement, *Essex County Standard*

1921–22 'Chesterfields, fly front single breasted. Evening dress overcoats with silk lapels. Single breasted Raglan overcoats with patch pockets. "Newbury" overcoat with velvet collar, fly front, half belt and inverted pleat at the back.'
Army and Navy Stores

HAIR

Throughout the period hair was worn short and neatly trimmed. In the earlier years it was generally parted at the side or centre: later a side parting, or no parting at all, with the hair brushed straight back, was popular. Brilliantines and hair-creams kept the hair in place.

Beards were dying out and by the 1920's were confined to the elderly, literary, artistic, and eccentric. At this time 'spotting a beaver' was a favourite game among the more irreverent of the young.

Moustaches, often heavy and drooping, were common up to 1914: during the war they tended to decrease in size, and in post-war years a clean shaven face was most often presented to the world.

Side whiskers (or 'sideboards') were definitely regarded with disfavour.

Wigs were unspeakable.

The decrease in the size of moustaches and an even closer cutting of the hair during the war was probably in some measure a hygienic move originating among the troops. The popular name for the mini-moustaches of the war-time officers was 'toothbrush'.

HATS AND CAPS

Some kind of headwear was essential to the gentleman on all occasions out-of-doors. A wide variety of hats and caps catered for most tastes and eventualities.

The most common were:

TOP HAT OR SILK HAT

Worn with frock coat, morning coat, and evening dress. As the first two were replaced by the lounge suit, the top hat consequently became less seen in the streets. Some grey top hats in the summer. Sides slightly concave; height about $5\frac{3}{4}$ inches.

T

ROUND CROWN HARD FELT

This was the *Bowler*, or, in America, the *Derby*. The brim in some cases curved up at the sides, in others comparatively flat. Black generally; sometimes brown, fawn or grey.

1909 'The Bowler hat is an abomination to the individualist.'

Tailor and Cutter

THE HOMBURG

A stiff felt with the crown dented in, from front to back, and a turned-up silk-bound brim.

THE TRILBY

Similar in shape to a Homburg, but of softer felt; brim silk bound.
  Trilby-shaped hats in velours, and for summer wear, of straw.

BOATER

A flat crowned, flat brimmed, straw hat.

THE OPERA HAT

Also known as a 'Gibus' after its inventor, was of corded silk or merino; the crown was supported by a spiral spring between the outer cloth and the lining. The spring could be collapsed, and the hat folded quite flat. When worn it had the appearance of a dull-surfaced silk hat. Worn with evening dress or, latterly, a dinner jacket.

  In addition there were tweed hats, some with ear-flaps ('deer-stalker'), tweed caps with the crown in eight segments, close fitting, and known as 'golf caps'; or looser, cloth caps, the crown cut in one piece and pouching over at sides and front, the front often fastened down to the peak with a press-stud. Soft felts with wide, unbound brims were known as 'wide awakes', and by a variety of trade names. Flat-topped, square cut hard felts were called 'Muller-cut-downs' after a murderer of the last century who had cut down the crown of his silk hat as a means of disguise. Panama straw hats were worn in summer at the seaside and in the country.

After the Great War the number and variety of hats and caps was greatly lessened. The top hat, except for formal occasions, disappeared; the 'boater' went out of favour, and the Trilby, together with soft felt hats with unbound brims, narrower than the old 'wide awakes', became increasingly popular. The bowler tended to be worn as a 'business' hat.

THE CITY   THE WEST END   THE COLONIAL

THE ROSEBERY

NEW GOLF CAP   THE BADEN-POWELL   LATEST TWEED HAT

HARD FELT

188. 1900 Hat types.

BOOTS, SHOES, SOCKS

BOOTS AND SHOES

At the beginning of the century with a long pointed toe – 'the tooth pick', black or tan in colour. Boots were correct for 'dress' wear, of light construction in kid, some with buttoned suede tops. Heavier boots in calf, laced. Some cloth-topped boots. There were some rubber soles and heels. Black was the correct colour in Town, but brown was permissible with some lounge suits. Boots and shoes for sport, such as shooting and golf, were generally brown and with rounder toes; tan and white together were favoured in some sporting circles.

From 1910 shoes became more popular than boots, and about this year also the American, Boston, or Bull-dog toe was introduced. This was a blunt round toe with an upward bulge.

After the war, brogues, first appearing about 1911 for sports wear and with flannel suits, were popularized by the Prince of Wales, who favoured fringed tongues.

Shoes now preponderated over boots.

From 1921 crêpe rubber was employed for soles, especially on golf shoes.

189. 1921 Footwear: (a) Patent Oxford walking shoe with broad laced ties. (b) Patent button day-dress shoe or boot with cloth or light kid top.

Tan and white sports shoes still appeared on certain feet. Throughout the period dancing pumps for wear with evening dress were low-cut in front with a flat black bow. As shoes replaced boots for dress wear the pump died out.

Sand shoes, or plimsols, for beach wear, of canvas with rubber soles: rubber Wellington boots, and galoshes to pull over the shoes were all in favour during the years under review.

SOCKS

Silk, wool, cotton. Plain colours or with self-clocks or clocks of differing colour. Colours mostly dark. Some coloured, embroidered fronts (1912). Coloured clocks on plain socks. Coloured, striped and checked socks (1921).

Socks came up to mid-calf and were supported by suspenders.

Stockings, some with fancy tops, for knickerbockers and plus-fours. They were knee-length and kept up by elastic garters below the knee, over which the tops were turned down.

ACCESSORIES

GLOVES

Essential for Town wear. Tan cape; kid; doeskin, etc. For evenings, kid, suede, fabric. Also gloves with leather palms and cotton and silk netted backs for driving or cycling. Lined gloves for winter. Generally two buttons or spring stud fasteners; sometimes only one. Lined with wool or fur for winter (1912).

Chamois, lavender kid, tan cape, fabric, all popular in 1921. Now mostly one button, sometimes two.

HANDKERCHIEFS

Linen or cotton. White or with coloured border. Patterned bandannas. Initials in corner.

Silk, white or coloured. Fancy borders. Bandannas. A red silk handkerchief was often worn as an ornament protruding from the bosom of the waistcoat with evening dress during the early years of the century.

As the outside breast pocket became more common it was increasingly fashionable to wear a white handkerchief carelessly thrust into it.

1915 'Practically all [lounge suits] have out breast pockets.'

Tailor and Cutter

SCARVES

Knitted in silk or wool. Some plain colours, including white and black; some striped. Fringed ends.

SPATS (SPATTS)

Drill or box-cloth. Drab, white or black. Covered top of shoe and ankle. Four buttons on outside, strap and buckle under foot.

By 1921 black spats were no longer listed; drab or grey for everyday, white for weddings, etc.

Gaiters and anklets were worn for country pursuits, shooting, golf, etc.

UMBRELLAS

Worn closely rolled. They had, in the 1890's, become a fashionable substitute in Town for a walking stick. Black silk or cotton. Mostly wooden sticks in the earlier years, but a few steel-tube sticks also. The steel stick enabled the umbrella to roll tighter and more neatly. Crook handles predominated, but before the Great War some crutch and plain straight handles were to be seen.

WALKING STICKS

Before the Great War were almost essential for the well-dressed man – and most men, within their means, aimed at dressing, if not stylishly, at least 'nobbily' or 'nattily'.

After the war, though still carried by many, the walking stick began to decline in favour. The increasing use of the motor car had a lot to do with this, as with other sartorial modifications in the inter-war years.

Canes such as rattan and malacca were favourites for Town use – with crook, crutch or straight handles, very often mounted with silver bands and tips. Ebony sticks, gold or silver mounted, for evening. Some canes ingeniously held in their recesses pencils, cigarettes, flasks, pipes, or even devices for measuring the height of horses.

In the country, plain sticks of ash, cherry, oak, hazel, etc. were correct.

JEWELLERY, etc.

WATCHES

Pocket type, open faced, half-hunters, and full hunter cases (i.e. with the glass protected by a metal cover; the half-hunter had a circular cut-out in the middle of the cover, with the hour-chapters engraved around it; the hands could partially be seen through this cut-out). Gold, silver, nickel, oxydized steel, etc. cases. Thin, dress watches. Matching Albert chains passed across the waistcoat, the watch in one pocket, the other end of the chain with perhaps a seal or charm on it in the other. The Albert generally passed through a chain-hole en route across the waistcoat. For evening dress some black or white silk straps in place of the chain.

Wrist watches on leather straps were seen in small numbers before the 1914 war – they were worn with motor-cycling kit, for instance – but did not become common until post-war years, possibly as a result of the popularity they had gained with men on active service.

TIE-PINS

Gold stick type for ties and scarves. Some with head in form of horseshoe, etc. Some mounted with small jewels. Safety-pin type and also clips to hold ends of long ties to shirt. Safety-pins in gold were also used to hold the fronts of soft collars together.

Small gold clips in the form of heart-shaped paper-clips with a protruding central boss or knob. These were used in pairs, clipped under the bottom of single stiff collars at each side of the neck, with the knob holding the top of the tie to prevent it riding up.

SIGNET RINGS

Of gold, often mounted with bloodstone or sardonyx, etc.

CASES, PURSES, ETC.

Cigarette cases and visiting card cases in silver, gold, leather, etc. Leather wallets and note cases and purses. Sovereign purses (up to 1916) in the form of leather wallets, or leather tubes; or spring loaded oval or watch-shaped in silver, etc.

STUDS AND CUFF-LINKS

Gold, silver, etc. Various forms. At the beginning of the century torpedo- and dumb-bell-shaped cuff-links were popular. Later oval or square were more fashionable. Sets of matching evening-dress cuff-links and waistcoat buttons: mother-o'-pearl was a popular material.

Key-rings, silver match-boxes, petrol and tinder lighters, cigar and cigarette holders of meerschaum, amber, etc. as well as pipes and tobacco pouches were all carried from time to time.

1926-1950

INTRODUCTORY REMARKS

The second quarter of this century showed little change in essentials from the first. Lounge suits continued in the greatest favour for ordinary wear; the morning coat was more and more confined to ceremonial and gala occasions; the frock coat was almost as dead as the golden sovereign, being 'relegated to elderly statesmen on special occasions'. The enthusiastic flush of the post-war years died to be succeeded by the anxiety of the Depression and the austerity of the Second World War. Dullness was the keynote, relieved occasionally by a flash of sports clothing of a more unconventional design, and by such minor features as an increase in coloured socks and shirts. Heads were topped by the almost universal soft felt hat, the brim turned down in front; the bowler was in less evidence. With the dinner jacket the opera hat was replaced by the black trilby, popularized for day wear also by Mr. Anthony Eden, and eventually acquiring his name.

The cinema had a certain effect on fashion, and some American features appeared. In 1926 the *Tailor and Cutter* commented on the transatlantic habit of wearing the trousers on the hips, with a consequent diminishing of the rise towards the waist. Shoulders became more square and a fuller, padded look appeared about the chest in 1930. In 1935 the *Tailor and Cutter* wrote that 'young men are undoubtedly influenced in dress by the screen'; another of the influences seems to have been the introduction of the turned-down, pointed collar and a soft shirt for wear with the dinner jacket, which by now was in greater demand than dress 'tails'.

The Prince of Wales continued to influence male fashion – he favoured the American style of trousers and to an extent revived the older fashion of wearing a white waistcoat with a dinner jacket. The Fair Isle pullover lost favour in the Thirties and was replaced in popularity by those of plain colours – yellow, perhaps, preponderating. Wind-cheaters, or lumber-jackets, from the blanket-cloth garments worn in the Canadian north, with waist and wristbands, pouching slightly and buttoned or zip-fastened to the neck, were replacing the conventional sports jacket on the golf links. Short-sleeved sports shirts were also appearing.

The majority of men's tailoring was in the hands of great multiple firms who produced factory-made, not only ready-to-wear, but made-to-measure, suits. These were of good quality and low price – about fifty shillings was the average – mostly in sober tones of greys and blues.

A very few eccentrics of more or less notoriety were seen about Town in sandals or open-necked shirts, and members of the 'hatless brigade' opposed the general tide by asserting the hygienic and aesthetic properties of the bare head. Among more conservative circles a tendency could be noted in the Thirties to wearing a dark lounge suit on social occasions, when a morning coat was generally accepted as being called for.

Rather high, square shoulders continued in fashion, and in about 1936 a draped cut to the lounge jacket was introduced: a fashion which passed to America, and returned to these shores in an exaggerated style in the immediate post-second war years. The Silver Jubilee had no effect on men's clothes: although a well-known store at this time spoke of 'the new shade of Dress wear cloth, midnight blue', this colour had in fact appeared in the form of 'a very dark navy' five years previously.

The years leading up to the Second World War, with the death of King George V, the accession of the Prince of Wales as the short-reigning Edward VIII, and the relinquishment of the Throne to his brother, were years of international crises and domestic unease and uncertainty. These conditions demanded a hope, even an unfounded one, of some form of security, and as women's clothes seemed to embody a return to maturity and womanliness after the fashions of the Twenties, so men's clothes in this country seem to have remained static in a desire to preserve the what-had-been.

The war of 1939–45 brought with it austerity and scarcity. As with women's, men's clothes were rationed from June 1941, and those men who were not in one of the Services were restricted to the minimum of replacement garments. Those in the Services had to be content with their uniforms and a microscopic issue of coupons for such non-issue essentials as handkerchiefs. 'Utility' garments appeared, made from Utility cloths. The Utility suit consumed 26 of the 60 precious annual coupons. The habit of 'dressing' either for day or evening events was well nigh discontinued, in many cases never to return.

One feature of the war years which was, to a large extent, to remain afterwards was the spread of the two-piece, waistcoatless, lounge suit. Waistcoats had, to a small degree, begun to be discarded before the war, in 'sports' or weekend and flannel suits, but the scarcity of cloth in the ensuing years dictated a rapid spread of the habit which persisted even after all controls were withdrawn.

In 1945 lounge jackets exhibited a moderate drape, and sports jackets based on the American battle jacket, with a pleated back panel, appeared.

In 1946 'supplies, however, are strictly limited', and firms hiring out formal dress clothes included shirts, ties and shoes to avoid any expenditure of coupons for special occasions.

By 1948 or 1949 the 'American' look of wide-shouldered, draped jackets was being rivalled by an 'Edwardian' look of slimmer-cut suits with narrower trousers, turned-back cuffs and some fancy waistcoats. By 1950 this was well established, to degenerate in the next few years to the 'Teddy boy' outfit. However, on the whole, men still continued to be conservative in their dress, and the majority remained faithful to the pre-war lines, including the many hundreds of thousands of conventional style 'demob' suits issued to the disbanded Forces.

During the war and increasingly thereafter the age-old concept of a gentleman declined in popular estimation and influence, and consequent upon this decline the traditional differences in dress that had marked the social distinctions of the past began to disappear.

Technical innovations in this second quarter-century do not seem to have been very great, the majority of these have occurred since 1950. However, the zip fastener which we have seen on lumber-jackets, is noted as applied to trouser flies in place of buttons in 1935, although its popularity in these regions took some time to establish and it has not yet completely conquered the older method.

The decreasing weight of suiting materials has been mentioned in the previous chapters, and in the years immediately before the second war an experimental suit of an acetate fabric was made, but it was not until many years later that the concept of man-made fibres for suitings became a commercial actuality.

Spun rayon shirts appeared just before the Second World War and in numbers from about 1945, and for some ten years had a success, though later they were superseded by other fabrics.

The twenty-odd years between the closing date of this book and the time of writing have seen rapid changes in the concepts and styles of dress for both sexes. Of the likely fate of modern fashions it is not within the province of recorders of past modes to prophesy. Some are here to stay; some, like the concept of 'Unisex' in dress seem already on the way out (in connection with this phenomenon it is interesting to see that as far back as 1950 there were advertisements for 'his' and 'her' matching knitted jerseys); but the chronicling of the last half of the Twentieth Century's clothes must wait for a future historian who can stand sufficiently far back from his subject to obtain a true picture.

DAY CLOTHES

THE FROCK COAT

Still seen in 1928 as an alternative to the morning coat for wear at funerals. But in 1930 'Now relegated to Elder Statesmen on special occasions' [The funerals of other Elder Statesmen?]. (*Tailor and Cutter.*)

H.M. King George V, however, remained a faithful adherent to the frock coat throughout his reign.

Details did not vary from the previous period.

THE MORNING COAT

Single breasted with V-notch lapels or wide, pointed, double-breasted style lapels. Centre back vent and two pleats with buttons at the head. One link button. Outside breast pocket. Inside breast and back-pleat pockets; sometimes inside ticket pocket. Cuffs generally slit and buttoned. Buttons black bone or composition. Some braided edges. Fronts sloping away fairly sharply to medium-narrow tails.

Correct wear for weddings, etc. Worn with single- or double-breasted grey waistcoat, or black waistcoat, and striped trousers.

1930 'Worn mostly for ceremony or gala.'

Tailor and Cutter

190. 1925 Morning coat; braided edges. Single-breasted waistcoat. Striped trousers. Wing collar. Bow tie. Spats. Silk top hat.

After the war almost only seen at weddings and Royal garden parties. The light grey waistcoat almost universal. Most morning-coat outfits were now hired by the day.

1931 'Morning coats, double breasted grey waistcoat, striped trousers. Bespoke, from £7.2.6.'

Army and Navy Stores

1934 Morning coat, single breasted. One button above waist seam. Fronts cut back in quite a sharp curve. Centre back vent and two pleats with buttons at the waist. Double-breasted lapels. Cuffs with slit and four buttons. Two pockets in back pleats, inside breast and ticket pockets, outside breast pocket.
      Six button, single-breasted black waistcoat, striped cashmere trousers.

London Museum

Materials for morning coats. Vicuna, diagonals and twills, cheviots, barathea, etc. Some with small herringbone pattern.

THE MORNING COAT SUIT

Still occasionally seen, generally in a light grey suiting for summer wear at weddings, the races, etc. A grey top hat was worn with it.

THE LOUNGE SUIT

The lounge suit was the predominating men's wear during the second quarter of the century. It appeared at events and in places where in previous decades more formal attire would have been *de rigueur*.

Normally consisting of jacket, waistcoat and trousers, by 1937 two-piece 'weekend suits' with no waistcoat and a slightly differing shade of trousers were advertised, and by 1940 two-piece suits were worn either with or without a pullover. In 1941 'some tailors favour abandoning the waistcoat instead of skimping the suit', and the war-time shortages led to the production of more and more two-piece lounge suits, a fashion which still prevails today.

The virtual disappearance of the frock and morning coats from everyday life led to an increase in the wearing of a black or very dark grey jacket and waistcoat with striped trousers. This outfit was advertised in 1931 for 'professional and business wear', and it was generally considered incorrect for social occasions. In some instances it was seen accompanied by a silk hat, but this was not a common usage.

The fashionable lounge jacket of 1926 was described as with a well defined waist, but not too close-fitting, three pockets outside and three-button cuffs. The single-breasted variety had softly rolling revers not pressed flat. Two or three buttons, the three-button style most popular, the middle one alone being done up. During the 1930's, one, two and three buttons were all in favour. Double-breasted models had four or six buttons.

191. 1925 Lounge suit. Single-breasted black jacket and double-breasted waistcoat with striped trousers.

192. 1928 Lounge suit. Single breasted, jetted pockets.

193. 1928 Double-breasted lounge suit or reefer. Grey, blue or brown flannel. From £5. 10. 0.

Fronts of single-breasted jackets were generally cut with rounded bottoms, but in 1928 a square-cut front was depicted, with three buttons rather close together, the middle one in the form of a link, and wide double-breasted pointed lapels.

Pockets were generally flapped at hip level and welted at the outside breast. However, welted or jetted hip pockets became popular, especially in double-breasted suits. Ticket pockets were generally inside the jacket or inset in an outside hip pocket.

In 1930 the *Tailor and Cutter* noted that jackets were now fuller in the breast, shoulders more square, closely fitting over the hips and with long rolling soft lapels. The waist was fairly high.

The double-breasted 'reefer' had a generous lap over, and the buttons were set closer together. In all cases the sleeves were cut to show at least half an inch of shirt cuff. The exposure of shirt cuffs has long been a class-distinctive mark of the gentleman, indicating that no manual work, likely to soil them, or likely to be incommoded by their presence around the wrists, was ever indulged in.

Double-breasted style lapels were a favourite cut with single-breasted jackets during the 1930's, although the narrow, notched lapel was also to be seen. Single-breasted jackets generally had a flower-hole in the left lapel, and double-breasted jackets had one in each lapel.

There was little alteration to the style of the jacket during this period. Mention has been made of a draped effect tentatively appearing in the later Thirties, but this did not have much significance until about 1942 when 'square shoulders and a semi-draped effect' are mentioned by the *Tailor and Cutter*. By this year the effects of the war were becoming noticeable. In 1941 jackets were being cut shorter and rationing was introduced. Various restrictions were imposed; the number of pockets limited; no outside breast pockets or buttons on the cuffs. In 1942 the Utility scheme had produced a more or less standard lounge suit incorporating these economies, and double-breasted jackets were prohibited.

1945 saw jackets with a moderate drape, easy over the chest, a natural shoulder line and a low waist. The black jacket

194. 1930 Lounge suit. Double breasted, jetted pockets. Snap-brim hat (see p. 335).

(see p. 335)

195. 1935 Lounge suit. Single breasted with wide, pointed, double-breasted lapels.

U

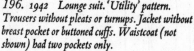

196. 1942   Lounge suit. 'Utility' pattern.
Trousers without pleats or turnups. Jacket without
breast pocket or buttoned cuffs. Waistcoat (not
shown) had two pockets only.

and striped trousers suit was very much less evident after the war.

This looser look continued during the rest of the decade, jackets aiming to be easy and not too fitting to the figure, particularly in country and leisure clothes. By the end of the period, double-breasted jackets, perhaps because of their prohibition during the war years, were becoming the more popular style. In 1946 a wide-shouldered, draped, double-breasted 'American' look had a certain favour; a look which, in a very exaggerated form, with much-padded shoulders and cut very long in the body, became associated with the 'spiv'. The 'spiv' was a wartime product: a wide-boy versed in all the intricacies of the Black Market and

197. 1949   *Lounge suits: (a) Double breasted. Draped American style jacket with low rolling lapels. (b) Single breasted, two-piece with fancy waistcoat.*

flourishing so long as shortages and rationing of all types continued. He was caricatured on the music hall stage by comedians of the day.

In about 1949 a narrower-cut single-breasted jacket with shorter lapels was heralding the 'Edwardian' look.

The many hundreds of thousands of demobilized Servicemen, resulting from the run-down of the Forces from the end of 1945, were each issued with a 'demob' suit, conservatively cut in a number of standard designs and materials. Demob suits were mass-produced, uniform and unadventurous, but generally speaking of a reasonably good material and make, if somewhat skimpily cut and finished. They appeared in double- and single-breasted styles and were non-Utility in that the side pockets were flapped; there were buttons on the cuffs and they had an outside breast pocket.

Most lounge jackets were made without a back vent or slit. Some 'sports' lounges cut with side vents. Grey flannel summer suits with unlined jackets.

EXAMPLES

1928 'Lounge suits. Single breasted lounge and double breasted Reefer style suits tailored from high grade worsteds, saxonies and tweeds in greys, browns, and blues. Ready to wear 6 gns. to 12 gns.'

Harrods

1929 'Men's suits in tweed. 50/- to 8 gns.'

Frank H. Page, Colchester

1937 ' "Weekend Suits." Jacket and trousers of Scotch cheviot. Trousers with a darker stripe. Brown, fawn and grey. £6.6.0.'

Harrods

1938 Black jacket and waistcoat, striped trousers. Single-breasted jacket with three buttons, and three buttons on each cuff. Flapped pockets at hip level, welted breast pocket. Double-breasted lapels. Double-breasted waistcoat with collar and broad lapels cut in a curve. Striped cashmere trousers with turnups.

London Museum

c. 1941 Blue worsted single-breasted lounge suit with faint white stripe. Flapped pockets at hip, but no outside breast pocket. Two inside breast, one ticket and one hip level pocket inside. Three button front. Three buttons on slit cuffs. Waistcoat with four pockets and six buttons (single breasted). Trousers with no turnups, side pockets, no back hip pocket.

London Museum

c. 1946 'Demob suit'. Double-breasted jacket and trousers in a dark grey flannel with white pin stripe. Six buttons, broad rolling lapels, two outside, hip-level, flapped pockets, welted breast pocket. Cuffs with slit and three buttons. Inside breast pocket. Ticket pocket inset in right hand outside pocket. Flower-hole in each lapel. Trousers with three pockets and turnups.

Holly Trees Museum, Colchester

1943 'Ready to wear Utility suits 80/- and 95/-.'

1950 'Worsted suits, ready to wear 9 gns. Sale price: Three piece tweed suits £4. grey, brown and fawn (usual price £6). Singlebreasted two-piece tweed suits, brown and grey, £5.10. (usual price £8).'

From local East Anglian advertisements

Materials for Lounge Suits: Serge, tweeds, saxonies, cheviots, flannel. Worsteds, including fancy pin stripe and bird's-eye weaves.

In 1926 it was said that there was 'more colour appearing in suiting' (*Tailor and Cutter*), but the usual range of dark blues, greys and browns remained firmly ensconced. In 1931 'Neat stripe patterns will be favoured, but there are dozens of weaves and patterns to choose from' (Harrods).

Dark clerical grey was very popular in the Thirties, and in 1937 'chalk stripes are favoured' (Harrods). It was noted in 1938 that brown was not fashionable, chalk stripes less popular, but narrow stripes and checks more so. Up to 1950, the greys, blues and fawns remained the most acceptable colours.

DAY WAISTCOATS

For frock coats, as before.

For morning coats, black or light grey or fawn, single breasted; or, increasingly, double breasted in the light colours for weddings.

For lounge suits, single breasted usually, but some double-breasted waistcoats seen in the late Twenties and early Thirties, and again in 1939 for a brief spell. Double-breasted waistcoats generally had square-cut fronts, but some had points as in the single-breasted style. Three or four buttons each side. Single-breasted waistcoats with five or six, the bottom button automatically left undone.

A fashion that started just pre-war was to leave off the waistcoat in summer, and the economies dictated by the war confirmed the habit.

In 1949–50 a few coloured and fancy waistcoats were appearing, and for sports wear chamois leather ones with a zip in place of buttons.

Pockets usually four, sometimes reduced to two in those wartime waistcoats that were made.

An adjusting strap and buckle at the back was customary.

DAY TROUSERS

Day trousers were striped cashmere, in most cases, with the morning coat and those frock coats that survived; also with the black lounge jacket and waistcoat. In the last case they may have been turned-up, otherwise the cashmere trousers were without turnups.

For lounge suits turnups were almost universal.

Oxford bags had left a legacy of trousers cut wider in the leg than in the earlier years of the century. In 1926 the *Tailor and Cutter* reported that although 'trousers are narrow again' (relatively speaking) they were cut with 'ample width in the legs, yet in no wise "baggy" '. Widths were about 20½ inches at the knee and 17 inches at the bottom, as against the Oxford bags' 24 and 23 inches. American style trousers, cut short in the rise, had proportions of 20 and 17½ inches.

By 1930 the measurements had become an average of 21¼ inches at the knee and 18 inches at the bottom. The waist was cut to a close fit with two pleats into the waistband.

Trousers were now of sufficient length to break slightly over the instep.

Zip fasteners instead of buttons on the fly-front appear in small numbers from about 1935. The waistband was often prolonged beyond the centre front closure into a tongue some three inches long. This tongue was usually secured by a flat metal hook engaging into a flat bar sewn into the opposite side of the waistband. A similar hook and bar often replaced the button on the waistband at the top of the fly.

Adjusting straps, either one at the back or one at each side, were general, and many trousers were fitted with belt loops of self material.

Leg widths increased somewhat and averaged 23 or 24 inches at the knee and 21 inches at the bottom in 1938: by 1942 they had decreased again to 20 inches at the knee, and bottoms of 18 or 19 inches.

False turnups appeared in 1941 in an endeavour to economize on material: by the next year no turnups at all on newly-made trousers.

Widths increased again after the war; in 1945, 22 inch knee and 21 inch bottoms, and a 'demob' suit of c. 1946 in Holly Trees Museum, Colchester, measures 23 inches at the knee and 20½ inches at the bottom. Photographs of the years 1946–48 show wide trouser legs breaking well over the front of the shoes.

However, with the 'Edwardian' look appearing in 1948, some trousers were again narrowing.

Pockets were usually one in each side seam with vertical openings, and one or two pockets opening horizontally at the back at hip level. These hip pockets were often omitted in war-time trousers. Sometimes a small fob pocket was inset at the right-hand side of the waist. Hip and fob pockets generally had a buttoned flap, but this was sometimes replaced by a zip fastener.

For a short while after the war, cross pockets were occasionally seen, especially on sports trousers. These were front pockets inset below the waistband, with almost horizontal, sloping openings, instead of the vertical opening in the side seam. They were considered easier of access when sitting in a motor car.

EXAMPLES

1929   'Striped trousers in cashmere, from £1.17.6.'

Army and Navy Stores

c. 1938   Trousers of lounge suit. Waistband cut with a 3 inch rise at the back. Six belt loops. Adjusting straps with white metal D-buckle, one each side. Six braces buttons inside waistband. Two pockets in side seams; one back hip pocket and one fob pocket at waist, right-hand front, both with buttoned flaps. Pockets and lining at waist white sateen. Fly-front with six buttons and a blued metal flat hook and bar at waistband. Permanent turnups. Length, outside leg waistband to bottom, 41 inches, inside leg 29¾ inches. Width at knee 24 inches, bottoms 21 inches.

Holly Trees Museum, Colchester

c. 1950   Trousers of Utility lounge suit. Waistband prolonged into tongue overlapping at front and fastened by white metal hook and bar. Waistband rises 1½ inches at back. Six braces buttons sewn on outside. Two sideseam pockets, one welted hip pocket, one flapped fob pocket. Fly-front with six buttons. Waist lined with white sateen. Pockets grey cotton. Narrow permanent turnups. Length, outside leg waistband to bottom 40 inches, inside leg 28½ inches. Width at knee 25 inches, bottom 19 inches.

Holly Trees Museum, Colchester

ODD JACKETS AND TROUSERS

Very popular. Generally tweed jacket and grey flannel trousers. Some fawn or sand-coloured flannels in the Thirties.

'Sports' jackets followed the lines of the single-breasted lounge suit with notched lapels. Blazers for summer wear, generally single breasted, sometimes double. Dark blue the usual colour, with gilt buttons. The blazer acquired considerable popularity for general wear after the war, and the double-breasted variety was much more frequently seen. It was worn all the year round.

Just pre-war and during the war years and for a short time after, the yoked sports jacket with a half belt at the back was again seen. Some versions had pleated backs. In 1945 draped sports jackets cut with a whole back.

By the end of the period lighter-weight materials such as gaberdine were rivalling, for summer wear, the traditional tweeds and homespuns.

198. 1938 Sports jacket with yoke, pleats and half belt. Pleated patch pockets. Flannel trousers, soft felt hat.

199. 1939 Sports jacket. Plus-fours.

200. 1939 Sports jacket, collarless. Three patch pockets. Soft felt hat with oval depression in crown.

Summer jackets in fawn or drab silk, cotton, etc.

Odd trousers were generally grey flannel. From about 1930 worsted flannel was becoming more usual than ordinary flannel. Light or medium shades of grey, with dark grey becoming increasingly popular in post-war years.

From about the mid-1940's odd tweed trousers, some quite colourful, plain, checked or striped, and by 1950 gaberdine, whipcord, corduroy and cavalry twill were increasingly favoured.

EXAMPLES

1928 'Blue Flannel Blazers, pure wool of a medium shade of blue – reliable dye. Lined sleeves. All sizes and fittings.
Single breasted 42/-, 63/-
Double breasted 45/-, 66/-.'
'All wool flannel trousers. White and three shades of grey. Every inch waist measurements from 30 ins. to 46 ins. and leg lengths from 27 ins. to 36 ins. 45/-, 30/-, 21/-.'

Harrods

1929 'Sports coats, tweed, 20/-.'
'Navy blazers in flannel, 17/11.'
'Grey flannel trousers, three leg lengths, belt loops, 8/11.'

Advertisements, *Essex County Standard*

1931 'Super quality flannel trousers. Light, medium and silver grey. Pleated waist band: belt loops: side straps. In a variety of leg lengths, 10/6.'

Fosters, Colchester

1938 'Flannels and Blazers. Ready to wear from 21/- each'.

Owen Ward, Colchester

1949 'Sports jackets 45/- to £6.5.0.'
'Cord trousers from £3.12.6.'
'Flannel trousers from 24/11.'

Advertisements, *Essex County Standard*

1942–52 Utility flannel trousers. Medium grey fine smooth flannel. Waistband prolonged into a tongue fastened with a composition button. Composition braces buttons inside; four belt loops. Two pockets in side seams, one jetted hip pocket with button. Waistband lined grey cotton, pockets unbleached cotton. Width at knee 24 inches, bottom 20 inches. Utility label.

Author's collection

EVENING DRESS

THE DRESS COAT

Altered little since the last period.

1930 'The fashionable dress coat fits the waist well at the back and has long skirts.
Square shoulders, wide back; waist seam not too straight in front. Bold lapels and ivory buttons with sunk centres.

*201. 1925   Evening dress
coat. Single-breasted waistcoat.
White gloves.*

*202. 1938 Evening dress coat,
long tails to mid-calf. Double-
breasted waistcoat.*

203. 1926 *Evening dress coat. Double-breasted waistcoat.*

The square shoulder effect is the outstanding feature of the present season.
Some gentlemen favour a very dark navy material for it is contended that
in artificial light [it] appears deeper black than actual black barathea.'

Tailor and Cutter

In 1935 as well as black the Army and Navy Stores were
advertising 'the new shade of Dress wear cloth, Midnight Blue'.

1938   'Modern Dress coat for the Dancing Man.
High shoulder line, bold fronts and lapels. Waist kept high . . . skirts long
and cut well away towards the bottom.'

Tailor and Cutter

The tails during this period were well below the knee in length.

1949   'Full formal dress is naturally left severely alone.'

Tailor and Cutter

By now tails were only reaching to the bend of the knee. Throughout the years slight variations of the slope at which the fronts of
the coat were cut are noticeable.

Increasingly the dress coat had given way to the dinner jacket,
and when the former was worn it was more and more usual to
hire it.

THE DINNER JACKET

Throughout the Thirties and Forties the double-breasted version
was perhaps the more popular. In 1926 with four buttons and
jetted outside pockets at hip level. Lapels rolled slightly higher
than formerly. Single breasted with one link button of bone or
composition.

1930   'There are more dinner jackets being ordered than dress coats.'

Tailor and Cutter

Dark navy or midnight blue as well as black.

1941   'Dinner jackets are still in evidence for dinner parties and dances. Boiled
[stiff starched] shirt and collar, but a soft collar and shirt are permissible.'

Tailor and Cutter

In this year single- or double-breasted jackets with wide pointed
lapels or deep shawl collars. The double-breasted style more
favoured, especially as there was 'no need for a waistcoat'.

204. 1939 Dinner jacket. Continuous roll collar, double breasted, two buttons only.

205. 1941 Dinner jacket, single breasted, wide 'double-breasted' lapels. Single button, jetted pockets.

206. 1941 Dinner jacket. Double breasted, continuous roll collar, jetted pockets.

Midnight blue was considered smarter than black and 'it is usual now-a-days to put on a black homburg with dinner clothes, which looks infinitely better than a gibus [folding opera hat]'. Backs were wide, and shoulders square.

In 1949 a variety of dinner jackets was shown, some flapped pockets, some with outside ticket pockets, and some with back vents.

MATERIALS FOR EVENING COATS

1926 'Materials for evening dress are veering from plainness to pattern . . . the neat barathea is still much to the front but . . . dress suits from fine fabrics with a canvas weave, a herring bone pattern, a silk stripe or a diamond or disc design.'

Tailor and Cutter

Barathea and fine worsteds continued in favour. Generally black, but also dark blue as noted above.

EVENING DRESS WAISTCOATS

Single breasted or double breasted, white marcella or piqué with the dress coat. Single breasted, matching black with the dinner jacket.

In 1930 the backless waistcoat, the two fronts joined behind by the collar and a strap at the waist, was noted as 'meeting with much favour'. (Can this be associated with the fashion for backless evening dresses for women appearing at this time?)

By 1941 the waistcoat was being discarded when a double-breasted dinner jacket was worn.

EVENING DRESS TROUSERS

Black or blue matching the dress coat or dinner jacket. No turnups. Braided down outside seam of legs: one row with the dinner jacket, two rows with a dress coat.

SMOKING JACKETS

As before. Also cut as a single-breasted dinner jacket in blue,
brown or black velveteen, with silk bound edges.

EXAMPLES

1928   'Dress suits 14, 12 and 10 gns.
        Dinner suits 12, 10, 8½ and 6 gns.'

                                                              Harrods

1931   'Dress suits £8.17.0. and £7.10.0.
        Dinner suits £9.5.0. and £6.7.6.'

                                                    Army and Navy Stores

KNITWEAR

1926   'Matching golf cardigan and stockings.'

1929   'Pure Botany wool cardigans in three colour effect in many pleasing shades,
        63/-.'

                                                    Army and Navy Stores

1931   'Pullovers in cashmere: Natural, Blue Lovat, Brown Lovat. With two
        inset waist pockets, 15/-.'

                                                              Harrods

1935   'Sleeveless slip-ons [pullovers] in two-colour pattern in blues, greys, fawns
        and browns, 16/6.'

                                                    Army and Navy Stores

1940   'Sleeveless pullover in pure cashmere. Reversable with different colour each
        side – green/lovat, grey/blue, etc. etc. 55/-.'
        'High neck sweater with long, raglan sleeves: plain knit outside, fleecy
        inside 39/6.'

                                                              Harrods

        'Khaki cardigans, pullovers and helmets in stock.'
                                              Owen Ward Ltd., Colchester

1950   'Smart matching jerseys' for men and women advertised.

Plain colour pullovers, cardigans and waistcoats were popular,
especially in a fairly light yellow. Some pullovers had a zip
fastener at the neck.

207. 1930–40   Sleeveless knitted pullover.

NECKWEAR

COLLARS

The soft double collar very much more popular. Either white, or matching a coloured or patterned shirt. Some with two button-holed tabs attached to the fronts to button on to the front stud, underneath the tie, and hold the collar in. Various celluloid stiffeners to insert into points of soft collars. Specially woven patented materials to give a firm semi-stiff finish.

x

Stiff linen double collars were also common. Both soft and stiff varieties had either long or short points. There appears to have been an increase in long-pointed collars from about 1936.

Single, wing collars for formal wear, including evening dress. But by 1930–31 soft double collars were being worn with the dinner jacket, and in 1941 the *Tailor and Cutter* noted that with the double-breasted dinner jacket 'most men . . . prefer soft collars with their black bow ties'.

Just after the war a fashion for American style, very long-pointed, soft collars.

TIES

For evening with the dress coat white piqué batswing or thistle-shape bows. With the dinner jacket black silk of similar design.

For day, bow ties of silk. Long four-in-hand ties the general wear. Spots, checks, club stripes (1928). Small quiet stripes and spots (1931). Checks and spots (1935). Artificial silk, silk, foulard, wool and poplin were all popular materials. Some knitted silk.

Uncrushable wool ties in 1940, 'especially suitable for wear with country clothes' (Harrods).

In 1949 small squares, diamond patterns, and stripes popular.

In 1950 artificial silk, barathea, cashmere, silk brocade, foulard ties in stripes, checks, spots, Paisley patterns and small floral patterns were advertised.

Some very vivid American designs, including painted motifs, appeared from about 1946–47.

With the morning coat the wide Ascot tie was worn, or a four-in-hand tie with a wing or double collar.

Ready-made ties were less common, but still seen, especially in bow ties.

CLOTHES FOR SPECIAL OCCASIONS

WEDDINGS

The morning coat outfit as before, or increasingly a lounge suit.

The gloves, stick and spats became obsolete.

In both morning coats and lounge jackets a white flower in the lapel and a white handkerchief in the breast pocket were general.

With the morning coat a grey top hat became the accepted wear.

MOURNING

Reduced in most cases to a dark suit and black tie at funerals.

PUBLIC OCCASIONS IN THE EVENING

In post-war years a dark lounge suit became more and more acceptable for restaurant dinners, the theatre, etc. and the dinner jacket replaced the formal dress tails, which tended to become fossilized on waiters, orchestra conductors and competitors in ballroom dancing contests.

COURT WEAR

The 1914–18 war alternative of evening dress coat with black breeches was retained.

In 1937 revised regulations were issued. The wearing of trousers with new style velvet dress was disallowed. With the cloth dress, trousers were to have gold lace on the side seams. Various other details were revised.

Although those revised Regulations still hold good, the virtual abolition of all Court functions during and after the 1939–45 war has made Court dress a very rare sight.

THE SECOND WORLD WAR (1939-45)

This had more impact, both physical and psychological, than the Great War of a generation earlier.

The clothes rationing and Utility schemes dictated changes and economies in men's clothes as well as in women's, and the social and political attitudes after the conflict have, as we have seen, resulted in a decline of formality in clothes, as in manners and customs generally, and a great levelling of class distinctions in matters of dress.

Rationing was introduced on 1st June 1941, with sixty-six coupons for a year's clothing. A suit used up twenty-six coupons, a pullover five.

The Utility scheme in 1942 produced the Utility lounge suit with a maximum of five pockets, single breasted only, no turn-ups, generally no waistcoat, and no metal fastenings of any kind.

In 1941 a suggestion was made, quoted in the *Tailor and Cutter,* that 'The Bank of England and other Banks can set a very useful example . . . by modifying the customary standard of dress . . .'

More and more capacity of tailors and manufacturers was taken up not only by Service uniforms but by the uniforms of civil bodies such as the Air Raid Precautions (Civil Defence) organizations, Auxiliary Fire Service, etc.

Prices increased (including the addition of purchase tax) and materials became scarcer.

1939   'Present prices cannot be repeated.'

1940   'Footwear is rising in price.'

1942   'Felt hats scarce.'

1943   'Utility suits to measure 80/- and 95/-.'
        'In co-operation with the Government Rubber Controller we are now equipped to repair your Wellingtons.'

1946   'Supplies [of raincoats] now, however, are strictly limited.'
                        Contemporary announcements and advertisements

Repairs, cleaning and turning services were all advertised.

208. 1941   *Gas-mask container. By courtesy of 'Punch'.*

A.R.P. WORKERS

1941. Dark blue drill combination suit with patch pockets on breast and at side of trouser leg. Belt. A.R.P. badge above breast pocket. Steel helmet. Also a dark blue battle-dress.

As with the Great War a certain amount of surplus Government clothing came on the market from about 1946–47. Also Service clothing was continued in use by individuals. The Army battle-dress had some influence on post-war fashions, as did the British warm overcoat and the naval duffel-coat.

SPORTS CLOTHES

GENERALLY

Sports jackets, blazers, wind-cheaters, flannel trousers. Plus-fours, getting less exaggerated in cut. Shorts for hiking and camping.

Collar-attached shirts in flannel, cotton, poplin, rayon, and from the end of the war nylon and other synthetics: some in plain colours, some in checks or stripes. Pullovers, cardigans, knitted and suede waistcoats.

Tweed caps, soft felt hats, and increasingly no hat at all: brogues, suede, and two-colour leather shoes.

FOOTBALL

As before, with a tendency towards increasing lightness in weight of materials, and shorter shorts.

CRICKET

As before.

TENNIS

Grey or white flannel trousers, and white shirt of flannel, silk, etc. Blue or white blazer. Shirt open-necked or with club tie (1926).

During the 1930's shorts began to appear in place of trousers on the tennis court, and by 1950 were almost universal.

White sweaters and pullovers.

The tie disappeared.

Some long double-breasted, belted overcoats in cream blanket cloth for wear after play.

GOLF

Plus-fours giving way to trousers. Shirt, pullover, collar and tie.

In the late 1920's, waist-length golf jackets of suede or cloth with close-fitting waists and wrists, the cuffs and waistband often knitted. Fastened at the front with buttons or zip fastener.

1929 'Golfer's overall blouse, rainproof, button front, ribbed knit border to hem and wrists. Two patch breast pockets.'
Army and Navy Stores

209. 1925   *Tennis outfit. Flannel trousers and blazer. Club scarf. Trousers 21/6d, blazer 26/6d.*

210. 1929   *Golf: Rainproof overall blouse (windcheater) and plus-fours. Blouse 40/-. Plus-fours 30/-.*

1935   '"Dalby" golf jacket. Made of Grenfell cloth which is wind proof and rain proof with zip fastening at the side to prevent pouching in front.'

Harrods

In fine weather, open-neck shirt and trousers.

SHOOTING

As before.

RIDING

'Hacking jackets' – full skirted lounge style, cut long in the skirt with a centre vent at back or two side slits. Breeches of cavalry

211. 1928 *Shooting: Plus-fours and jacket under waterproof cape. Boots and short gaiters.*

212. 1942 *Riding: Hacking jacket, Jodhpurs, soft felt hat. Button-down shirt collar.*

twill, whipcord, moleskin, tweed, etc. Riding boots or ankle boots and gaiters, or Jodhpurs in place of breeches.

Soft or hard felt hat, or cloth cap, or reinforced velvet riding cap. String netted gloves.

HUNTING

As before. In 1926 single-breasted frock coats, double-breasted swallow-tail coats, and full-skirted morning coats are all mentioned.

SEASIDE WEAR

Flannel trousers and blazer, 'Palm Beach' suits of light coloured linen, etc. Shorts and open-necked shirt or, after the war, 'bush-jackets' worn with a scarf tucked in the neck. The bush jacket was modelled on the Services' tropical uniform, of drill or similar material, with a shirt type collar and short sleeves, generally worn without a shirt underneath. Linen or cotton trousers and polo-necked shirts.

In 1931 one- or two-piece bathing costumes, some with an overskirt attachment. Black or navy blue with coloured trimming.

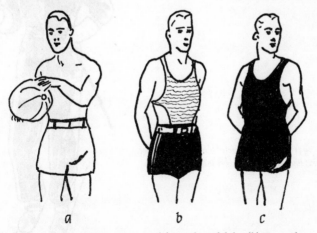

213. *1936 Swimming costumes: (a) Trunks with belt. (b) Two-colour suit with cut-out back, and belt. (c) One-piece costume with skirt attachment.*

In 1935 costumes cut out at the sides forming a Y at the back. Black, navy, maroon, royal blue. Sun-bathing trunk drawers.

Short bathing trunks gradually ousted the bathing costume from about the mid-1930's.

MOTORING

In 1926 lounge jacket or leather coat. Single-breasted waistcoat, trousers or plus-fours. Double-breasted ulster; cap, boots. Leather overcoats.

As motoring moved from being a sport to a way of life special clothes declined in use. The effects of the modern motor car were towards the abandoning of hats, overcoats and umbrellas and walking sticks. From after the war, however, a fashion for short, thigh-length overcoats modelled on the American war-time 'jeep-coat' appeared.

214. 1931 Ski-ing: Proofed blue gaberdine jacket. Trousers lined with wool, rubber inter-lining at seat.

SKI-ING

In 1928, breeches, stockings, boots, gloves, woollen sweaters, knitted caps with close turned-up brims. Scarves.

Later, trousers tucked into short socks and boots, jackets of weather-proof material, and similar caps with peaks.

YACHTING

Traditionally a blue reefer suit, or a white single-breasted suit, or reefer jacket and white trousers. Yachting cap, with glazed peak and white top, white canvas shoes. Oilskins in bad weather.

As the days of the big yachts declined and the small boat and dinghy replaced them, the amateur sailor wore trousers or shorts, shirt, woollen jersey, oilskins.

In almost all cases there was a progressive tendency towards more and more informality, and even unconventionality, in the dress of both participants and spectators of sports and games.

OUTDOOR CLOTHES

The Chesterfield continued as the favourite form of overcoat, single or double breasted. Usually now without a velvet collar. In 1930 it was either just below the knee in length, or longer, to the calf. By 1935 it was generally of medium length.

From 1946–50 it was seen in both forms, single breasted, with or without a fly: double breasted with six buttons, with or without a half belt at the back.

Ulsters, double breasted with an all-round belt and inset or patch pockets were also much worn. From about 1929 a fawn camel-fleece type was popular. A variety of this type, bulky, with thick, deep pile, was known as the 'Teddy bear': it had disappeared from favour in 1939. Raglan cut coats also worn throughout the period under review. Some evening cloaks.

After the war, duffel-coats had some years of popularity. The

215. 1925 Single-breasted Chesterfield in tweed or Saxony. From 5 gns.

216. 1928 Double-breasted Chesterfield.

217. 1938 Double-breasted Ulster, with half belt and lapped seam at back.

219. 1928 Macintosh.
Single breasted with full skirt
and belt. Wrist straps. Fawn
parramatta. 52/6d.

218. 1941 Single-breasted fly-fronted
Raglan overcoat with patch pockets.

220. 1946 Raglan raincoat; lined check material.
Back vent and multiple-stitched seam. Inside tongue
and jigger button to keep bottom of fronts together.

duffel-coat was originally a protective naval garment, dark blue or fawn, loose fitting and fastened with wooden toggles and rope loops in place of buttons. It had two patch pockets at the sides and generally an attached hood.

'British warms' and coats cut in a similar style, with shoulder straps, were also to be seen.

Dark greys, blues, browns and black were popular overcoat colours, as well as the camel or fawn mentioned. Some checked patterns ; some herringbone design.

MACINTOSHES AND RAINCOATS

As before, generally. The *Tailor and Cutter* in 1926 noted a preponderance of ready-made raincoats.

From 1946 nylon and other synthetic macintoshes.

EXAMPLES

1929   'Sports overcoat in thick camel fleece. Double breasted with belt all round. Ideal for watching all forms of sport during the winter or for wear after the game. £12.12.0.'

Army and Navy Stores

'Ready to wear overcoats 37/6.'

Lawrence's, Colchester

1935   'Covert raincoats, raglan or set-in sleeves. Single breasted, fly front. Horizontal or vertical pockets.'
'Teddy Bear pile camel "an ideal motoring coat" '.

Army and Navy Stores

1939   Dark blue-grey herringbone tweed fly-front single-breasted Chesterfield. Four bone buttons. Flower-hole in left lapel. Small button and tab inside near the bottom to hold fronts together when walking. Two flapped pockets outside at hip level; ticket pocket inset in right pocket. One outside breast pocket, one inside. Lined in body and sleeves with black silk. Hip-level pockets lined velveteen. Cloth loop coat hanger at neck. Slit cuffs with four buttons.
Length 45 inches. Chest 45–46 inches. Style width $8\frac{1}{2}$ inches. Waist $18\frac{1}{2}$ inches from base of collar. Vent in back seam 20 inches long.

Author's collection

1950 'Double breasted Ulster style with belt. Two patch pockets. Six buttons. Sale price £5.10.0.'

Local advertisement, Ipswich

HAIR

Usually short and well brushed; left side partings. Brilliantines and hair creams were used.

Punch noted an increase in the popularity of moustaches in 1928, but they were generally less popular than in earlier years. During the war, a large, straight moustache was favoured by many R.A.F. pilots, and also by some Army officers in the North African campaign. This style persisted in civilian life for some years after the war.

HATS AND CAPS

An increasing degree of hatlessness, especially after the war, was evident, particularly among younger men. The growing number of motor cars perhaps contributed to the hat's loss of favour, as, no doubt, did freedom from the compulsion to wear 'headgear' which had ruled in the Services.

The top hat was now more usually seen in grey cloth at weddings and races. The black silk variety rarely seen, then mostly with evening dress, but also with the morning coat on occasion. The crown became lower, and the sides less concave.

The bowler and Homburg declined in favour of the trilby during the 1930's, although the former always retained a following. The black trilby, popularized by Sir Anthony Eden (Lord Avon), and eventually succeeding to his name, was worn on formal and business occasions with dark suits, black jacket and striped trousers, and also with the dinner jacket in place of the opera hat. Grey and fawn trilbies were also worn with lounge suits.

'Snap brim' felt hats, trilby shape, but with a narrow binding or an unbound brim that could be turned, generally, down in front and up at the back, became increasingly popular in town and country.

Harrods' catalogues of 1928 showed silk top hats, trilbies (grey, brown and fawn), adaptable brim soft felt sports hats (in the same colours), bowlers, tweed sports hats and caps and collapsible opera hats.

In 1931 the 'adaptable' soft felt hat was described as 'snap or curl brim', and 'sports' was omitted.

221. 1929 Hats: (a) Bowler. (b) Snap brim. (c) Trilby.

Later in the 1930's this style acquired a circular instead of a longitudinal dent in the crown and was called a 'pork pie' hat.

'Pork pie hats, rough felt, green, brown or grey mixtures, 21/-.'
                                                        Harrods

In 1942 'felt hats scarce' due to war conditions.

At about the end of our period, light-weight felt hats with un-bound brims in every shade were available, and the Anthony Eden was almost universal among professional and business men. The bowler was worn by Guards' officers, with plain clothes, in London, which helped to confirm its smartness and formality.

Cloth caps continued in popularity: the Panama was occa-sionally worn, but the boater disappeared, except for a minor revival about the mid-1930's, perhaps influenced by the great French film star, Maurice Chevalier.

BOOTS, SHOES, SOCKS

BOOTS AND SHOES

Fashions continued much the same up to the war of 1939–45. Black or brown laced, leather shoes. Brogues, becoming heavy-looking in the 1930's. Some two-colour sports shoes. 'Monk' shoes, some in suede, with a high tongue and strap and buckle fastening. Suede was becoming more acceptable.

Boots less in favour and mostly worn by older men, workmen and in the country.

Rationing and Utility during the war discouraged extravagance and innovation, but from 1947 new styles were appearing, although the traditional laced shoes continued in most favour for some years. Among the new styles were thick crêpe-soled shoes, some with a strap and buckle fastening; and ankle-high boots with elastic gussets at the side.

Rubber galoshes declined in popularity, but the rubber Wellington boot continued, especially for wear in the country.

Some sandals for holiday and leisure wear.

SOCKS AND STOCKINGS

Generally as in the previous quarter-century.

During the war socks were restricted in length to reach just above the ankle, a most distressing feature, and could not be supported by suspenders.

Evening dress socks in black rayon had been in production for some time, and about the end of the half-century nylon socks for evening wear were making their appearance.

Knee-length stockings with turn-over tops for wear with plus-fours.

Y

ACCESSORIES

GLOVES

Much as previously. After the war kid and chamois gloves became less fashionable, and gloves became less worn as a fashion accessory and more purely as protection and for driving a motor, when string or leather driving gloves were worn. Gloves almost disappeared from the scene in the summer months.

One button as fastener now usual, but some gloves with a strap at the wrist.

HANDKERCHIEFS

No change. Perhaps more coloured borders. Coloured silk handkerchiefs in the breast pocket.

SCARVES

Knitted or woven silk or wool. White for evening. Plain coloured or patterned by day. Club stripes.

SPATS

Fawn and grey box cloth. White, biscuit or drab canvas. White canvas for weddings. By 1939 were almost extinct. Just after the war a few pairs seen at weddings but this fashion also died in most cases.

UMBRELLAS

Unchanged. A cane handle with pronounced joints became very popular. Some leather-covered handles.

WALKING STICKS

Like spats suffered a great decline during this period, and in post-war years were used only by the infirm and one or two eccentric conservatives (of which the male author is one).

JEWELLERY, etc.

WATCHES

The wrist watch well-nigh universal, some square or oblong in shape. Pocket types now mostly open faced; some half-hunters. The pocket watch was considered correct for dress wear, however, and some octagonal models appeared.

As the dress coat declined, wrist watches were more and more worn with the dinner jacket.

TIE-PINS

Less worn. A safety-pin type to keep the long tie in place, often concealed by the waistcoat or pullover. With the advent of the semi-stiff collar the safety-pin could be dispensed with at the neck.

CASES, PURSES, ETC.

Cigarette cases as previously: declining in popularity after the war. Visiting card cases and purses all but extinct.

CUFF-LINKS

Still worn extensively, but the increase of button-cuff shirts was eroding their usefulness.

The petrol lighter superseded the silver match box, and the increase in motor cars led to a corresponding increase in key-rings, many with a charm or amulet attached to propitiate the gods of the road.

GENERAL

Do nothing with this page until told what to do

A	A1	A2	A3	A4
B	B1	B2	B3	B4
C	C1	C2	C3	C4
D	D1	D2	D3	D4
E	E1	E2	E3	E4
F	F1	F2	F3	F4

CLOTHING BOOK 1946-47

General CB 1/9

CLOTHING BOOK 1946-47

GENERAL CB 1/9

This book must not be used until the holder's name, full postal address and National Registration Number have been written below. Detach this book at once and keep it safely. It is your only means of buying clothing.

HOLDER'S NAME
(in BLOCK letters)

ADDRESS
(in BLOCK letters)

HOLDER'S NATIONAL REGISTRATION No.

IF FOUND please take this book to any Food Office or Police Station

FOOD OFFICE CODE No.

THIS BOOK IS NUMBER

H 389735

HOLD Pages I—VIII in one hand and
TEAR ALONG THIS LINE

Appendix I

CLOTHES RATIONING

Rationing of clothing was introduced on 1st June 1941, and lasted effectually until 1st February 1949, when the controls over the majority of garments were removed. Average annual allotment of coupons was sixty-six.

On the 1st June 1941 the following numbers of coupons had to be surrendered:

MEN	Unlined macintosh	9
	Overcoat	16
	Coat, Blazer, etc.	13
	Waistcoat, pullover or Cardigan	5
	Trousers	8
	Trousers, Corduroy or fustian	5
	Collar	1
	Tie	1
	Socks	3
	Shoes or Boots	7
	Suit	26
WOMEN	Coat or unlined macintosh	14
	Jacket or short coat	11
	Dress, wool	11
	Dress, other material	7
	Blouse, jumper or cardigan	5
	Skirt	7
	Stockings	2
	Shoes or Boots	5
	Suit	18

Underclothing, knitting wool, material by the yard, etc. were all subject to rationing by coupons.

222. (*opposite*) *Two pages from clothes ration book as issued to civilians from 1941 to 1949.*

Appendix II

PURCHASING POWER OF THE POUND STERLING (1900–1971)

1900	100	1950	36
1910	90	1960	24
1920	34	1970	16
1930	53	1971	15
1940	46		

The Authors are indebted to Barclay's Bank Economic Intelligence Unit for the preparation of the above figures.

GLOSSARY

ACCORDION PLEATS. Close-pleating enabling a garment to expand its shape on movement: umbrella pleats.

ALPACA. Cloth made from the wool of the alpaca with silk or cotton. It has a shiny surface.

ANGOLA; ANGORA. Material made from the wool or hair of the angora goat.

APPLIQUÉ. Applied decoration of one flat material sewn down onto another.

APRON SKIRT. (1) An overskirt to a dress simulating or giving the effect of an apron. (2) For riding, a half-skirt concealing the breeches when mounted.

AQUASCUTUM. A proprietory brand of rainwear.

ART NOUVEAU. From c.1890, a decorative style using free-flowing, exaggerated curves and natural forms.

BAKST, Leon (1866–1924). Russian stage designer who was renowned for his ballet settings and use of strong massed colours.

BANDANA; BANDANNA. A yellow or white-spotted dark handkerchief originally from India.

BANDEAU. A band worn round the head to bind the hair in place.

BANGKOK (1927). Woven straw plait of Oriental make used for hats.

BARATHEA. Twill or diagonal weave fine dense worsted.

BARRETTES; BARRETTER PINS. From BARRETTE, a little flat cap: a metal pin with an ornamental head to secure the hair – a hair grip.

BASKET BUTTONS. A button covered in silk in a basket-work pattern.

BASQUE. Extension of the bodice below the waist. Also applied to fulness or flare in the skirt of a woman's jacket.

BATIK. A process of dyeing in successive colours to produce a marbled effect: fabric so treated.

BEAVER CLOTH. Heavy woollen overcoating with a raised nap.

BELLOWS POCKETS. Patch pockets applied with pleated sides and bottom giving a box-like appearance when extended.

BERTHA. A deep fall generally of lace or silk covering the shoulders and sometimes the neck. Now usually attached to the dress.

BIRD'S-EYE. A weave giving an overall effect of small dots.

BISHOP SLEEVE. A full roomy sleeve gathered into a tight wrist-band or cuff.

BLANKET CLOTH. Thick soft woollen cloth having the pile raised by teazing.

BLAZER. Unlined flannel jacket, in club colours or plain navy, etc. worn for games, and, later, leisure wear.

BOA. A snake-like stole of feathers or fur.

BOAT NECK. A wide, medium deep eliptical neck line.

BOATER. Hard straw hat with a flat brim and fairly shallow flat crown.

BOLERO. A short jacket ending above the waist, square or rounded fronts, worn loose and unfastened. With or without sleeves.

BOUCLÉ. Any fabric woven or knitted from a yarn which has knots or loops in it, thus producing an uneven or curly surface.

BOXCLOTH. Woollen fabric with a dressed face resembling felt. Originally used for driving coats in the nineteenth century.

BOX PLEAT. Two parallel pleats made in contrary directions behind the face of the material.

BRETON; BRETON SAILOR. A type of hat with a close fitting round crown and a deep upturned brim. Made of felt or straw.

BRETTELLES. Shoulder straps: ornamental strappings over the shoulders on the surface of a bodice, starting and ending at the waist.

BRIDGE COAT. A woman's loose open jacket of lace, brocade, velvet, etc. worn over an evening or afternoon dress.

BRILLIANTINE. A pomade or hair-grease to fix the hair in position and to impart a lustrous effect.

BROCADE. A plain or figured silk material woven with a raised coloured pattern.

BROCHÉ SATIN. With a pattern on the surface.

BRODERIE ANGLAISE. A cut-out design in white material consisting of holes arranged in patterns with button-hole stitch round the edges.

BROGUE. Stout, heavy shoes with a decoration of punched patterns.

BUSTLE. A device for thrusting out the skirt at the back of the waist: drapery bunched or applied at that point.

CAMBRIC. Fine linen or cotton fabric.

CANTON. A cotton or cotton/wool mixture fabric.

CAP SLEEVE. Very short sleeve just covering the point of the shoulder.

CAPE. Skin of Cape of Good Hope sheep, used in glove making.

CAPE SLEEVE. A very flared short sleeve.

CARDIGAN. A close-fitting knitted wool, collarless jacket.

CASHMERE. Fine woollen twill fabric originally made from Tibetan goats' hair.

CELANESE (1923). Trade name of artificial silk made by British Celanese Ltd. (from cellulose).

CHAPLET. Wreath or garland for the head, usually of flowers.

CHARMEUSE (1907). Smooth, satin-like, soft silk.

CHEMISETTE. Lace or material filling in the décolletage of a dress.

CHEVIOT. Fine quality tweed somewhat coarser than Saxony.

CHIFFON. A delicate, sheer, soft and filmy silk.

CHIGNON. Hair coiled or folded at the nape of the neck; generally in conjunction with a pad.

CLOCHE. Bell-shaped, close-fitting hat worn well down over the forehead and eyes.

COAT FROCK. Made of costume or coating material, varying with the season, for outdoor wear without an overcoat.

COATING CLOTH. Medium or light-weight woollen fabric used for women's wear.

CORDUROY. Thick ribbed cotton cloth.

CORSELET. Skirt with a boned, high waist line, or later, with a deep petersham waistband.

COWL NECKLINE. Bodice draping in soft folds at the front of the neckline.

CRAPE. A variant spelling confined to transparent black silk crêpe used solely for mourning.

CRAVENETTE. A waterproofing process patented by Bradford Dyers Ltd.: used in raincoats and covert coats.

CRÊPE. Material with the alternate weft threads having a left- and right-hand twist. When shrunk a crinkled surface is produced.

CRÊPE DE CHINE. Finely crinkled, soft silk crêpe.

CRINOLINE HAT. Made from crin, a mixture of horsehair and vegetable fibre, or from fibres of a palm known as *crin végétal*.

CRINOLINE MATERIAL. A stiff material originally of horsehair and wool or cotton for making a stiff petticoat to support the skirt.

CROMWELL SHOE. With a large tongue and a bow or buckle in the front.

DÉCOLLETAGE. The degree of lowness of a neckline.

DÉCOLLETÉ. Low necked.

DELAINE. A light soft, plain woven wool fabric.

DERBY SHOE. A shoe with the facings carrying the lace holes stitched on top of the front part, or vamp.

DIAGONAL. Twill weave: generally a left to right twill, as in gaberdine.

DIAMANTÉ. Applied decoration of white paste or glass resembling diamonds.

DICKY. A false shirt front often with an attached collar.

DIRECTOIRE LINE. High waisted style with a broad sash often swathed and sewn about the waist line.

DIRECTOIRE SKIRT. Tight fitting: sometimes slit for easy walking.

DIRECTOIRE SUIT. Had a long cut-away coat with tight sleeves.

DOLMAN SLEEVE. Cut all in one with bodice to give an extremely deep arm-hole, reaching almost to the waist.

DOROTHY BAG. Open-topped handbag secured by a drawstring, by the loops of which the bag can be hung on the wrist.

DRILL. Stout twilled cotton or linen material.

DUCHESSE. A highly lustrous and rich satin.

DUCK. Heavy canvas-like cotton or linen.

DUNGAREES. Working overalls of stout cotton. From 'dungaree', an Indian calico.

DUST COAT. A long light overcoat to protect the clothes when driving or motoring in summer.

EMPIRE LINE. Very high-waisted dress with a close-fitting skirt, often trained.

EPAULETTES. Ornamental shoulder pieces.

ETON JACKET. A waist-length tailless jacket, worn open.

FAIR ISLE. Intricate knitting patterns carried out in multi-coloured wools.

FICHU. A triangle or length of material, generally soft and light, worn round the neck and shoulders.

FILLET. A narrow band or ribbon to tie around the hair.

FILL-IN. *See* MODESTY PIECE.

FLANNEL. Soft woollen cloth of loose texture made with a slightly twisted yarn. Worsted flannel was made from a similar worsted yarn.

FLARE. Gradual widening, especially in a skirt, to give fulness at the bottom.

FLY-FRONT. Device for concealing a row of buttons by an overlap of material, as in trousers and some overcoats.

FROGGING; FROGS. Ornamental braiding and braid loops used as a fastening, together with toggle-shaped buttons.

FRONTS. Front part of a coat or waistcoat covering the chest, etc.

GABERDINE. A fine worsted or worsted/cotton mixture twill, tightly woven and water repellent. There are also all-cotton gaberdines.

GALLOON; GALON. A narrow closely-woven braid.

GAUFFERED; GOFFERED. Set in small pleats as in an edging or frill: material with a crimped appearance obtained by heating or other means.

GAUGING. Taking up fulness by gathering with equidistant parallel rows of stitches, as in smocking.

GEORGETTE (1914). A filmy silk crêpe, less dense that crêpe de Chine. Also (imitated) in cotton, rayon etc.

GHILLIE SHOE. One where the lacing is through a number of separate tabs at each side of the front opening, not through holes all cut in one piece of leather.

GIGOT SLEEVE. Very full at the shoulder, narrowing towards the elbow and then becoming tight to the wrist; the 'leg o' mutton'.

GODET. Piece of fabric sewn into the lower part of a skirt or sleeve etc. to give a fluted-like fulness.

GOFFERED. *See* GAUFFERED.

GORE. Wedge-shaped panel of material. Used in skirt construction to narrow the waist, avoiding gathers or pleats.

HALTER NECK. A bodice with back décolletage, the front supported by a strap of material passing round the neck.

HAND POCKETS. A term unknown to tailors today. Possibly vertical slit pockets.

HAREM SKIRT. A divided skirt caught in about the ankles, resembling Turkish trousers: often with a shorter tunic overskirt.

HARRIS TWEED. Firm, heavy, rough, hand-woven tweed. Made in the Outer Hebrides.

HEEL. Cuban: the sole terminates at the top of the heel.
    French: high, with a straight front and a curved back.
    Louis: the sole continues under the arch and down the front of the heel.
    Spanish: like the French but with a larger base area.

HOLLAND. A linen cloth.

HOMBURG. A stiff, felt hat with a longitudinal dent in the crown and a ribbon-bound brim curled upwards at the sides.

HOMESPUN. Locally-made tweeds originating in Ireland or the Western Highlands.

HOPSACK. Plain weave, fine dense worsted.

HORSESHOE NECKLINE. Opening out downwards in a widening curve to give a horseshoe appearance.

INVERTED PLEAT. The reverse of a box pleat: the folds of the opposed pleats meet in front of the face of the material.

ITALIAN CLOTH. A wool/cotton mixture lining with a glossy surface.

JABOT. A made-up cravat of lace, etc. worn in front of the neck and bosom; frilling down the front opening of a bodice or blouse.

JAP SILK. A plain weave, flat-faced silk originating in Japan.

JERSEY. A fine elastic, plain knitted fabric.

JETTED POCKET. Also known as a piped pocket. The opening is piped or bound with a narrow strip of self material.

JODHPURS. Riding pantaloons cut as breeches to the knee and thence continuing downwards to the ankle as narrow, close-fitting trousers finished with a turnup. Worn over ankle boots.

JULIET CAP. Made of mesh or net, close-fitting, often with bead or jewel trimming.

KICK PLEAT. Short pleat in the back of a tight, straight skirt to facilitate walking.

KID. Dressed leather from the skins of young goats, etc.

KIMONO. Originally a long, loose Japanese robe, the sleeves cut all in one with the main body of the garment. The name is applied to various Oriental-type dressing gowns, etc. and to a sleeve cut in the Kimono manner.

KNICKERBOCKERS. Easy-cut knee breeches of tweed etc., fastening with a band below the knee. Worn with a Norfolk or other type of sports jacket for golf, etc.

LAMÉ. Silk with metallic gold or silver threads woven into it.

LAPELS. The turned back upper part of a coat, etc. front, below the collar or neck line.

LEGHORN. Wheat straw from Tuscany used for hat-making.

LEG O' MUTTON SLEEVE. *See* GIGOT SLEEVE.

LISLE. Fine twisted cotton thread used for stockings particularly. Often with a mercerized finish.

LUVISCA (1915). Soft artificial silk with a sheen. Made by Courtaulds.

MAGYAR SLEEVE. Cut in one with the bodice with a closer fitting arm-hole than the dolman.

MANTLE. A cloak-like outer garment, sometimes with a cape, often with sleeves.

MARCELLA. A cotton piqué with a diamond-shaped pattern used for evening dress waistcoats and shirt fronts.

MAROCAIN. A crêpe of silk, silk and wool or wool.

MEDICI COLLAR. A collar standing up fairly high at the back of the neck and sloping away to nothing at the front.

MELTON. A woollen overcoating of a firm appearance and dense nap, produced by shrinking and milling during manufacture.

MERCERIZED. Cotton treated to give a silky effect, especially in lisle stockings.

MERINO. Fine twilled cloth from the wool of the Merino sheep.

MERVEILLEUX (MERVE). A rich satin, but not so lustrous as DUCHESSE (q.v.).

MOCCASIN. A type of shoe originating with the North American Indians in which the leather of the uppers is wrapped around the foot from underneath.

MOSS CRÊPE. A crêpe weave with an irregular effect.

MODESTY PIECE, VEST. An insertion, or a separate piece, of lace, etc. in the décolletage to cover the bosom.

MOUSQUETAIRE SLEEVE. A full sleeve with a turned-back cuff.

MOUSSELAINE DE SOI; MOUSSELINE. Chiffon.

MUSLIN. Fine gauzy cotton fabric of various types. Includes organdie.

NINON. Sheer, soft silk similar to chiffon but firmer.

NORFOLK JACKET. Tweed jacket with box pleats running down back and fronts, with a self belt or belted waistband.

NUTRIA. Fur of the coypu.

NYLON. The first synthetic man-made fibre. Made entirely from mineral sources, mostly petroleum or coal based chemicals.

ORGANDIE; ORGANDY. Crisp finished fine muslin.

OTTOMAN SILK. A strong, corded silk stuff.

OXFORD SHOES. A tie shoe with the vamp or front part stitched on top of the facings which carry the lace holes.

PAGODA SLEEVE. A long narrow sleeve opening about six inches above the wrist with a small undersleeve or detachable 'sleevette'.

PAILLETTE. A lustrous silk, least rich of the satins.

PALETOT. A long, fitted overcoat.

PANAMA. A hat made from plaited fibres of the toquilla leaf.

PANIERS. Drapery of the skirt or overskirt bunched upon the hips.

PANNE. (1) Velvet with a flat pile. (2) Soft silk between satin and velvet.

PARAMATTA; PARRAMATTA. In Australia in the early nineteenth century a coarse woollen cloth perhaps made at or connected with the female prison at Parramatta, New South Wales. Also a silk and worsted or cotton mixture.

PEU DE SOI. A silk with a dull satiny finish.

PELERINE. A short cape with long stole-like ends in front.

PEPLUM. An overskirt cut away to hang in points: an extended basque to give a partial overskirt effect.

PETERSHAM. A ribbed belting used for skirt tops and to stiffen waistbands. Also a heavy woollen cloth.

PETERSHAM RIBBON. Thick ribbed ribbon often used as hat trimming.

PICTURE HAT. Large wide-brimmed hat of straw or light material, generally trimmed with ribbons, artificial flowers etc. and worn in the summer for garden parties and the like.

PINAFORE DRESS. A sleeveless dress with a bib-front worn over a blouse.

PIQUÉ. Material, usually cotton, woven with a raised rib, often in a honeycomb or diamond pattern: also in straight lengthways or crossways ribs.

PLACKET. An opening or slit to make getting into and out of a garment easier. Generally at back or side waist of skirts, dresses, etc. Can also be in the sleeve or bodice from the neck. Generally with concealed right-over-left fastening.

PLASTRON. Front panel of a bodice differing from the rest, or accentuated by decoration, etc.

POCHETTE. A flat, oblong handbag like an envelope. Handleless or with a strap-handle on the back through which the hand was thrust.

POLONAISE. An overskirt bunched up behind.

POPLIN. Fine transverse ribbed fabric of silk, cotton or wool; or worsted and silk (Irish poplin).

PRINCESS LINE. A fitted dress with no waist seam, the bodice and skirt being cut in one.

PRUSSIAN COLLAR. A high turn-over or stand-fall coat collar, the ends nearly meeting in front.

RAGLAN. A sleeve cut in one with the shoulder, eliminating a shoulder seam at the junction, thus making it waterproof. A coat or macintosh with Raglan sleeves.

RATINE. Cotton or wool sponge cloth with a rough uneven surface.

RAYON (1924). 'Artificial silk.' A man-made cellulose fibre derived from wood pulp.

REP; REPP. Transverse ribbed fabrics of silk, cotton, worsted, and cotton/worsted mixtures.

REVERS. The turned-back front edges of a coat or bodice. Now often applied to the 'lapel'.

ROULEAU. A length of material cut-on-the-cross and made into a long tube. Rouleaux are applied in various patterns as trimming.

RUCHE; RUCHING. Narrow straight strips of material gathered lengthways by various means and applied as trimming.

RUFFLES. Frilled cuffs. Also frills down a shirt front, etc.

SAC; SACK; SAQUE. Loose dress or jacket, or short overcoat.

SATEEN. A cotton fabric with a shiny surface resembling that of satin.

SAXONY. Fine wool tweed, soft and smooth made from Botany, Saxony, etc. wools.

SERGE. Twilled worsted used in suits, etc.

SHANTUNG. Originally a Chinese silk of rather coarse and irregular appearance, used in its natural undyed brownish colour. Also imitations of cotton and man-made fibres.

SHINGLE. Hair cut so that all the ends are exposed.

SHIRRING. Rows of gathers similar to gauging. From about 1940 very fine elastic thread was often used.

SLIPS. White edgings buttoned into each side of the waistcoat 'V' and slightly protruding. Perhaps to prevent soiling the shirt, or probably the vestigial remains of an under waistcoat. The fashion is said to have originated with King Edward VII. Correctly worn only with a morning coat.

SNOOD. A fine cord hair net to retain the chignon. Worn outdoors with or without a hat. Also made in material and attached to a hat.

SOI DE CHINE. A lightweight silk.

SPATS; SPATTS. Short gaiters reaching just above the ankle, buttoning on the outer side and with a strap going under the foot.

STEPPED COLLAR. A collar meeting the lapel with a plain 'V' notch.

SUEDE CRÊPE. A rayon fabric.

SUNRAY PLEATS. Pleats radiating out from a common point of origin.

SUSPENDER (Male). (1) Braces for supporting trousers. (2) A type of garter of elastic at the front of which is attached a metal and rubber clip to grip the top of the sock. The length around the leg is adjustable and the garter is fastened by a metal clip.

SWALLOW TAIL. A coat with the fronts cut away at the waist, leaving only 'tails' below the waist at the back, as in the evening dress coat.

SWEETHEART NECKLINE. A fairly wide square neck descending into a curved 'V' resembling the top of a conventionalized heart.

TABLIER. A decorated front panel to a skirt.

TAFFETA. Rather stiff, rich plain silk. Imitated in rayon, etc. also.

TAGEL. Type of straw used in hat making.

TAM O' SHANTER; 'TAM'; 'TAMMIE'. A cloth, crocheted or knitted, soft round flat cap or hat, brimless with a bobble on top.

TIE-SILK. Firm yarn-dyed silk fabric, usually 'weighted' by steeping in a compound of tin solution. Originally produced for men's ties, tie-silk is also used for scarves, etc. and for women's dresses.

TOILETTE. Mode or way of dressing; hence a dress, costume, etc.

TOQUE. A close-fitting brimless hat.

TRICOLINE. A proprietory rayon dress material made by Tricoline, Watling Street, London, E.C.4.

TULLE. A fine silk net.

TUNIC DRESS, -FROCK. With a blouse-bodice coming down over the skirt.

TUSSORE. A 'wild' silk of brownish, irregular appearance.

TWEED. A woollen cloth in a variety of grades from coarse and rough to fine and smooth.

TYROLESE HAT. Felt hat with a pointed crown and up-and-down turned brim, worn with a feather.

ULSTER. (Male) Overcoat with a belt or half-belt; sometimes with a hood or a cape.

(Female) A long overcoat, caped. Later becoming a generic term for an overcoat.

VANDYKING. Decorative border or edging cut into points.

VELOUR. Wool or wool mixture cloth, soft and smooth with a closely-cut pile or nap.

VELOURS. A heavy, smooth silk or silk and hair mixture with a pile, used for hats, etc.

VELVET. Silk fabric with a dense vertical pile.

VELVETEEN. Cotton or cotton and silk fabric with a pile resembling velvet.

VENT. A vertical slit up from the hem of a coat, etc. for convenience of movement in wear.

VEST. Tailor's name for a waistcoat.

VICUNA. Cloth made from the hair of a type of llama. It is also made of a hair/wool or wool/worsted mixture.

VOILE. A very light wool or cotton fabric. Is also made of rayon.

VYELLA. Proprietory brand of wool/cotton mixture, manufactured by William Hollins & Co. Ltd., Nottingham.

WELTED POCKET. A slit pocket finished with a welt about an inch deep and the width of the pocket.

WIND CUFFS. Cuff with a strap to tighten round the wrist or with an elasticated inset fitting closely round the wrist.

WORSTED. Wool cloth, the yarn of which is made from long stapled wool, combed straight before spinning.

YOKE. A shaped piece covering the shoulders of a bodice blouse, etc. to which the lower part is sewn.

YOKE, SKIRT. A deep shaped band at the top of a skirt.

ZEPHYR. A fine, light cotton gingham.

ZOUAVE. A short jacket with rounded fronts, fastened at the neck only.

SOURCES OF ILLUSTRATIONS

'Cunnington' refers to *English Women's Clothing in the Present Century* and is given where no original attribution is listed in that work.

Women (1900–10)

1. Cunnington.
2. Cunnington, from *Hearth and Home*.
3. Army and Navy Stores Ltd.
4. Thornton's *Sectional System of Ladies Garment Cutting*.
5. Thornton's *Sectional System*.
6. *West End Gazette*.
7(a) 'La Belle Epoche' *(Ladies Realm)*.
7(b) 'La Belle Epoche' *(Strand Magazine)*.
8. Thornton's *Sectional System*.
9. Army and Navy Stores Ltd.
10. Cunnington.
11. Cunnington.
12. Thornton's *Sectional System*.
13. Army and Navy Stores Ltd.
14. *The Cult of Chiffon*.
15. *The Cult of Chiffon*.
16. Army and Navy Stores Ltd.
17. Thornton's *Sectional System*.
18. Thornton's *Sectional System*.
19. Army and Navy Stores Ltd.
20. Army and Navy Stores Ltd.
21. Army and Navy Stores Ltd.
22. Army and Navy Stores Ltd.
23(a)
23(b) } Private photographs.
24. Northampton Museum.
25. Army and Navy Stores Ltd.
26. Army and Navy Stores Ltd.
27. Army and Navy Stores Ltd.

Women (1910–20)

28.   Army and Navy Stores Ltd.

29(a) }
  (b) } Cunnington.

30.   *Woman's Weekly.*
31.   Army and Navy Stores Ltd.
32.   *Ladies' Tailor.*
33.   Army and Navy Stores Ltd.
34.   Cunnington from the *Ladies' Tailor.*
35.   Army and Navy Stores Ltd.
36.   Army and Navy Stores Ltd.
37   Army and Navy Stores Ltd.
38.   Army and Navy Stores Ltd.
39.   *Weldon's Practical Crochet.*
40.   Harrods Ltd.
41.   Harrods Ltd.
42.   *Vogue.*
43(a)   Army and Navy Stores Ltd.
43(b)   *Daily Mail.*
44.   Army and Navy Stores Ltd.
45.   Army and Navy Stores Ltd.
46.   Army and Navy Stores Ltd.
47.   *Essex County Standard.*
48.   Army and Navy Stores Ltd.
49.   *Pan.*
50.   *Pan.*
51.   *Pan.*
52.   Army and Navy Stores Ltd.
53.   Army and Navy Stores Ltd.

Women (1920–30)

54.   *Woman's Weekly.*
55.   Cunnington.
56(a), (b), (c) Harrods Ltd.
57(a), (b)   *Essex County Telegraph.*
58.   Cunnington.
59.   *Tailor and Cutter.*
60.   *Essex County Telegraph.*
61.   *Essex County Telegraph.*
62.   Army and Navy Stores Ltd.
63.   *Woman's Life.*
64.   *Woman's Life.*
65.   *Woman's Weekly.*

66. *Vogue.*
67. Harrods Ltd.
68(a) *Vogue.*
68(b) Private photograph.
69. Army and Navy Stores Ltd.
70. Private photograph.
71. *Daily Mail.*
72. *Woman's Weekly.*
73. Army and Navy Stores Ltd.
74. *Vogue.*
75. *Tailor and Cutter.*
76. *Essex County Telegraph.*
77. *Daily Mail.*
78(a), (b), (c) *Woman's Life.*
78(d) *Woman's Weekly.*
79(a), (b), (c) *Essex County Telegraph.*
80. Army and Navy Stores Ltd.
81. Army and Navy Stores Ltd.

Women (1930–40)
82. *Good Needlework.*
83. *Good Needlework.*
84. *Ladies' Companion.*
85. *Good Needlework.*
86. *Woman's Pictorial.*
87(a) *Woman's Pictorial.*
87(b) *Woman's Pictorial.*
88. A. J. Lucking and Company Ltd.
89. A. J. Lucking and Company Ltd.
90. *Good Needlework.*
91. Harrods Ltd.
92. *Good Needlework.*
93. *Vogue.*
94. *Woman's Own.*
95. *Good Needlework.*
96. *Woman's Pictorial.*
97. *Woman's Pictorial.*
98. *Vogue.*
99. *Good Needlework.*
100. *Woman's Pictorial.*
101. *Woman's Own.*
102. *Woman's Pictorial.*
103. *Good Needlework.*

104.   *Good Needlework.*
105.   Harrods Ltd.
106.   *Daily Mail.*
107.   Harrods Ltd.
108.   *Weldon's Good Taste.*
109(a)   *Good Needlework*
109(b)   *Good Needlework.*
109(c)   *Woman's Friend.*
110.   *Good Needlework.*
111.   *Good Needlework.*
112.   Harrods Ltd.
113.   A. J. Lucking and Company Ltd.
114.   *Essex County Standard.*
115.   A. J. Lucking and Company Ltd.
116.   *Woman's Pictorial.*
117.   A. J. Lucking and Company Ltd.
118.   A. J. Lucking and Company Ltd.
119(a), (b) Army and Navy Stores Ltd.
119(c)   *Good Needlework.*

Women (1940–50)
120.   *Vogue.*
121.   *Vogue.*
122.   *Wife and Home.*
123.   A. J. Lucking and Company Ltd.
124.   *Woman's Weekly.*
125.   A. J. Lucking and Company Ltd.
126.   Cunnington (Joy Ricardo).
127.   *Vogue.*
128.   A. J. Lucking and Company Ltd.
129.   *Vogue.*
130.   *Vogue.*
131.   A. J. Lucking and Company Ltd.
132.   A. J. Lucking and Company Ltd.
133.   *Vogue.*
134.   A. J. Lucking and Company Ltd.
135.   *Vogue.*
136.   *Vogue.*
137.   *Ladies' Journal.*
138.   A. J. Lucking and Company Ltd.
139.   *Wife and Home.*
140.   Harrods Ltd.
141(a)   *Vogue.*

141(b)   *Vogue.*
141(c)   Private photograph.
142.   *Vogue.*
143.   *Wife and Home.*
144.   *Vogue.*
145.   *Vogue.*
146.   *Vogue.*
147.   *Vogue.*
148.   A. J. Lucking and Company Ltd.
149.   A. J. Lucking and Company Ltd.
150.   A. J. Lucking and Company Ltd.
151.   *Vogue*
152.   *Vogue.*

Men (1900–25)
153.   *Tailor and Cutter.*
154.   *Tailor and Cutter.*
155.   *Tailor and Cutter.*
156.   Wallis & Linnell Ltd.
157.   *Tailor and Cutter.*
158.   Wallis & Linnell Ltd.
159.   Wallis & Linnell Ltd.
160.   *Tailor and Cutter.*
161.   Army and Navy Stores Ltd.
162.   Private photograph.
163.   Army and Navy Stores Ltd.
164.   Army and Navy Stores Ltd.
165.   *Tailor and Cutter.*
166.   *Tailor and Cutter.*
167.   Army and Navy Stores Ltd.
168.   *Tailor and Cutter.*
169.   *Punch.*
170.   Wallis & Linnell Ltd.
171.   *Tailor and Cutter.*
172.   Army and Navy Stores Ltd.
173.   Army and Navy Stores Ltd.
174.   Army and Navy Stores Ltd.
175.   *Tailor and Cutter.*
176.   Army and Navy Stores Ltd.
177.   Army and Navy Stores Ltd.
178.   Army and Navy Stores Ltd.
179.   Wallis & Linnell Ltd.
180.   *Tailor and Cutter.*

181.   *Black and White.*
182.   *Tailor and Cutter.*
183.   Wallis & Linnell Ltd.
184.   *Tailor and Cutter.*
185.   *Tailor and Cutter.*
186.   Wallis & Linnell Ltd.
187.   Army and Navy Stores Ltd.
188.   *Tailor and Cutter.*
189.   Army and Navy Stores Ltd.

Men (1926–50)
190.   Army and Navy Stores Ltd.
191.   Army and Navy Stores Ltd.
192.   *Essex County Standard.*
193.   Harrods Ltd.
194.   *Tailor and Cutter.*
195.   *Tailor and Cutter.*
196.   *Tailor and Cutter.*
197.   *Tailor and Cutter.*
198.   *Tailor and Cutter.*
199.   *Tailor and Cutter.*
200.   *Tailor and Cutter.*
201.   Army and Navy Stores Ltd.
202.   *Tailor and Cutter.*
203.   *Tailor and Cutter.*
204.   *Tailor and Cutter.*
205.   *Tailor and Cutter.*
206.   *Tailor and Cutter.*
207.   Bestway Knitting Pattern.
208.   *Punch.*
209.   Army and Navy Stores Ltd.
210.   Army and Navy Stores Ltd.
211.   Harrods Ltd.
212.   *Tailor and Cutter.*
213.   Harrods Ltd.
214.   Army and Navy Stores Ltd.
215.   *Essex County Standard.*
216.   *Tailor and Cutter.*
217.   *Tailor and Cutter.*
218.   Harrods Ltd.
219.   *Ambassador.*
220.   Army and Navy Stores Ltd.
221.   Army and Navy Stores Ltd.
222.   Author's collection.

BIBLIOGRAPHY

BOOKS

The following books are a selection of primary and secondary sources covering all or part of the period for further reading. Publication, unless otherwise stated, is in London.

ADBURGHAM, A., *Shops and Shopping, 1800–1914,* 1964.

ARNOLD, J., *Patterns of Fashion,* 1964.

BALMAIN, P., *My Years and Seasons,* 1964.

BRADFIELD, NANCY, *Costume in Detail: Women's Dress 1730–1930,* 1968.

BROOKE, IRIS, *English Costume 1900–1950,* 1951.

BUTTERICK PUBLISHING CO., *Making Smart Clothes,* 1930.

COHN, NIK, *Today there are no Gentlemen,* 1971.

CORSON, R., *Fashions in Hair,* 1965.

COSTUME SOCIETY, *La Belle Epoche,* 1968.

CUNNINGTON, C. W., *English Women's Clothing in the Present Century,* 1952.

CUNNINGTON, C. W. & P., *Picture History of English Costume,* 1960.

FORBES, LADY ANGELA, *How to Dress for all Ages and Occasions,* 1926.

GARLAND, M., *The Changing Form of Fashion,* 1970.
    The Indecisive Decade, 1968.

GORDON, L. W. D., *Discretions and Indiscretions* (The Autobiography of Lucile), 1932.

INNIS, I., *Scientific Dressmaking & Millinery,* 1913.

JACK, F. B. (ed.), *The Woman's Book,* 1911.

JOY, L., *The Well Dressed Woman,* 1907.

LANE, M. R., *Half a Century of Fashion,* 1950.

LATOUR, A., *Kings of Fashion,* 1958.

LAVER, J., *Taste and Fashion,* 1945 edition.
    Women's Dress in the Jazz Age, 1964.

LINKS, J. G., *The Book of Fur,* 1956.

MASON, GERTRUDE, *Tailoring for Women,* 1946.

M. M., *How to Dress and What to Wear,* 1903.

MOORE, DORIS LANGLEY, *Fashion Through Fashion Plates 1771–1970,* 1971.

PRITCHARD, E., *The Cult of Chiffon,* 1902.

SILK & RAYON USERS ASSOCIATION, *The Silk Book*, 1951.

THORNTON, J. P., *Sectional System of Ladies' Garment Cutting*, 1901.

VINCENT, W. D. F., *The Cutter's Practical Guide to the Cutting of all Kinds of Ladies' Garments* (n.d., c.1920).

WAUGH, NORAH, *The Cut of Women's Clothes 1600–1930*, 1968.

WILSON, EUNICE, *The History of Shoe Fashions*, 1969.

PERIODICALS

Ambassador
Country Life
Drapers' Record
Good Needlework
Harper's Bazaar
Illustrated London News
Lady, The
Ladies' Companion
Ladies Tailor
Punch
Queen, The
Tailor and Cutter
Vogue
Weldon's Good Taste
Weldon's Ladies' Journal
Weldon's Practical Crochet
Weldon's Practical Knitting
Weldon's Practical Needlework
Wife and Home
Woman's Friend
Woman and Home
Woman's Life
Woman's Own
Woman's Pictorial
Woman's Weekly

Also national and local newspapers

Paper Patterns
Bestway
Butterick's
Vogue
Weldon's

INDEX

Page numbers in *italics* indicate an illustration in the text, but in the case of articles of clothing, where written reference is made on the same page as an illustration ordinary type is generally used.

Named garments or parts of garments are indexed under the main headings, e.g. 'Angel Sleeve' under 'Sleeves', 'Chesterfield' under 'Coats, Men's outdoor'.

214, 218; angel, 34; bell, 112, 125, 150; bishop, 112, 150, 170, 178, 202, 212, 227, 229; cap, 216; cape, 21, 168; dolman, 178, *201, 203,* 212, *226,* 227; elbow, 106, 112; Gigot or leg-o'-mutton 22, 74, 142, 168, 218; handkerchief, 82; kimono, 22, 70, 202, 203, 208, 209, 212; Magyar, 26, 65, 70, 75, 80, 105, 113, 150, 178, 203; raglan, 75, 150, 178, 208, 212

Slip, 249

Slip-on, 163, 320

Slip-over, 163

Sloppy-Joe, 212

Smocks, 155, 173, 174, 220

Smoking jacket, *see* Coats, men's indoor

Smoking suit, *see* Suit

Snood, 184, 220, 232

Socks, men's, 292, 337; women's, 225, 236; *see also* Ankle-socks

Spats, *95,* 274, 294, *301,* 303, 338

Spiv, 195, 306

Sports clothes, 38–42, 85–8, 121–4, 174–7, 223–5, 277–83, 325–31

Sports coats, women's, *76,* 77, 87

Standard suit, 243,

Stockings, 51, 95, 135, 187, 194, 235, 277, 279, 293, 320, 337; Nylon, 194, 236; short, 187

Stole, *79,* 97, 136, 188, 236, 237

Style width, 246

Suffragette Movement, 19, 56

Suits, men's, demob, *see* Demob suit; golf, *278;* knicker, 283; lounge, 251–258, 275, 297, 298, 302–9, 323; morning coat, 247, *248, 250,* 302; shooting, *280;* smoking, 270; tennis, 277; twopiece, 299, 302; utility, 299, 304, *306,* 309, 324; weekend, 302

women's, 27–32, 66–72, 108–11, 155–60, 206–10; cardigan, 163, 209;

jumper, 109, *110,* 212; siren, *see* Siren; smoking, 114, 119; trouser, 161, 213

Sun dress, 225

Sunshade, *see* Parasol

Sun top, 225

Suspenders, *see* Braces

Suspenders, sock, 292

Sweater, 113, 163, 166, 271, 277, 320, 326

Swim suit, *see* Bathing dress

Sword, 276

"Tailor made", 21, *30, 59, 67,* 70

Tails, coat, 247, 264, 317

Tea gown, *see* Dress

Teddy Boy, 299

Tennis clothes, 40, 85, 122, 174, *175,* 225, 277, 326, *327*

Tie, *see* Necktie

Tie pins, 295, 339

Toque, *see* Hats, women's

Train, 34, 78, 64, 106, 120; court, 38, 85, 120, 173

Transformation, 47

Trench coat, 91, *92,* 180, 230, 286

Trimming, general, 23, 24, 26, 28, *33,* 34, 36, 39, 42, 46, 50, 62, 65, 71, 73, *79,* 82, 88, 104, 107, 116, 118, 125, *127,* 133, 146, 148, 152, 164, 166, 168, *169,* 170, 178, 180, 196, 200, 216, 227; millinery, 48, 93, 94, *129,* 184, 185, 232, 233

Trousers, men's, 246, 247, 257, 276, 278, 300, 301, 329; crease in, *251,* 261; day, 261–64, 310, 311; flannel, *see* Flannels; evening dress, 269, 319; odd, 313; peg top, 242, 261; *see also* Knickerbockers; Oxford bags; Plusfours

women's, 85, *86,* 114, 122, *123,* 160, 162, 174, 175, 176, *177,* 213, 214, 220; turkish, 56, 114, 119